W9-CPF-403

The
Importance of
SCIENTIFIC
THEORY

The Importance of Cell Theory

John Allen

ReferencePoint
Press®

San Diego, CA

About the Author
John Allen is a writer living in Oklahoma City.

© 2016 ReferencePoint Press, Inc.
Printed in the United States

For more information, contact:
ReferencePoint Press, Inc.
PO Box 27779
San Diego, CA 92198
www.ReferencePointPress.com

Picture Credits:
Cover: Thinkstock Images; Maury Aaseng: 28; Associated Press: 45; © Lester V. Bergman/Corbis: 19; © Blue Images Online/Masterfile/Corbis: 37; A. Barrington Brown/Science Source: 40; © Burger/Phanie/phanie/Phanie Sarl/Corbis: 55; CNRI/Science Source: 67; Depositphotos: 7; © GraphicaArtis/Corbis: 22; © Waltraud Grubitzsch/epa/Corbis: 49; © Ralph Hutchings/Visuals Unlimited/Corbis: 65; © Lucy Nicholson/Reuters/Corbis: 9; David M. Phillips/Science Source: 26; Science Source: 61; © Leif Skoogfors/Corbis: 53; Thinkstock Images: 6; Animalcules, including sperm, after Leewenhoek (1632–1723) 29 & 30. Observations of human spermatazoa from warm cadaver 31–40 (Leeuwenhoek). Hand-coloured engraving c1795. /Universal History Archive/UIG/Bridgeman Images: 15; Simulium damnosum/Natural History Museum, London, UK/Bridgeman Images: 33

LIBRARY OF CONGRESS CATALOGING-IN-PUBLICATION DATA

Allen, John, 1957- author.
  The importance of cell theory / by John Allen.
    pages cm. -- (The importance of scientific theory series)
  Audience: Grades 9 to 12.
  Includes bibliographical references and index.
  ISBN-13: 978-1-60152-888-9 (hardback)
  ISBN-10: 1-60152-888-4 (hardback)
  1. Cells--Juvenile literature. 2. Cytology--Juvenile literature. 3. Medicine--Research--Juvenile literature. I. Title. II. Series: Importance of scientific theory.
  QH582.5.A43 2016
  571.6--dc23
                                                        2015021278

CONTENTS

FOREWORD

What is the nature of science? The authors of "Understanding the Scientific Enterprise: The Nature of Science in the Next Generation Science Standards," answer that question this way: "Science is a way of explaining the natural world. In common parlance, science is both a set of practices and the historical accumulation of knowledge. An essential part of science education is learning science and engineering practices and developing knowledge of the concepts that are foundational to science disciplines. Further, students should develop an understanding of the enterprise of science as a whole—the wondering, investigating, questioning, data collecting and analyzing."

Examples from history offer a valuable way to explore the nature of science and understand the core ideas and concepts around which all life revolves. When English chemist John Dalton formulated a theory in 1803 that all matter consists of small, indivisible particles called atoms and that atoms of different elements have different properties, he was building on the ideas of earlier scientists as well as relying on his own experimentation, observation, and analysis. His atomic theory, which also proposed that atoms cannot be created or destroyed, was not entirely accurate, yet his ideas are remarkably close to the modern understanding of atoms. Intrigued by his findings, other scientists continued to test and build on Dalton's ideas until eventually—a century later—actual proof of the atom's existence emerged.

The story of these discoveries and what grew from them is presented in *The Importance of Atomic Theory*, one volume in ReferencePoint's series *The Importance of Scientific Theory*. The series strives to help students develop a broader and deeper understanding of the nature of science by examining notable ideas and events in the history of science. Books in the series focus on the development and outcomes of atomic theory, cell theory, germ theory, evolution theory, plate tectonic theory, and more. All books clearly state the core idea and explore changes in thinking over time, methods of experimentation and observation, and societal impacts of these momentous theories and discoveries. Each volume includes a visual chronology; brief descriptions of important people; sidebars that highlight and further explain key events and concepts; "words in context" vocabulary; and, where possible, the words of the scientists themselves.

Through richly detailed examples from history and clear discussion of scientific ideas and methods, *The Importance of Scientific Theory* series furthers an appreciation for the essence of science and the men and women who devote their lives to it. As the authors of "Understanding the Scientific Enterprise: The Nature of Science in the Next Generation Science Standards" write, "With the addition of historical examples, the nature of scientific explanations assumes a human face and is recognized as an everchanging enterprise."

IMPORTANT EVENTS IN THE HISTORY OF CELL THEORY

ca. 1590s
Hans and Zacharias Jansen, a father-son team of spectacle makers in the Dutch city of Middelburg, invent the first microscope.

1839
German physiologist Theodor Schwann formulates the first cell theory by stating that all living things are made of cells and the cell is the basic unit of structure in living things.

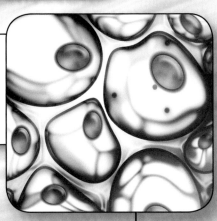

1665
English scientist Robert Hooke uses a microscope to discover cells in a slice of cork. Hooke coins the term *cells* for the tiny compartments he sees.

1833
Scottish botanist Robert Brown discovers the nucleus in plant cells.

1650	1700	1750	1800	1850

1837
German botanist Matthias Schleiden proposes that cells are the fundamental building blocks of plants.

1840
Swiss anatomist Albrecht Koelliker recognizes that the sperm and egg are modified cells.

1670s
Dutch scientist Anton van Leeuwenhoek uses his own improved microscope to observe living cells in pond water.

1858
German physiologist Rudolf Virchow adds the final tenet to classical cell theory: all cells come from preexisting cells.

1859
French chemist Louis Pasteur disproves the theory that cells can be created through spontaneous generation.

1953
American biologist James Watson and British physicist Francis Crick discover the structure of DNA.

1902
German biologist Theodor Boveri confirms that chromosomes include hereditary material.

1984
British geneticist Alec Jeffreys develops the basic method of genetic profiling.

1945
American cell biologist Keith Porter produces the first image of a tissue cell.

1900	1925	1950	1975	2000

1931
Ernst Ruska invents the first electron microscope.

1998
American cell biologist James Thomson isolates embryonic stem cells.

1951
Cells removed from an African American woman named Henrietta Lacks develop into an important tool for modern medicine.

1963
Canadian scientists James Till and Ernest McCulloch identify blood stem cells.

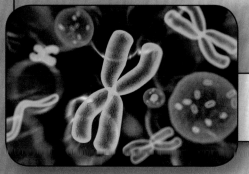

1879
German scientist Walther Flemming is the first to identify chromosomes.

Cell Theory

THE CORE IDEA

The cell theory is a scientific theory about the structure of living things. It is a basic principle in the study of biology. Classical cell theory consists of three ideas. First, all living things are made up of cells. Second, cells are the basic units of structure and function in living things. Third, all new cells come from preexisting cells. Modern cell theory adds three further observations. First, energy flow takes place within cells. Second, cells contain DNA, which is passed on to new cells during cell division. Third, all cells are essentially identical in chemical composition.

The properties of tiny human cells can have a huge impact on a person's life. Take the case of Kevin Durant, pro basketball superstar for the Oklahoma City Thunder. After Durant underwent surgery for a broken bone in his right foot, the fracture failed to heal properly because of a lack of blood supply to the bone. On March 31, 2015, a doctor in New York performed another surgery, repairing the fracture with a bone graft—a sliver of bone from Durant's hip. Cell theory was key to the surgical procedure. "One of the benefits of bone grafting," writes medical expert Stephania Bell, "is that it directly places cells with a healthy blood supply in an underserved area, which may, ultimately, enhance the healing potential of the bone."[1] In the days and weeks after such a surgery a machine called a bone stimulator is applied to the foot to stimulate boneforming cells with ultrasound or electrical impulses. Other athletes with similar fractures have received enriched bone cells and resumed their careers with no further problems. Durant's outlook for returning to the court better than ever is much brighter today due to detailed knowledge about how cells work.

Peering into a Hidden World

Cell theory first arose with the invention of an improved microscope in the seventeenth century. The ability to peer into a previously hidden world, one beyond the limits of human vision, was a revelation for early scientists. Society at large was not prepared for what they described. The first advocates of cell theory were attacked as insane for their claims that living organisms were made up of tiny honeycomb-like chambers. Nevertheless cell theory helped to affirm the scientific method—the process of testing and comparing the

In 2015 Kevin Durant underwent a bone graft to repair a broken bone in his right foot. The grafting of the healthy bone chip—taken from his hip—allowed the imported blood cells to improve blood flow in the injured area.

results of experiments—and eventually was used to demolish widely accepted ideas. For example, the study of cells disproved the idea of spontaneous generation, which held that nonliving matter could generate living tissue. Cell theory also established that plants and animals share the same basic microscopic structure, thus linking the studies of botany and zoology. Perhaps cell theory's greatest effect on society, at least before the discovery of DNA in the twentieth century, was the revolution it brought about in diagnosing and treating illness. Certainly it formed the basis for French chemist Louis Pasteur's germ theory of disease, which posited that many diseases were caused by infectious microorganisms within the body.

WORDS IN CONTEXT

DNA

Deoxyribonucleic acid, the molecule containing a biological blueprint of a living thing.

The development of classical cell theory in the nineteenth century focused on the cell as the basic unit of life. Scientists realized that cells determine the structure and function of all living things. Study of the chemical processes of cells, and their importance as the building blocks of life, caused a major shift in society's view of life and religion. Scientists concluded that cells perpetuate life without divine intervention. Nobel Prize–winning genetic scientist Paul Nurse calls cell theory one of the five big ideas in biology. "Cell theory—this is crucial for us understanding biology because cells form the basis of all life," says Nurse. "[And] cell division, the division of a cell from one, to two, to four, forms the basis of growth and development of all living things."[2]

In the twentieth century, cell theory expanded further due to the invention of much more powerful microscopes. With the ability to examine separate parts of a cell, scientists began to detail the integral role cells play in reproduction and energy storage. Modern notions about human development took their cue from the latest cellular research. By midcentury cell theory was helping to produce increasingly sophisticated medical treatments, such as a vaccine for polio. The discovery of DNA—the coded blueprint of all living things—in cells opened new possibilities for studying human origins and treating hereditary disease. At the same time it raised thorny questions about the wisdom of tampering with human life on the cellular level.

Cell Theory Today and in the Future

Today some of the main issues related to cell theory involve DNA and stem cells. Research on DNA has shown it to be a useful tool for identification. It is now widely used to determine parentage and to identify suspects in criminal investigations. DNA in cells found at crime scenes has been used to track down lawbreakers and also to exonerate prisoners who were wrongly convicted. Stem cells are undifferentiated cells that can be stimulated to form new tissue. One source of stem cells is the human embryo, but today many oppose harvesting these cells on ethical grounds. In the future, research on cells promises to create amazing new treatments and technologies—and many new questions for society.

CHAPTER ONE

The History of Cell Theory

Before the discovery of cells, there were many theories to account for the complexities of living things. Some scientists—or natural philosophers, as they were called in the 1600s—believed that the bodies of people and animals were composed of different types of fibers. The varied properties of these fibers explained why tissues differed from each other in form and function. Other scientists suggested that bodies were made up of some kind of fundamental units, just as matter is formed from atoms. However, the most popular theory of how life developed was called spontaneous generation. According to this idea, living things simply sprang up from inanimate matter. Observations that seemed to support spontaneous generation were found everywhere in nature. After all, mold grew on food, maggots appeared on rotting meat, and mushrooms sprouted in the roots of dead trees. Development of an improved theory about the makeup of living things required a new invention and a new way to scrutinize tissue.

The Invention of the Microscope

In their studies of plants and animals, early scientists were limited by what the naked eye could see and what the imagination could surmise. This changed around 1590 with the invention of the microscope. Zacharias Jansen and his father, Hans, were Dutch makers of spectacles and magnifying glasses. In an experiment they aligned several convex lenses inside a tube and made a key discovery. The device produced a two-stage magnification. An object near the end of the tube appeared to be significantly enlarged, magnified much more than a single lens could accomplish. The Jansens' compound microscope was somewhat crude, with a blurry image, and it could magnify objects only three to nine times their true size. However, news about this important tool for looking at very small things quickly spread across Europe.

In the following decades the microscope underwent a series of slight improvements. Robert Hooke, a self-educated English scientist with a brilliant mind and a prickly personality, tinkered with the height and angle of microscopes to achieve magnifications of fifty times actual size. He also adjusted light sources for better illumination. Using his improved microscope, Hooke made a historic discovery. Peering at a thin slice of cork, he noted that the magnified substance looked like a honeycomb pattern of empty pores or boxes enclosed by a surrounding wall. He referred to these boxes as cells, since they reminded him of the small rooms in a monastery. (The word *cell* is short for the Latin *cellula*, meaning a small compartment.) Hooke observed similar arrangements in wood and other plants. In 1665 Hooke published *Micrographia*, in which he described his magnified observations of everything from flint to fabric to frozen urine. He also included detailed drawings of what he had seen. Hooke touted the microscope as a tool "only to promote the use of mechanical helps for the Senses, both in the surveying the already visible World, and for the discovery of many others hitherto unknown."[3] *Micrographia* became the equivalent of a best seller, with learned readers marveling at the miniature world it revealed.

An Unlikely Scientist Looks at Cells

Hooke's illustrated book inspired a Dutch tradesman named Anton van Leeuwenhoek to pursue his own research. Leeuwenhoek began to grind lenses and make microscopes as a pastime. The single-lens instruments he made were simpler in design than the Jansens' and Hooke's compound microscopes and less like microscopes used today. Nonetheless Leeuwenhoek ground each lens with great skill and was ingenious in his use of lighting. The microscopes he built could achieve magnifications of 200 times or more in clear, bright images. Leeuwenhoek also possessed remarkable eyesight, boundless curiosity, and a passion for detail. "For his studies," writes the art historian Jonathan Lopez, "he interposed the specimen between lens and light source, much as children of later generations would do when holding their toy kaleidoscopes up to the sky. No prior microscopist, not even the great Robert Hooke, had ever thought simply to look at a droplet of water lighted from behind."[4]

In the 1670s Leeuwenhoek set about studying every substance he could think to peer at through the eyepiece. This included the plaque scraped from his own teeth. As Leeuwenhoek described it in a letter to the Royal Society, a renowned group of scientists in London, "I then most always saw, with great wonder, that in the said matter there were many very little living animalcules, very prettily a-moving. The biggest sort . . . had a very strong and swift motion, and shot through the water (or spittle) like a pike does through the water."[5] What Leeuwenhoek called animalcules, or little animals, were single-celled bacteria. He also observed blood cells, sperm cells, and intestinal protozoa. Unlike Hooke, Leeuwenhoek seemed to perceive that cells were not merely empty compartments. His description of globules within blood cells probably referred to cell nuclei. Although no artist himself, he also oversaw precise illustrations of his many findings.

WORDS IN CONTEXT

protozoa
Tiny one-celled animals that are parasites.

Isolated in his hometown of Delft, Holland, and lacking formal education, Leeuwenhoek tried to reach out to other scientists for advice. A Dutch diplomat wrote to Hooke on Leeuwenhoek's behalf, but Hooke never replied. Over the years, however, the former cloth merchant gained fame for his work. In 1680 Leeuwenhoek was named a full member of the Royal Society, although he never traveled to England for a single meeting. He continued to use the microscope to examine everything from crystals to fossils, and was the first person to see all sorts of microscopic animals. Leeuwenhoek, the unlikely scientist, made discoveries related to cell theory that would be unsurpassed for 150 years.

Preparing the Way for Cell Theory

Before cell theory took shape, scientists continued to learn more about cells. In France biologist and chemist Francois-Vincent Raspail made important discoveries about the structure and function

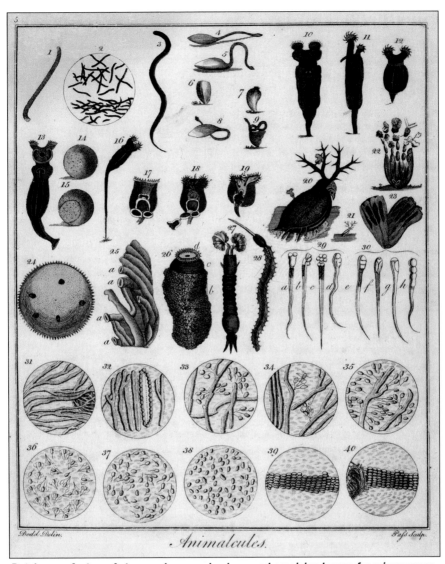

Dutch manufacturer Anton van Leeuwenhoek ground precision lenses for microscopes. His instruments achieved powerful magnification, permitting scientists to clearly see and identify living bacteria, various body cells, and tiny protozoa.

of plant cells. It was Raspail who in 1825 coined the Latin phrase *omnis cellula e cellula*—every cell is derived from another cell. Raspail combined chemical analysis with microscope work by adding iodine-starch color reaction to the cell. He used this technique to examine processes within cells, such as how the membrane of the cell wall serves as a selective gateway: "[Cell walls] thus have the property of

The Globule Error

Before cell theory took shape in the late 1830s, several influential scientists thought all living things were made of globules, or tiny globe-like particles. In 1823 French scientist Henri Milne-Edwards proposed the best-known statement of globule theory in his master's degree thesis. Building on the work of earlier scientists, Milne-Edwards had examined a variety of animal organs from many species. He concluded they all consisted of minute globules, about 1/300 of a millimeter in diameter. English scientist Everard Home agreed with the globule hypothesis. Once skeptical about the ability of microscopes to show clearly the details of animal tissue, Home came to believe that improved instruments revealed globules in blood and tissues of the nerves and brain. Home's 1823 lectures on anatomy at the College of Surgeons in London helped spread his own ideas about globules.

However, Joseph Lister's invention of the achromatic microscope in the late 1820s exploded the globule theory. The new microscope featured lenses that produced higher magnification with less distortion. Lister and his associate Thomas Hodgkin observed that what looked like globules through the old microscope lenses were actually optical illusions. As science historian John Baker writes, "The fact that the excesses of the globulists were exposed by Lister's microscope seems significant; for the particular advantage of his instrument was that spherical aberration was corrected and the 'ring' appearance round small particles thus reduced." As a result a better microscope led scientists closer to the truth about cells.

Quoted in Giora Hon, Jutta Schickore, and Friedrich Steinle, eds., *Going Amiss in Experimental Research.* New York: Springer, 2009, p. 29.

acting as a sorter, of admitting certain substances and preventing the passage of others, and consequently of separating the elements of certain combinations in order to admit only a portion of them."[6] Raspail was thus the first person to systematically investigate the chemistry of a cell. He also noted how disease originates in the basic cell and spreads through cell division, a fundamental point in cell pathology. The main flaw in Raspail's work was his continued belief in the old theory of spontaneous generation. Nevertheless, many of his observations about cells were years ahead of their time.

Other French scientists did important work on cells. In 1809 a French botany professor named Charles-Francois Brisseau-Mirbel noted that all plants are made up of cells. That same year French naturalist Jean-Baptiste Lamarck published a book with an entire chapter devoted to cellular structure in plants. In 1824, years before German scientists popularized the idea, Henri Dutrochet declared that the cell is the fundamental unit of organization in life forms. Dutrochet also named and described the process of osmosis. That is how molecules of fluid—usually water—move through a cell's semipermeable membrane from an area of low concentration to one of higher concentration. In 1832 French scientist Barthélemy Dumortier described cell division in plants. Dumortier noticed how a middle line of partition formed between an original cell and a new cell, which resulted in division into two complete cells. Dumortier wrote that this process, called binary fission, "seems to us to provide a perfectly clear explanation of the origin and development of cells, which has hitherto remained unexplained."[7] These discoveries would not gain wider acceptance in the world until they were affirmed by German scientists in the following decades.

The Basic Unit of Life

In the 1830s Germany became the center for cell research. This was largely due to the availability of improved microscopes in Germany. In 1832 Joseph Jackson Lister, an English wine merchant and amateur in microscopy, invented a spaced system of lenses for microscopes. This system corrected a problem called chromatic aberration—a distortion that occurs when wavelengths of colored light are not on the same focal plane. Lister's microscope produced sharper images with greater magnification. It caused scientists to realize that the microscope was no longer a novelty but a reliable tool for research. A decade later Carl Zeiss started an optical company in Jena, a university town in Thuringia, Germany, dedicated to the manufacture of high-quality scientific instruments. Zeiss's microscopes, employing Lister's ideas, were the finest in the world but not widely distributed. With their cutting-edge instruments, German universities began to attract the greatest minds in the fields of botany and biology.

Several of the best young scientists were students of a professor at Berlin University named Johannes Peter Müller. Accomplished in the study of physiology—how living organisms function—Müller promoted the use of the microscope and chemical analysis in research. He also urged his students to combine the quest for facts with philosophical thinking—to think beyond the accepted truths of the time. In 1837 two of Müller's students, Matthias Schleiden and Theodor Schwann, were dining out in Berlin when their discussion turned to a recent discovery about plant cells. Schleiden, a botanist himself, noted that the Scottish botanist Robert Brown had found that various types of plant cells all had nuclei. This got Schwann, an animal physiologist, to thinking about similar structures in animal tissues. The next day Schwann and Schleiden examined a rod-shaped tissue called a notochord—the embryonic spinal cord in vertebrates—under the microscope. Indeed they saw that the cells of the notochord contained nuclei. Schleiden was inspired to examine a variety of plant tissues with the microscope, sketching the cells and nuclei of an orchid, a palm, and a cherry rice-flower. He affirmed in an article that cells and their nuclei are the fundamental building blocks of plants. Schwann found the same kind of structures in various animal tissues, from the pith of bird feathers to the aorta of a pig fetus. He suggested that all animal tissues are made of cells. More important, Schwann proposed that the cell is the basic unit of structure for all living organisms. He wrote in 1839, "It may be asserted that there is one universal principle of development for the elementary parts of organisms, however different, and that this principle is the formation of cells."[8] Schwann called his proposition the cell theory.

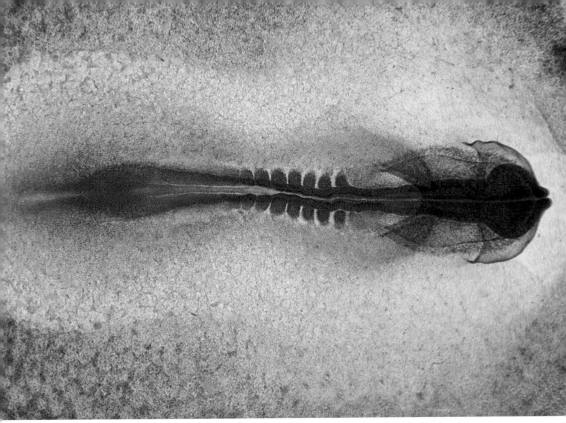

In the 1830s Matthias Schleiden and Theodor Schwann examined the notochord (embryonic spine) of vertebrates under a microscope and discovered that the tissue was made up of cells. Schwann, a physiologist, went on to propose that all living things were made up of cells.

Working in the lab of the influential Müller, Schleiden and Schwann soon found their ideas the talk of the scientific world. Müller himself contributed to their success by writing about cell theory in his *Handbook of Human Physiology*. "From the 1840s to the 1880s it was probably the most important physiology textbook in Europe," says Laura Otis, author of a book about the professor and his students. "Everyone read Müller."[9] Müller also employed cell theory in his own work on the cell structure of cancerous tumors, creating in the process a new branch of medical study. Cell research was spawning a period of upheaval in science, with new discoveries arriving at a rapid pace.

The Generation of Cells

Although Schleiden and Schwann played major roles in developing two major tenets of cell theory—that all living tissues are composed of cells and the cell is the basic unit of structure and function in life—their ideas on the third would soon be rejected. They believed, as did many of their colleagues, including their teacher, Müller, that living cells appeared and spread due to a kind of spontaneous generation called free cell formation. They differed on how this occurred. Schleiden suggested that new cells arose within old ones by crystallizing around a newly formed nucleus. Schwann declared that cells formed from some featureless material that surrounded existing cells. It was left to two of their fellow students to correct this final plank of the original cell theory.

In 1852 Robert Remak, once an unpaid research assistant in Müller's laboratory and now a practicing physician, published his ideas on the origins of new cells. Remak insisted that Schleiden and Schwann's ideas about free cell formation were wrong, as were all theories related to spontaneous generation. Instead Remak declared that new animal cells were produced by binary fission, or cell division. He based his idea on a decade of work observing embryos and studying the question of how new cells appeared. Remak's view gained acceptance through the efforts of another former Müller student, Rudolf Virchow. In lectures and a successful 1858 book, *Cellularpathologie*, Virchow detailed his ideas about cells and cell division. Although Virchow's conclusions were almost identical to those of Remak, he failed to acknowledge his colleague's work. Virchow also became known for the Latin phrase *omnis cellula e cellula*, which he presented as his own but which had originated with the French scientist Raspail years before. In the field of cell biology, the self-promoters and colorful personalities tended to get most of the credit. At any rate Remak and Virchow added the last tenet to classical cell theory: All cells come from preexisting cells.

Pasteur Disproves Spontaneous Generation of Cells

Despite the work of Remak and Virchow, many scientists refused to give up their belief in spontaneous generation. Finally in 1859 a young French chemist named Louis Pasteur performed an experiment to settle the issue. Pasteur prepared a soup-like broth and divided it equally between two flasks, one with a straight neck and the other with a neck bent into an S shape. Next, Pasteur boiled the broth

Cells and Disease

For centuries disease was often attributed to demons or evil spirits or to special punishment sent by the gods. Another explanation for disease was contagion—the idea that disease was always passed on simply by physical contact. As European cities grew, the causes of disease were thought to be in miasmas—noxious atmospheres—which were associated with bad smells, airborne particles of rotting plants and animals, and swamps or fetid waters. Ignorance about the true causes of disease allowed epidemics of plague, typhus, cholera, smallpox, and influenza to rage unchecked.

Beginning in the 1860s scientists found the cellular cause of many diseases: single-celled microorganisms, or germs. Germs had been identified two centuries before, and were viewed as a kind of seed. In fact, the word *germ* comes from a Latin verb meaning "to sprout." French chemist Louis Pasteur found that germs caused fermentation in liquids such as beer. He also discovered that killing germs in milk by heating the liquid—a process, named after him, called pasteurization—could prevent milk from curdling. It was a small step for Pasteur to propose that multiplying germs caused not only decay in bodies but also disease. Pasteur used germs to create vaccines—weakened forms of germs that when introduced into a body helped it develop immunity to disease from those germs. Robert Koch, a German physician and scientist, discovered that certain bacteria cause specific diseases, including anthrax, cholera, and tuberculosis. Pasteur and Koch's breakthroughs helped save lives and did away with many superstitions about the causes of disease.

in both flasks to kill any living matter in the liquid. He then left each flask with its sterile broth to sit at room temperature, open to the air. After several weeks the broth in the straight-neck flask had turned cloudy and discolored, while the broth in the S-curve flask was unchanged. Pasteur decided that germs in the air had fallen down the straight-neck flask unobstructed in order to contaminate the broth. Germs in the S-curve flask, however, had been trapped in the curved neck. This prevented the germs from reaching the broth and left it

Louis Pasteur performed experiments that disproved the theory that new cells form through spontaneous generation. Pasteur also established that many diseases are caused by the presence and activity of germs.

unchanged. Pasteur declared that if spontaneous generation were real, germs in the S-curve flask would have appeared regardless and infected the broth. The fact that they did not supported the idea that germs—living microorganisms—come only from other germs.

Pasteur's famous experiment not only affirmed an important tenet of cell theory but also established the scientific method for testing a hypothesis, or proposal. He began with a hypothesis, conducted a careful step-by-step experiment to test it, and compared the results to his original observation. This method would become the standard approach for scientific experiments of all kinds. Pasteur went on to do other groundbreaking work related to cell theory. For example, he established that many diseases are caused by the presence and activity of germs. Over time this theory revolutionized the practice of medicine.

Original Cell Theory and Society

By proving that cells do not appear by spontaneous generation but instead arise only from other cells, Pasteur added to the nineteenth-century idea that all of nature is unified. Scientists began to realize that each tiny cell is a link in the endless chain of life. Ernst Haeckel, another of Müller's brilliant students, insisted on this interconnectedness in nature. He and many other scientists and thinkers touted nature as a creative force and no longer saw a place in the universe for the traditional God. Haeckel called his approach to nature *monism* and viewed the universe as an enormously complex machine that runs on fixed and unchangeable laws. Haeckel's ideas, inspired by Charles Darwin's theory of evolution, became popular by the end of the nineteenth century. Materialism—the doctrine that all existence can be explained in terms of matter and natural laws—rose to challenge traditional religion in every corner of society. Geologists declared that Earth is much older than the biblical account of creation allows. Popular books such as Andrew White's *The Warfare of Science with Theology in Christendom* argued that religion had hindered scientific progress for centuries.

Discoveries about cells also were linked to ideas about government. "The cell theory held sociopolitical messages," notes science writer Jan Sapp. "Like the theory of evolution, it was sometimes portrayed as a description for our social world for how to best define the individual and organize the state."[10] Leading nineteenth-century biologists often pushed the analogy between cells and citizens. The politically liberal Theodor Schwann insisted on cell theory as an example of the importance of individuals: nutrition and growth resided in individual cells, not in the organism as a whole. Rudolf Virchow compared the organism to "a society of living cells, a tiny well-ordered state."[11] These ideas spread throughout European society. The discovery of cells and their relation to life changed the way many people looked at the world.

CHAPTER TWO

Modern Cell Theory

Biologist Lynn Margulis was passionate about cells, particularly lowly single-celled bacteria. A Distinguished Professor of Geosciences at the University of Massachusetts from 1997 up to her death in 2011, Margulis was not afraid to challenge the commonly held ideas of her day. In the late 1960s she proposed a theory that contradicted an important point of evolution science. She suggested that complex cells such as those that make up the human body evolved from simple bacteria. According to her theory, bacteria joined together billions of years ago, early in the development of life on Earth. They formed symbiotic relationships, in which organisms that mutually benefit each other unite, and were able to reproduce. Margulis believed that bacteria partnerships evolved into at least two of the major organelles, or parts of the cell. This meant that evolution actually began long before the major theories allowed. At first, prominent scientists scoffed at the idea, but today it is an accepted part of the evolution story. "She talked a lot about the importance of micro-organisms," says Margulis's daughter, Jennifer. "She called herself a spokesperson for the microcosm."[12] Margulis's work is an example of how modern cell theory continues to impact many branches of science today.

From Classical to Modern Cell Theory

Modern cell theory builds on classical cell theory, which established that all living things are made of cells, that cells are the basic units of structure and function in living things, and all cells come from preexisting cells. Due to the limitations of their microscopes, mid-nineteenth-century scientists could do little more than describe the spherical nucleus of a cell and the protoplasm, or semifluid substance, within a cell. But just as improvements in the microscope led to the formation of the classical cell theory in the 1830s and 1840s, further innovations in the late nineteenth century and in the twentieth century enabled researchers to identify previously unseen parts of cells. Like Lynn Margulis, many of the scientists who have contributed to modern cell theory have studied the organelles inside a cell and their various roles in the cell's structure and function. Scientists learned about the chemical processes in cells that make them integral to how living things reproduce, pass on characteristics, and make and store energy. They learned how different cells are configured to perform specific functions. They found relationships between cells of widely varying organisms. Each new discovery affirmed the cell's central role in sustaining life. Modern cell theory reveals the cell to be an amazing microscopic factory, warehouse, power plant, clinic, and library all rolled into one.

Cells and Reproduction

A key line of modern cell research is the cell's role in the process of reproduction. The stage was set by discoveries in the nineteenth century. As early as 1840 Swiss anatomist Albrecht Koelliker recognized that the sperm and egg were modified cells. In the mid-1870s the stages of cell division were described, first for flatworms and later for various plants. In 1879 German scientist Walther Flemming first observed chromosomes in the dividing cells of salamander larvae. Chromosomes are the structures in cells that contain and transfer information about the heredity of

an organism, although Flemming was mostly unaware of this. Using what was still a rather primitive light microscope, Flemming was able to see tiny, faint threads within the nuclei that appeared to be

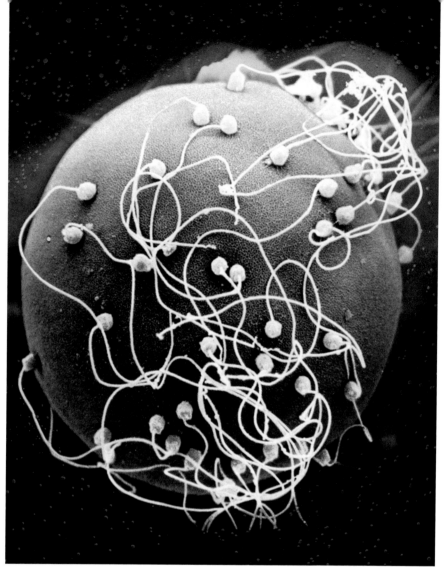

The nineteenth century witnessed the development of reproductive cell theory. Early observations proved that sperm and egg cells (shown here) were distinct and that the nuclei and their chromosomes are involved in cellular division during embryonic development.

dividing lengthwise. Flemming called this division *mitosis*, from the Greek word meaning "thread." As science writer Neidhard Paweletz explains, Flemming was amazingly perceptive about the beautifully logical process of cell division:

> Flemming described the processes in the nucleus as we know them today, and he made a distinction between the "progressive" and "regressive" phases of cell division. The progressive

phase started with the appearance of the threads in the nucleus of the mother cell and continued as far as the arrangement of the threads in the center of the cell. The regressive phase, by contrast, began with the separation of the threads into two groups and ended with the reappearance of the daughter nuclei.[13]

In 1883 Belgian scientist Edouard van Beneden added to Flemming's discovery of chromosomes. Van Beneden discovered the process of meiosis, through which the number of chromosomes in a cell nucleus is halved during the formation of reproductive cells. (In 1876 German biologist Oscar Hertwig had also observed meiosis in sea urchin eggs but had not fully perceived the movement of chromosomes.) Van Beneden proposed that an egg and a sperm, which are mature gamete (reproductive) cells, each containing half the number of chromosomes found in somatic (nonreproductive) cells, fuse to form a single cell called a zygote. This enables the zygote to have the proper number of chromosomes. The fusion of the sperm and egg to produce a single new cell is called fertilization.

The 1880s saw other breakthroughs in the study of cell division. The cell nucleus was identified as the genetic center of the cell. Chromatin, the substance of chromosomes, was proposed as the main agent of heredity. A remarkable number of discoveries about chromosomes and cell division were made in a period of about forty years. They helped shape and connect several areas of scientific study, including cytology (the study of cells), embryology (the study of embryos), biochemistry, and evolution.

> **WORDS IN CONTEXT**
>
> *mitosis*
> The process by which a cell nucleus divides into two identical sets of chromosomes.

Chromosomes and Cell Division

The next great figure in the study of cells and chromosomes was American biologist Edmund B. Wilson. Wilson attended Yale University in the 1870s, where he first learned about evolution and heredity, sparking an interest that lasted his entire life. In 1891, before accepting a professorship at Columbia University in New York,

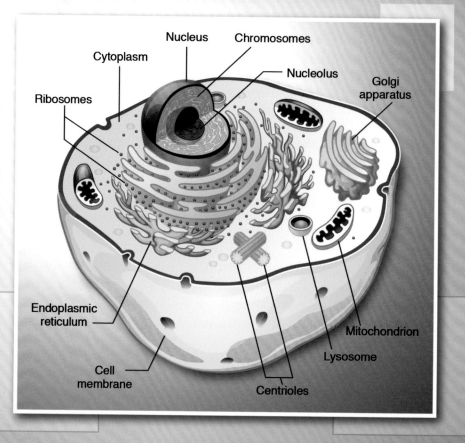

Source: Alexandra Villa-Forte, "Cells," Merck Manual. www.merckmanuals.com.

Wilson traveled to Europe, where he worked with German biologist Theodor Boveri in Munich and embryologist Hans Driesch in Naples, Italy. A budding friendship with Boveri convinced Wilson to focus on cell biology and experiments with embryos. Back in the United States Wilson threw himself into research on cell division. He affirmed Boveri's conclusion about the chromosomes' role in heredity, seeing heredity as basically a chemical process inside the cell. "And thus we reach the remarkable conclusion," Wilson wrote in 1896, "that inheritance may perhaps be affected by the physical transmission of a particular chemical compound from parent to offspring."[14] This would become a key tenet of modern cell theory.

In the 1890s, with cell theory widely accepted, researchers sought to connect biology with Darwin's theory of evolution. They asked why the embryos of vastly different species had such similar characteristics. They marveled at the fact that people, porpoises, horses, and bats all have very similar bone structures in their forelimbs. German biologist Ernst Haeckel proposed that individual life forms pass through the same stages in their development as species did in their past evolution—from a simple cell to more complex cells to wormlike or fishlike forms, and so forth. They climbed their own family tree, as evolutionary biologist Stephen Jay Gould often said. Wilson refuted Haeckel's idea about how life forms develop with his own groundbreaking work on cell lineage—the closest studies yet of cell division. Wilson and his colleagues carefully traced the egg as it divided into two cells, then four, then eight, and on to its further development. Wilson concluded that cell division was a product of both heredity and influence from other surrounding cells. Basically this is the modern view of how a cell develops.

In addition to his laboratory work, Wilson excelled as a teacher and writer. In 1895 he teamed with a Columbia University photographer to produce a book containing the first published photos of cell division, including detailed images of chromosomes dividing. A year later Wilson published *The Cell in Inheritance and Development*, dedicated to his friend Theodor Boveri. For years it remained the key text introducing students to cell biology. Wilson had a knack for presenting difficult concepts with force and clarity, as in this description of the common descent of cells: "Now, if the cells of the body always arise by the division of pre-existing cells, all must be traceable back to the fertilized egg-cell as their common ancestor. Such is, in fact, the case in every plant and animal whose development is accurately known."[15]

> **WORDS IN CONTEXT**
>
> *meiosis*
> The process by which the number of chromosomes in a cell nucleus is halved during the formation of reproductive cells.

Mendel, Boveri, and Inheritance

In 1900 Wilson and other cell biologists were startled by an amazing rediscovery. That year three of the world's top botanists, including Dutch researcher Hugo de Vries, independently found papers on heredity written by Gregor Mendel in 1866. Mendel, a German-speaking friar from Moravia (Czech Republic), had set down many of the rules of heredity through his experiments on growing pea plants. Mendel had noted that various pea plants had dominant and recessive *factors*—what would later be called genes. In light of the discovery of chromosomes and their effect on inheritance, Mendel's laws now had a solid basis in biology.

In 1902 Wilson's friend Boveri confirmed that chromosomes include hereditary material. In effect he placed Mendel's work on a cellular level. In an experiment with the double fertilized eggs of sea urchins, Boveri found that each chromosome in a cell carries a different set of genetic elements. The lengthwise splitting of the chromosomes during cell division ensures that these elements are divided equally between the parent cell and daughter cell. As Boveri wrote in 1903, the probability is "extraordinarily high that the characters dealt with in Mendelian experiments are truly connected to specific chromosomes."[16] In other words, Boveri had traced the transmission of genetic characteristics, as described in Mendel's studies, directly to chromosomes. Scientists were at first divided over the value of Boveri's chromosome theory. One skeptic was American embryologist Thomas Hunt Morgan. However, it was Morgan who in 1910 proved the theory to be correct. His experiments on the sex and eye color of fruit flies established beyond a doubt that genes are located on chromosomes. This also marked the beginning of the field of genetics.

Cell Theory and Eugenics

In the early twentieth century, ideas about genetic inheritance from cell theory and evolution theory were used to support the controversial pseudoscience of eugenics. Charles Darwin's half-cousin Francis Galton had coined the word *eugenics* in 1883 from Greek word parts meaning "well born." Two decades later new findings about the laws of heredity and the workings of chromosomes were linked to the Darwinian notion of survival of the fittest. Eugenicists sought to improve the racial stock of the human species through selective breeding and sterilization of those deemed mentally or physically inferior. Many colleges in the United States and Europe provided classes on

What's in a Name?

The word *cell* to denote the structural units of living things was first used by English scientist Robert Hooke in the 1660s. The term came into general usage only at the beginning of the nineteenth century. A cell was thought to be a little chamber containing some kind of fluid or glutinous material. The important part of the unit, to the pioneering scientists of cell theory, was the cell wall.

By the mid-1800s microscopes with higher magnifications and less distortion changed this view. The ability to see cells more clearly shifted the focus to the contents of the cell. In 1840 Czech scientist Johannes Purkinje referred to the living substance within the cell as protoplasm. This word came from the term *protoplast*, which means "the first formed" and was used by theologians as a name for Adam, the biblical first human. As microscopes continued to improve, scientists realized that the cell was not a rigid compartment of material. It was thought of instead as a mass of protoplasm containing a nucleus. The word *cell* suggested a metaphor that no longer applied. However, replacement terms such as *bioblast* and *energid* never caught on. As American cell biologist Edmund B. Wilson admitted in 1896, "Nothing could be less appropriate than to call such a body a 'cell'; yet the word has become so firmly established that every effort to replace it by a better has failed, and it probably must be accepted as part of the established nomenclature of science."

Edmund Beecher Wilson, *The Cell in Development and Inheritance*. New York: Macmillan, 1896, p. 19.

eugenics, and politicians from both the left and right supported it as a forward-looking policy.

Eugenics was also at issue in the 1927 Supreme Court case *Buck v. Bell.* The Court surprisingly upheld a Virginia law authorizing the forced sterilization of so-called mental defectives. In his opinion Justice Oliver Wendell Holmes thundered, "It is better for all the world if, instead of waiting to execute degenerate offspring for crime or to let them starve for their imbecility, society can prevent those who are manifestly unfit from continuing their kind. . . . Three generations of imbeciles are enough."[17] After this infamous case, eugenics as a movement began to decline in the United States. It was further discredited by Adolf Hitler's attempt to create a master race through murderous racial policies in 1930s Nazi Germany. The rise of eugenics in the West demonstrates how scientific ideas such as cell theory and genetic inheritance can be twisted and abused for dubious social ends.

Impact of the Electron Microscope

Genetics mostly focused on one part of the cell—the nucleus, and particularly the chromosomes within the nucleus. In the nineteenth century, scientists had identified other parts of the cell in sketchy fashion, being limited by what current microscopes could achieve using visible light. For example, in 1857 Swiss scientist Albrecht Koelliker noted granule-like structures in muscle cells. Thirty years later German researcher Richard Altman used a dye technique to study the granules. Altman proposed that the granules are vital to cell activity. In 1898 another German scientist, Carl Benda, named these granules mitochondria. In succeeding decades mitochondria were discovered to have several functions, including their role as the power plant of the cell, transforming food into chemical energy. The observation that this flow of energy occurs within cells would become another important tenet of modern cell theory. Also in 1898 Italian neurologist Camillo Golgi found a special method, called the black reaction, for staining nerve cells to produce black outlines. Golgi used the technique to isolate a delicate network within the cell that transmits information between cells. This network became known as the Golgi apparatus.

WORDS IN CONTEXT

mitochondria

Tiny structures inside a cell that convert food into chemical energy to power the cell.

Such breakthroughs in knowledge about cell structure received a tremendous boost in 1931 with the invention of the electron microscope. German engineer Ernst Ruska realized that ordinary microscopes were limited by the longer wavelengths of light used to view tiny specimens. Working with his mentor, Max Knoll, Ruska built an electron lens— an electromagnet capable of focusing a beam of electrons as if it were a beam of light. Two years later he produced a much more powerful design. The device passed a stream of electrons through a thin slice of a specimen. The electrons were then deflected onto photographic film or were projected onto a fluorescent screen as a highly magnified image. The technique gave the electron microscope much greater resolution

Invented in 1931, the electron microscope uses the incredibly short wavelength of electron beams to capture images of even the tiniest of objects in amazing detail. The resolution of this electron micrograph of the head of a black fly is about five thousand times greater than that offered by the best optical (i.e., visible light) microscopes.

Boveri and the Cellular Basis of Cancer

At the beginning of the twentieth century, little was known about how deadly cancerous tumors appeared and spread. Effective cancer research was still decades away. Yet in 1914 cell biologist Theodor Boveri published, in his native German, an article on cancer that seemed to see into the future. In "Concerning the Origin of Malignant Tumours," Boveri drew on his groundbreaking work on cells and chromosomes to theorize about the causes of cancer. He insisted that cancer is a cellular problem and that it originates with a single cell. He further proposed that chromosomes in a cancer cell are somehow defective, causing it to proliferate rapidly. As Boveri wrote,

> The essential elements of my point of view may therefore be summarized as follows. A malignant tumor cell is a cell with a specific defect; it has lost properties that a normal tissue cell retains. . . . A cell in this drastically altered state reacts differently to its environment, and it is possible that this alone might account for its tendency to multiply without restraint.

Boveri went on to suggest that cancer cells lacked key cell attributes—actually genes—that should suppress the formation of tumors. He thus thought inheritance might play a key role in susceptibility to cancer. Boveri's proposals about cancer were remarkably accurate. Although he died a year after the article appeared, his insights were not lost. His wife, Marcella, herself an accomplished biologist, translated the great article into English and brought it to a wider audience.

Theodor Boveri, "Concerning the Origin of Malignant Tumours," translated and annotated by Henry Harris, *Journal of Cell Science, 2008.* http://jcs.biologists.org.

than any previous microscope could achieve. The new device allowed scientists to study things too tiny to be seen with light microscopes. It took fifty years, but in 1986 Ernst Ruska finally received the Nobel Prize for his invention. The Nobel committee called the electron microscope one of the twentieth century's most important innovations.

Studying Cell Structure and Function

In 1945 American cell biologist Keith Porter used an electron microscope to produce the first image of a complete tissue cell. Porter published his micrograph (photograph made through a microscope) in the *Journal of Experimental Medicine* to great fanfare. Porter saw that the new microscope called for radically different methods of preparing a specimen for study. To be most useful, the cells had to be incredibly thin and dry. Porter's success at producing images of cells revitalized the field of cell biology, which had reached the limits attainable with light microscopes. Porter's breakthrough united the study of cell structure and function, creating whole new areas for research. Porter himself was the first to identify several parts of the cell, including the endoplasmic reticulum, cilia, and microtubules. As microbiologist Peter Satir wrote in 1997, "To many, [Porter] was the father of cell biology, who helped establish many of the enduring institutions and ideas in the field."[18]

Steady improvements to the electron microscope, especially the scanning electron microscope in 1965, have allowed scientists to explore the interior world of the cell with remarkable detail and clarity. Later versions have magnified objects more than a million times their actual size, enabling scientists to study proteins, viruses, and even atoms within cell parts.

Modern Cell Theory

Discoveries in the later nineteenth and twentieth centuries added ideas to classic cell theory. Scientists found that cells contain information about heredity and pass it on from cell to cell during the process of cell division. They noted that the production and flow of energy takes place within cells. They affirmed that all cells are basically the same in chemical composition. These tenets make up modern cell theory and formed the basis for the explosion in research on cell biology beginning in the 1950s. As biologists learned to grow, maintain, scrutinize, and experiment with cells outside of living organisms, they began to unlock deeper mysteries about the cell. From the discovery of the many uses for stem cells to the manipulation of DNA, this work has transformed modern life.

CHAPTER THREE

Using Cell Research to Solve Crimes

On April 9, 1974, police found the body of seventeen-year-old Mary Jayne Jones in a remote Iowa farmhouse. Jones, a waitress at a drive-in in Ottumwa, had been beaten, sexually assaulted, and shot in the face and heart with a high-powered rifle at close range. Despite strong suspicions about the murderer's identity, investigators lacked evidence for an arrest. Items from the crime scene, including a blood-soaked blanket, were placed into storage in hopes that new facts would be discovered.

Ten years after the murder, a young scientist in Leicester, England, made an important discovery that would eventually enable police to reopen the case. The discovery was the use of DNA "fingerprinting" to solve crimes. The method rapidly went from novelty to serious crime-fighting tool around the world. Nevertheless, it was not until 2010 that a special cold case unit in Iowa took another look at Jones's murder. Officers plugged a DNA sample taken from the bloody blanket into a national database of samples from convicted felons and got a match. The sample pointed to Robert Gene Pilcher, the Ottumwa man whom police had originally suspected. Pilcher was a cousin of the farmhouse's owner and was known to use the residence. In the years since the murder he had been arrested many times, ensuring that his DNA was in the national database. The cellular evidence helped send Pilcher to prison four decades after the original crime. "For a case this old, it's difficult to have enough evidence to prove the case to a jury," says Wapello County attorney Gary Oldenburger. "This family has been waiting for 40 years for a resolution."[19]

Isolating the DNA Molecule

Pilcher's conviction and those of many other criminals was made possible by a breakthrough in cell research that occurred in the mid-1900s. This was the discovery of the molecule that contains all of a person's genetic information: DNA. Swiss chemist Friedrich Miescher was actually the first to identify DNA—or what he called nuclein—in 1869 while studying the proteins in pus-filled bandages at a surgical clinic. However, Miescher's discovery was barely known for fifty years. In 1928 Frederick Griffith, a British medical officer, made a discovery that drew more attention. In an experiment with mice and cells infected with pneumonia virus, Griffith concluded that a chemical

Forensic units scour crime scenes for hair, blood, and other materials containing human DNA to collect as evidence. These samples can be used to identify potential perpetrators by matching the DNA against that of suspects or running it through a national database of known felons.

component in cells could change nonvirulent cells into a different, lethal form. This was accomplished by what Griffith called a "transforming principle"—which was actually DNA.

Canadian-born American researcher Oswald Avery took Griffith's experiment a step further. In 1944 Avery and two colleagues at the Rockefeller Institute in New York set out to test how one type of pneumonia could change into another in live mice. They were able to systematically remove certain organic compounds from the streptococcus bacteria. Then they tested each resulting strain to see if it caused the transformation as in Griffith's study. Only when the bacteria were treated with an enzyme that removed the DNA did the strain stop transforming to the lethal kind. Avery and his team concluded that DNA was the carrier of genes in cells.

Avery published his team's results in the *New England Journal of Medicine*. Avery's claims were controversial, as many scientists insisted that such a powerful and complex transformation had to be the work of proteins with a much more complex structure than DNA. Nonetheless, American biologist James Watson, who was soon to affirm Avery's findings, knew the value of his predecessor's work. "Both Francis [Crick] and I had no doubts that DNA was the gene," Watson said years afterward. "But most people did. And again, you might say, 'Why didn't Avery get the Nobel Prize?' Because most people didn't take him seriously. Because you could always argue that his observations were limited to bacteria, or that . . . the DNA was just scaffolding."[20]

Other contributions had come from Russian biochemist Phoebus Levene and Austrian biochemist Erwin Chargaff. Levene had discovered the order of the chemical components of DNA and had determined how these components combine to form units called nucleotides. Chargaff formulated rules about the chemical composition of DNA that proved basically correct. As Chargaff said of his research, "Avery gave us the first text of a new language, or rather he showed us where to look for it. I resolved to search for this text."[21]

A Model of DNA

In 1953 Watson and his colleague, British physicist Francis Crick, made an extraordinary breakthrough regarding this new language by describing the structure of the DNA molecule. Watson and Crick employed cardboard cutouts that represented the chemical components of DNA to fashion models of the molecule. They kept shifting the parts in different arrangements, much like solving a three-dimensional puzzle. Finally, with a hint from Jerry Donohue,

Touch DNA

Today the testing of DNA in human biological fluids such as blood, semen, and saliva is an everyday occurrence in crime labs worldwide. One example of improved technology is Touch DNA, which involves genetic material recovered from skin cells. This DNA is left behind when someone touches or comes into contact with clothing, a weapon, a utensil, or other objects. Of the approximately 400,000 skin cells that a person sheds each day, it is the deeper skin cells that offer the most helpful DNA profile. These cells are usually found at a crime scene when force or a struggle is involved. They can be recovered from a weapon or from the victim's clothes. They might even be found under the victim's fingernails. Investigators can lift these skin cells with tape, swab them with a Q-tip, or scrape them from objects or clothing. As few as five to twenty skin cells are sufficient to produce a Touch DNA sample.

Touch DNA has been used to convict murderers, exonerate the wrongly accused, and reopen cold cases from years ago. Nevertheless Touch DNA remains controversial. The technique has become so routine that many police departments use it to investigate not just murders and assaults but lesser property crimes. They collect DNA samples and add them to enormous databases. "Some people have called it a lifetime of genetic surveillance," says Michael Risher of the American Civil Liberties Union. "We don't believe that innocent Americans should have their genetic blueprint in a giant database."

Quoted in Forensic Genetics Policy Initiative, "The DNA Difference: Debate over Crime-Fighting Tool," December 30, 2013. http://dnapolicyinitiative.org.

an American chemist, they hit upon the correct structure of hydro-gen bonds and chemical bases. They proposed that the DNA mol-ecule is shaped like a double helix—twin strands that wind around each other like a spiraling ladder. This structure, with its complex repeating "codes" of nucleic acids, is crucial to the way in which cells store and pass on genetic information. The structure also sug-

James Watson (left) and Francis Crick (right) pose near a model of a partial DNA molecule. The intertwined strands of nucleotides make up the double helix structure, and each carries the same genetic pattern so that they can separate and replicate with the help of cellular enzymes.

gests how form follows function. The double helix form of the DNA molecule enables it to replicate itself by unwinding into two single strands. On the day of their discovery, Watson recalls, Crick burst into a pub near Cambridge University and announced to the crowd in his booming voice, "We have discovered the secret of life."[22]

Crick's boast was not far from the truth. DNA is basically the chemical code of life. It explains how a brain cell "knows" how to help produce thoughts and sensations. It explains how various cells in the body "know" how to grow, reproduce, specialize, and fend off disease. The significance of Watson and Crick's announcement was recognized at once. Editorialists, philosophers, and social critics weighed in on the far-reaching effects of this discovery. Some predicted great improvements in medicine and the treatment of disease. Others focused on potential dangers. "[It] will lead to methods of tampering with life," declared Arne Tiselius, president of the Nobel Foundation, "of creating new diseases, of controlling minds, of influencing heredity—even, perhaps, in certain desired directions."[23] Religious leaders were divided between those who thought DNA revealed the complexity and beauty of God's creation and others who feared that the discovery would fuel more arguments against God's existence. The only point of agreement among critics and commentators was that the new knowledge about DNA would change modern society forever.

> **WORDS IN CONTEXT**
>
> *double helix*
> A form like a spiraling ladder.

Alec Jeffreys and the Genetic Fingerprint

In the decades following Watson and Crick's discovery, research into DNA spread rapidly to many fields, from medicine to agriculture. One unexpected application was devised by Alec Jeffreys, a professor of genetics at the University of Leicester in Great Britain. Beginning in 1977 Jeffreys worked with part-time lab technicians to study genes and their inherited variations. While testing the DNA of his assistants and some of their family members, he discovered that one of the technicians had an inherited DNA sequence variation.

A variation occurs when a nucleotide, which is one of the building blocks of DNA, differs between members of a species or between the chromosome pairs in a person. Jeffreys worked on mapping genes, seeking highly variable DNA. After several failed approaches, he began to study how genetic variations evolved. The breakthrough came when Jeffreys focused on so-called minisatellites—specific segments in DNA that have a high rate of mutation and a high rate of diversity in the population. In other words, he looked at the 1 percent of DNA sequences that make an individual's DNA different from that of all other people. As Jeffreys says, "We had found a way of detecting lots of minisatellites variable enough to provide extremely informative genetic markers."[24]

One morning in September 1984, Jeffreys experienced his "eureka" moment of discovery. Examining a developed X-ray blot of DNA from one of his assistants and her parents, he at first saw only a complicated mess. Then he began to see patterns, and he realized that the amazingly varied patterns of DNA he was finding constituted the world's first genetic fingerprint. It was clear that certain parts of the genetic makeup of each person's cells are unique and, with scientific expertise, can be distinguished from those of every other person except an identical twin. Jeffreys also found that every person's DNA is a composite of the patterns in his or her parents' DNA.

Jeffreys quickly saw possibilities for his discovery. "Not only have we got access to these really good genetic markers for mapping genes and chromosomes and so on, but we've got a method of biological identification," he recalls. "And so [I] immediately started thinking of forensics, you know, could you use this in criminal investigations, you know, could DNA survive in crime scene samples? Could you match samples with suspects and so on?"[25]

Uses for DNA Profiling

Jeffreys had established the basis for what would be called DNA profiling. Besides forensics, he and his assistants thought of other possible uses for the technique. These included testing the paternity of a child

The Supreme Court Weighs in on DNA Profiling

In 2013 the debate over DNA profiling reached the US Supreme Court. At issue was whether the collection of a DNA sample from a person in police custody is an unreasonable search and seizure under the Fourth Amendment to the Constitution. In *Maryland v. King*, the Court heard the case of Alonzo Jay King Jr., who was arrested in Maryland in 2009 for assault. While being booked, King was required to submit to a cheek swab to collect DNA from cells in his cheek lining. King's DNA sample was matched to DNA from an unsolved 2003 rape. He was charged with that crime and subsequently convicted of rape. The Maryland Court of Appeals set aside his conviction on the grounds that the Maryland DNA Collection Act authorizing DNA collection from felony arrestees was unconstitutional. The state of Maryland appealed the case to the Supreme Court.

In oral arguments, Maryland's attorney general Katherine Winfree insisted the procedure was routine—"the fingerprinting of the 21st century, but it's better." She noted that it helped solve many rapes and murders. But some of the justices were skeptical. "Under your theory, there's no reason you couldn't undertake this procedure with respect to anybody pulled over for a traffic violation," said Chief Justice John Roberts. In the end, the Court ruled 5–4 that DNA collection, like fingerprinting and photographing, is a legitimate booking procedure for persons arrested for a serious offense. The dissenting opinions, however, were scathing—a hint that the issue may arise again.

Quoted in Robert Barnes, "Supreme Court Weighs DNA 'Fingerprinting,'" *Washington Post*, February 26, 2013. www.washingtonpost.com.

(to determine the child's biological father), finding out if siblings are actually related by blood, and determining whether newborn twins are identical or fraternal. Jeffreys also realized DNA testing could be used to establish proof of relatedness for immigrants seeking visas to join their families. Indeed the first case pursued by Jeffreys and his lab in 1985 helped to reunite a young boy from Ghana with his family in England. "If our first case had been forensic [i.e., a criminal case] I believe it would have been challenged and the process may well have been damaged in the courts," says Jeffreys. "But our first application was to save a young boy and it captured the public's sympathy and imagination. It was science helping an individual challenge authority. Of all the cases this is the one that means most to me."[26]

In 1985 Jeffreys and the Leicester University lab took their first criminal case. In the nearby village of Narborough two young girls had been raped and murdered three years apart. Richard Buckland, a teenaged suspect in police custody, confessed to the second crime, but detectives had doubts about his guilt. Police enlisted Jeffreys to compare semen samples from both murders against Buckland's blood sample. DNA tests proved that the same person had committed both crimes—and it was not Buckland.

At this point police employed the first so-called DNA dragnet, testing a total of 4,582 men in three nearby towns against the killer's type A blood. The 10 percent with that blood type were then given Jeffreys's DNA profiling test. When no match was found, the case seemed to be in limbo. Months later, however, detectives learned that a local baker named Colin Pitchfork had paid a friend to submit his own blood in place of Pitchfork's. Jeffreys' test of Pitchfork's blood against the crime scene samples produced a perfect match. In 1987 Pitchfork pled guilty to both murders and was sentenced to life in prison. He was the world's first person to be identified, arrested, and prosecuted with the use of DNA evidence.

Expansion of DNA Profiling

Publicity about Pitchfork's conviction opened the floodgates for requests for DNA tests at the Leicester University lab, according to Jeffreys. DNA profiling as an investigative technique spread to law enforcement agencies around the world. It was used to convict murderers, exonerate those wrongly accused, and occasionally reopen cases and bring justice to those who had been imprisoned for crimes they did not commit. Further breakthroughs in the early 1990s made

DNA testing methods more sensitive and required smaller samples. In 1995 the Forensic Science Service started a national DNA database in the United Kingdom, and three years later the FBI in the United States launched its own DNA database. The FBI database compiles DNA samples of convicted offenders, subjects in custody and facing federal charges, and non–US citizens detained under federal authority. Commercial laboratories specializing in DNA profiling sprang up in many cities. On a local level DNA profiling played a large part in such celebrated cases as the O.J. Simpson murder trial in Los Angeles in 1995 and the investigation of the 1996 murder of six-year-old

Blood found near the murder victims and submitted as evidence in the 1995 trial of suspect O.J. Simpson was found to contain Simpson's genetic markers. However, Simpson's defense attorneys argued that the collection methods were sloppy and that contamination ruined the DNA evidence.

JonBenét Ramsey in Boulder, Colorado. In the Ramsey case DNA testing was used to clear members of the girl's family from suspicion. More recently forensic scientists have developed new techniques such as Touch DNA or Contact Trace DNA to test genetic material in skin cells gathered at crime scenes. In 2008 this method was used to exonerate Tim Masters, who had been convicted of a 1987 murder that took place in Fort Collins, Colorado, when Masters was fifteen. Masters had served nine years of a life sentence when he was finally freed. A lawsuit filed against the authorities in Larimer County, Colorado, resulted in Masters receiving $4.1 million in damages.

Lawyers, law enforcement officials, and spokespersons for women's rights groups have pointed out that DNA profiling has been particularly helpful in solving crimes against women. As attorney Katie Lachter explains, "Ninety percent of the victims of crimes involving DNA identification are . . . women. The tests are most useful in sex crimes, traditionally the toughest to solve and among the most under-reported. . . . DNA has made it a lot harder for violent offenders to prey on women with impunity."[27]

Controversy and Privacy Issues

The overall success of DNA profiling has led some politicians and law enforcement officials to call for national DNA databases containing samples from every citizen. Such suggestions are cause for alarm among concerned social critics. Many point to problems with DNA profiling and vast databases of genetic material. For example, defense attorneys have repeatedly insisted that DNA evidence is not nearly as reliable as prosecutors claim and that it can lead to the conviction of innocent people. One of the main objections is that DNA samples can be contaminated due to sloppy police procedures or faulty laboratory work. In the O.J. Simpson murder trial, defense attorney Barry C. Scheck cast doubt on how DNA evidence was collected and handled, and he also claimed that as many as 1 to 4 percent of DNA matches found in laboratories were incorrect (a statistic many labs disputed). Attorneys also stress that DNA evidence can be planted at a crime scene. Other critics point out that persons in certain isolated groups or tightly knit immigrant communities can be so genetically similar that a DNA match becomes more likely for samples drawn from within the group. They also say DNA profiling offers only statistical probability, not certainty. As a safeguard against mistakes, some legal experts have suggested sample splitting, or sending samples to two different forensic laboratories for testing. Some have proposed that DNA laboratories undergo tests of their own proficiency so juries can evaluate their error rates.

DNA profiling has also led to concerns about privacy and civil liberties. One main complaint is that DNA databases designed to contain information on convicted criminals actually are now used to compile and store data on many people who have never been charged with a crime. Critics warn that DNA data could be used to find out about a person's medical history or risk of genetic disease. Such information could then be used by an employer as grounds to fire a worker or by political foes to raise questions about a candidate's fitness for office. DNA databases compiled by hospitals, research laboratories, and insurance companies have been criticized for the same reasons.

One person who questions current policies about DNA databases is the inventor of DNA profiling, Alec Jeffreys. While he supports the gathering of criminals' DNA into large databases, Jeffreys questions the need to retain DNA samples from those acquitted of a crime or never charged. "My view is, that is discriminatory," says Jeffreys. "It works on a premise that the suspect population, even if innocent, is more likely to offend in the future."[28] In response to such concerns, in 2012 Britain's Parliament passed a bill that caused 1,766,000 DNA profiles of innocent adults and children to be deleted from the national database. In addition, almost 8 million DNA samples, including nearly one-half million from children, were destroyed because they contained sensitive personal biological data. By contrast, the US national DNA database is expanding and now is maintained in all fifty states.

Modern cell theory and its discoveries about the chemical basis of heredity has brought about a revolution in crime detection. It has also enabled governments to stockpile personal information about the cells of citizens. Time will tell whether privacy concerns will lead to new laws restricting this controversial process.

CHAPTER FOUR

Cells in Medical Research and Treatment

Henrietta Lacks was a poor African American tobacco farmer who died in 1951 of cervical cancer at age 31. She is also, in a sense, immortal. After Lacks died, George Gey, a cancer researcher at Johns Hopkins Hospital in Baltimore, discovered something he had never seen before: tumor cells that surgeons removed from Lacks's body went on to thrive, and replicate, in the laboratory. While most cells divide about fifty times before dying out, these cells—dubbed HeLa cells, from the first two letters of Lacks's first and last name—

WORDS IN CONTEXT

replicate

To duplicate or reproduce.

showed the ability to divide indefinitely with amazing speed. Gey shared the HeLa cells with a few colleagues. Later he began shipping them to labs all over the world, where their unusual properties became familiar to generations of research technicians.

Breakthroughs and Questions

The cells proved to be one of the most important tools in modern medicine. Remarkably hardy, HeLa cells have been used in more than seventy-four thousand medical studies, and they have played a vital role in the study of cell biology and viruses, development of the polio vaccine, cloning, gene mapping, in vitro fertilization, and much more. Untold billions of them are still in use, with vials for sale to researchers at $250 each.

Widespread usage of HeLa cells raises questions about who owns biological assets such as human cells. Henrietta Lacks's cells have helped produce astounding breakthroughs in such fields as medicine and genetics, leading to enormous profits along the way. For all the lives Lacks's cells have helped save, they have provided nothing for her family. Living in poverty in Baltimore, Maryland, the Lacks family has had no control over the distribution of Lacks's cells—which doctors originally took without her permission—and the family has never received any payment for their use. According to *New York Times* reporter Carl Zimmer, "It was not until 1973, when a scientist called to ask for blood samples to study the genes her children inherited from her, that Ms. Lacks' family learned that their mother's cells were, in effect, scattered across the planet."[29] In 2013 the Lacks family made an agreement with the National Institutes of Health, giving family members some control over how the cells are used in the future. But they still have no rights to any earnings from research on Henrietta's unique cells. Many scientists argue that once human tissues such

A sophisticated device that combines a microscope, a camera, and an incubator is used in some in vitro fertilization research. Human fertilization is just one of the fields that has benefited from the studies of the amazingly useful yet controversial HeLa cells.

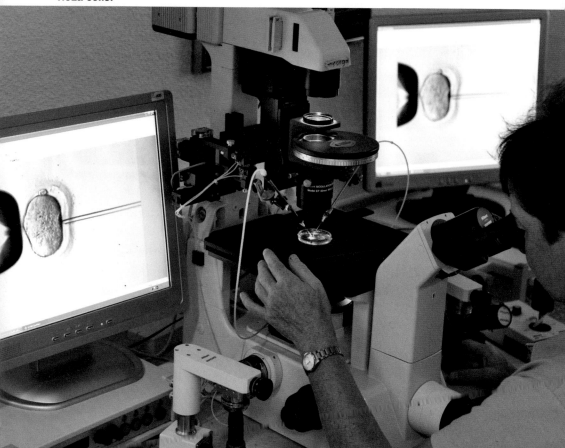

HeLa Cells and Privacy Issues

Another twist in the story of HeLa cells involves the issue of privacy. In 2013 a team of scientists in Heidelberg, Germany, led by geneticist Lars Steinmetz, sequenced the genome of a line of HeLa cells. Sequencing a genome is like decoding the history of a cell line. Several laboratories had tried for years to unlock the secrets of the DNA within the HeLa cell line, but Steinmetz and his team were the first to succeed. They confirmed that the genome for HeLa cells, as with many tumor cells, is highly unusual and filled with errors. HeLa cells feature one extra version of most chromosomes, and as many as five copies of some. Scientists suspect that the cells have also developed additional errors in their decades-long journey around the world.

Steinmetz and his team found the results fascinating and had them published—again without the permission of the Lacks family. Experts at once pointed out that this was a huge invasion of the Lacks family's privacy. As science reporter Ewen Callaway explains, the report contained "data with the potential to reveal some very private information about Ms. Lacks' descendants, including their risks of various diseases. After outcries from the Lacks family, scientists, bioethicists, and many others, the HeLa genome sequence was removed from a public database." Aside from their value as a medical tool, Henrietta Lacks' remarkable cells may also change the way society regards the commercial use of human tissues and personal information derived from them.

Ewen Callaway, "Most Popular Human Cell in Science Gets Sequenced," *Nature*, March 15, 2013. www.nature.com.

as cells are removed from a patient for any reason, they no longer belong to that person.

HeLa cells were also used to develop techniques for isolating stem cells. Unlike HeLa cells, which are cancer cells incapable of change, stem cells can develop into many different kinds of cell, including nerve cells, skin cells, bone cells, liver cells, and so forth, depending on their environment. A stem cell is an undifferentiated cell, like a utility player capable of playing a variety of positions in the body. Researchers are finding that stem cells harvested from a person's own body can be adapted to fight disease and repair serious injuries. Stem cells might one day be used to produce insulin-making cells for patients with type 1 diabetes or to replace heart muscle cells for people recovering from a heart attack. The ability of stem cells to regenerate organ tissue could make organ transplants unnecessary. Advocates for stem cell research consider this technology among the most promising in modern medicine.

Blood Stem Cells and Bone Marrow Transplants

Research on stem cells is based on key ideas from cell theory, including that cells control metabolic (life) processes in the body and that some cells are germinal—able to produce other cells. Basic knowledge of stem cells dates back more than one hundred years. In 1908 Russian cell biologist Alexander Maximov was first to use the phrase *stem cell* in his study of hematopoiesis, or how blood cells form and develop. In a 1917 article, American medical professor Florence Sabin described how blood cells and vessels originate in what she called "angioblasts," which later came to be known as stem cells.

The first widely seen description of stem cells did not appear until 1963, when Canadian scientists James Till and Ernest McCulloch published an article in the journal *Nature* identifying blood stem cells. Their discovery came during a study of how radiation affects the bone marrow of mice. When mice treated with radiation were injected with bone marrow cells, colonies of new cells arose in the spleens of the mice. Till and McCulloch theorized that various kinds of cells also originate from blood stem cells in bone marrow. Research soon confirmed that blood stem cells, which are found in bone marrow, are able to copy themselves and produce the various types of specialized cells found in the blood. These specialized cells include both red blood cells and the many kinds of white blood cells that make up the body's immune system.

Worries about nuclear war led to further breakthroughs in stem cell technology. In the 1960s doctors began working on ways to save people exposed to radiation. High levels of radiation can destroy a person's bone marrow, so they sought ways to transplant healthy bone marrow from donors. In 1972 American physician E. Donnall Thomas performed the first bone marrow transplant on a patient with aplastic anemia, a blood disorder in which white blood cells attack blood stem cells, causing dangerously low counts of red cells, white cells, and platelets. First, Thomas killed off the patient's diseased bone marrow using a form of chemotherapy. Thomas then replaced the diseased bone marrow with the healthy version. The procedure was a success, proving that stem cells can be used to treat blood diseases. Today thousands of patients around the world receive bone marrow transplants for a range of conditions, including many forms of cancer. Leukemia has been transformed from an incurable disease to one that is highly treatable, with survival rates approaching 90 percent.

> **WORDS IN CONTEXT**
>
> *leukemia*
>
> A type of cancer that usually starts in the bone marrow and produces unusually high numbers of white blood cells.

Payment for Stem Cells

The advent of bone marrow transplants raised new questions about the value and use of human tissues. Bone marrow donors have to be matched genetically to the patient so that his or her immune system does not sense the new blood stem cells as foreign and destroy them. Typically donors are sought among family members, especially siblings, who may share the same human leukocyte antigens (HLA). These are special proteins on the surface of cells that monitor what does and does not belong in a person's body. However, only about 30 percent of patients have an HLA-matched sibling. The chances of receiving usable bone marrow from an unrelated donor with a very similar HLA system are better, at about 50 percent. The urgent need for such donors inevitably raises the question of possible payment for the tissue. That is why bone marrow was one of the parts of the body included in the 1984 National Organ Transplant Act (NOTA).

NOTA makes it a criminal offense to accept compensation for donating various parts of a person's body, from a liver to a kidney to bone marrow. The law set off a heated debate among bioethicists—those who deal with ethical issues involving medical treatments and research—a debate that continues to this day. Supporters of the law fear that offering payment for donations of tissue would result in an unregulated market. "Once you insert monetary gain into the equation of organ donation, now you have a market," says Dr. Francis L. Delmonico, a transplant surgeon in Newton, Massachusetts. "Once you have a market, markets are not controllable, markets are not something you can regulate. The problem with markets is that rich people would descend upon poor people to buy their organs, and the poor don't have any choice about it."[30] However, opponents of the law claim the issue is one of property rights. They insist that a person, whether rich or poor, should have the right to accept payment for his or her own tissues if that person chooses. Many also see compensation as an

A surgeon extracts bone marrow from a cancer patient. After the patient undergoes toxic chemotherapy, the marrow will be replaced with untainted donor marrow. Such operations raise ethical concerns about donors receiving payment for bone marrow donations.

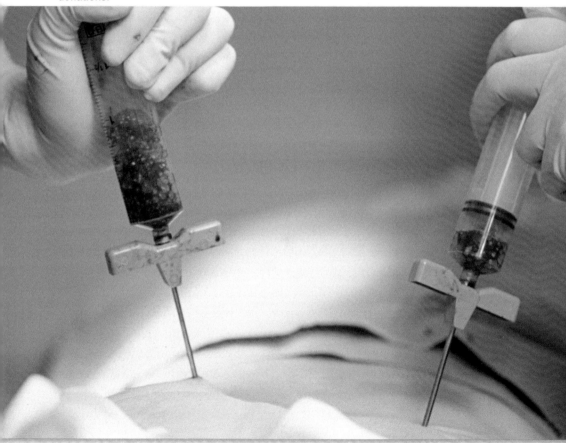

important incentive to get more people to donate tissues such as bone marrow. They urge that donors at least be paid for any lost work time and for any medical treatment they might need due to complications from donating.

In December 2011, those in favor of a market-based system for bone marrow donation won a small victory. The US Court of Appeals ruled that NOTA's ban on selling bone marrow does not include blood stem cells obtained by a new and much less invasive method called apheresis. At the time NOTA was passed, extraction of bone marrow required anesthesia and the insertion of long needles into the donor's hip bones. Apheresis, however, calls for the donor to have five days of injections of a drug that speeds up blood stem cell production in the bone marrow. The marrow then can be harvested from the donor's blood. According to Mary Vitale, an expert on bone marrow transplant law, "Arguably, the biggest sacrifice marrow donors must make . . . is their time and the minimal discomfort they may experience during injections and extractions."[31] The court ruled that since this new procedure did not exist in 1984, the original law does not apply to stem cells obtained through its use. Apheresis makes donating bone marrow almost as simple as donating blood, and NOTA does not ban payments for blood donations.

Stem Cells from Cord Blood

Bone marrow is only one source of stem cells. In 1978 blood stem cells were discovered in something that was once scrapped as waste material: the umbilical cord. Following a birth, cord blood is left in the umbilical cord and placenta. This blood can be collected with relative ease and with no risk to the mother or baby. Blood stem cells obtained from cord blood are used to treat blood diseases such as leukemia in children. They are easier to collect than bone marrow and can be frozen and stored until needed. Stem cells from cord blood also have properties that lessen the likelihood of immune rejection and other complications. They have even been used to treat adults with some success, but in general, blood from a single umbilical cord contains fewer blood stem cells than are needed for an adult.

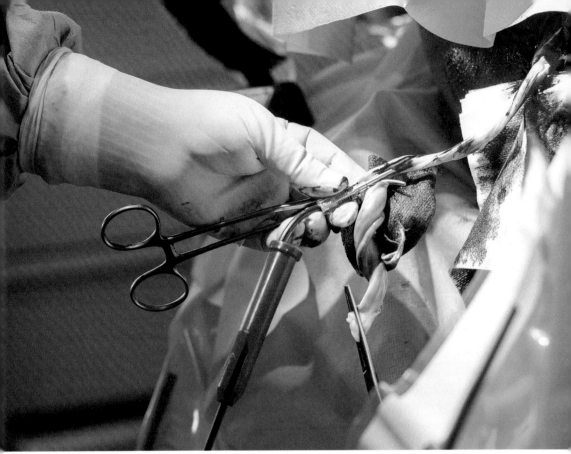

In the past the umbilical cord connecting mother to infant was scrapped after birth. In 1978, however, researchers discovered that the cord contains stem cells that could be harvested and frozen for future use in fighting blood diseases such as leukemia.

Early success in the use of stem cells from cord blood led some physicians to make exaggerated claims about the cells' ability to treat a number of conditions. Nonetheless, more than eighty different diseases have been treated with stem cells from cord blood. Researchers are studying the possibility that cord blood stem cells may one day be used to replace nerve or heart cells. Excitement about their potential has threatened to create a black market for umbilical cords. In 2011 a midwife from Texas was prosecuted for selling stem cells from umbilical cords to patients with terminal cancer.

Controversy over Embryonic Stem Cells

The most controversial source of stem cells is the human embryo. In 1998 University of Wisconsin cell biologist James Thomson isolated cells from embryos to create the first embryonic stem cell lines. These cells are especially useful because they are pluripotent, which means they are able to differentiate into all the body's specialized cells, such as nerve cells or skin cells. The cells were harvested from embryos that were created for infertility treatments but never implanted. In the course of gathering these few hundred cells, each embryo was destroyed, which became a source of controversy. Supporters insisted it was better to use the embryos for research and treatment rather than simply discard them as had been done before. Opponents likened the process to abortion and branded it as unethical and immoral. What many scientists viewed as an immensely promising development, others saw as something that devalued human life in its most basic and vulnerable form. Celebrated American evolutionary biologist Stephen Jay Gould understood the ethical concerns but strongly believed that embryonic stem cell research should proceed. In 2001 Gould wrote,

> "[We] must use embryonic stem cells if we wish to pursue a large body of enormously important, highly promising and deeply humane research in how specific tissues and organs grow from the broad potential of early cells derived from the fertilized ovum. Speaking personally, I do not grant the status of a human life to a clump of cells in a dish. . . . But I also have no desire to offend the sensibilities of those who disagree. Thus, if I could derive cells of similar flexibility in a different way, I would gladly do so, even at considerable extra time and expense."[32]

In August 2001 President George W. Bush announced a compromise policy, allowing research to proceed on embryonic stem cells but only on those cell lines already created before he took office. Many scientists were frustrated by the limitations. Polls suggest that the American public has come to support the research by large margins, but a later discovery seeks to preclude the need for embryonic stem cells. In 2006 Japanese researcher Shinya Yamanaka announced

WORDS IN CONTEXT

pluripotent
Able to differentiate into various types of cells.

a method for converting ordinary somatic cells—any cells from the body except sperm and egg cells—into pluripotent stem cells, the kind that can develop into every other cell type in the body. "Human [embryonic stem] cells created this remarkable controversy," says James Thomson, who also has worked with the new cells, "and [induced pluripotent stem cells], while it's not completely over, are sort of the beginning of the end of that controversy. Having a hand in both is very satisfying."[33]

A Database for Bone Marrow Donors

A crucial part of stem cell treatment is matching each patient with the right donor. Doctors must ensure that the donor's cells match in several ways with those of the patient so that the patient's body does not reject the new cells. In 1979 ten-year-old Laura Graves, a leukemia patient, was transferred to the Fred Hutchinson Cancer Research Center in Seattle, Washington, for treatment. Tests showed that none of Laura's family members was a matched donor, a situation that occurs for about 70 percent of patients. Doctors finally turned to a member of the laboratory staff who proved to be an acceptable match. Although Laura's transplant was a success, her leukemia returned and she died two years later. Seeing the importance of finding suitable donors for cancer patients, the Graves family led an effort to start a national registry of volunteers for bone marrow donations. "With the time it saves, it's going to save lives," said Laura's mother, Sherry. "You're just lost unless you can find a suitable donor."

In 1986 the federally funded National Bone Marrow Donor Registry was begun. Today this registry, now operating from Minneapolis, Minnesota, and called the Be the Match Registry, has grown into the world's largest and most diverse donor database, with more than 12 million potential donors listed in 41 countries. Be the Match has also collected more than 200,000 umbilical cord blood units from parents' donations, making it a leader in promoting stem cell treatment.

Quoted in *New York Times*, "National Bone Marrow Registry Is Seeking Donors," October 13, 1987. www.nytimes.com.

A Regulatory Sweet Spot

Researchers and medical reporters alike have often portrayed stem cells as nothing less than a miracle treatment for all sorts of ailments and injuries. Nevertheless, while stem cell research certainly shows great promise in several areas, many of the projected therapies are still far from becoming reality. To date, the Food and Drug Administration (FDA), which regulates stem cells in the United States, has approved only one stem cell product for sale. The FDA has said that it "is concerned that the hope that patients have for cures not yet available may leave them vulnerable to unscrupulous providers of stem cell treatments that are illegal and potentially harmful."[34]

At the same time, doctors in stem cell clinics continue to use non–FDA approved stem cell products on patients. These doctors argue that stem cells are not drugs and therefore do not belong under FDA jurisdiction. Yet even some supporters of the technology urge a more cautious approach. "The goal of stem cell advocates, including myself, is to find a regulatory sweet spot where science-based, innovative stem cell medicine can advance expeditiously," says Paul Knoepfler, a biomedical scientist. "On the other side we have largely physicians and lawyers along with some patients arguing for drastically-reduced regulation and acceleration of for-profit stem cell interventions to patients, even without concrete data supporting safety or efficacy."[35] With so much at stake regarding stem cells, it seems certain that their use in research and treatments will continue to be a source of controversy.

CHAPTER FIVE

The Future of Cell Research

Will Martin was two years old when his parents, Lori and Neil, discovered that their son has Leigh's disease, a rare genetic disorder. The disease is caused by a mutation in Will's mitochondrial DNA that he inherited from his mother. The Martins learned that the disease is killing Will's cells and that the child is unlikely to survive beyond his seventh birthday. As the couple concentrate on caring for their son, they also realize that any child they might have in the future would almost certainly suffer from the same condition. What Lori finds particularly frustrating is that a new cellular technology exists that quite likely could address the problem and possibly allow her to give birth to a healthy child. However, the therapy is controversial and has yet to be approved for research in the United States. Lori knows that approval, if it ever comes, will probably be too late for her and Neil. "It's not in my timeline," she says. "But the fact that other women might have that opportunity, I just think that's an incredibly meaningful gift."[36] For families like the Martins, cell research is not just an abstract concept but a vital attempt to improve their lives.

A Continuing Debate on MRT

The cell technology that could help the Martins is called mitochondrial replacement therapy (MRT). Mitochondria contain a tiny fraction of a cell's total DNA, but a mutation in mitochondrial DNA can be passed on from a mother to her children, for whom it can be deadly. Mutations can cause conditions ranging from blindness, deafness, or diabetes to the Leigh's disease that affects Will. MRT replaces mutated mitochondria with healthy mitochondria, greatly increasing the likelihood that couples like the Martins will have healthy children.

However, ethical questions have focused on one aspect of MRT. The tiny fraction of healthy mitochondrial DNA—less than 0.01

percent—must be donated by another woman. Critics of the procedure argue that this is unnatural. They assert that any child produced after MRT would actually have DNA from three parents and would thus be the creation of genetic engineering. News reports about MRT tend to feed the controversy by focusing on this idea of three parents for one baby. Many scientists, however, think such criticism is misguided. They see MRT research as a potential lifesaver that the federal Food and Drug Administration should approve at once. Robert Klitzman, director of a bioethics program at Columbia University, says the arguments about having a child with three parents are misleading. Instead, he insists MRT should be seen in the context of organ donation. "If I receive a kidney from a donor," says Klitzman, "no one says that I then consist of two people. . . . Similarly, to replace less than one out of every 100,000 bits of DNA in an individual with DNA from someone else makes no major difference to the recipient's identity other than to allow him or her to survive."[37]

While the debate over MRT continues in the United States, both houses of Parliament in Great Britain voted in February 2015 to allow research on the procedure. Research biologists are hoping that closely regulated clinical trials in the United Kingdom will demonstrate that MRT is safe and effective, and that the results from these trials will soon lead to widespread acceptance of the therapy.

A Not-So-Bright Future for Stressed Cells

The debate about MRT shows how cell theory and new discoveries related to cells continue to be crucial to medical research. Some of the most promising ideas are found in so-called regenerative medicine, in which stem cells are used to repair or replace damaged tissue. With this goal in mind, the search goes on for the holy grail of cell research: a way to make pluripotent stem cells that does not involve embryos and all the controversy that accompanies their use. Shinya Yamanaka's apparent breakthrough with a technique to reprogram adult cells into pluripotent stem cells—a discovery that won Yamanaka and his colleague John Gurdon the 2012 Nobel Prize—has been slow to pro-

WORDS IN CONTEXT

regenerative

Having to do with replacing a body part with new tissue.

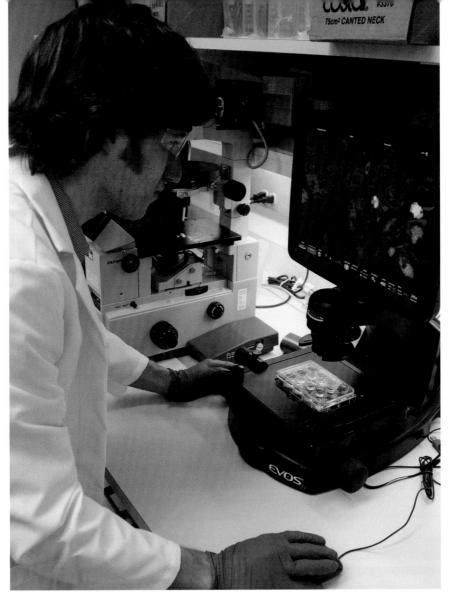

A researcher at the National Institutes of Health works with stem cells in hopes of making breakthroughs in tissue repair. One aim is to create stem cells that can differentiate into any cell of the body so that research does not have to rely on pluripotent stem cells taken from embryos.

duce actual therapies. The four genes Yamanaka and Gurdon used to reprogram the cells also introduced a risk of switching on genes that cause cancer, forcing researchers to proceed with caution.

In January 2014, however, a research team led by Charles Vacanti at Harvard Medical School and Haruko Obokata at the Riken Center in Kobe, Japan, claimed to have discovered a simpler method to reprogram adult cells to be ultraversatile, a method that would leave

Reversing MS with Stem Cells

Multiple sclerosis (MS) is a crippling nerve disease with no cure. It attacks the brain and spinal cord, causing painful inflammation, disability, and eventually death. Medical experts have long disagreed about the possibilities of treating MS with stem cells. Critics point to overhyped therapies that have failed in clinical trials. But a new experimental treatment in England appears to be the first to actually reverse the symptoms of MS. The therapy has normally reserved doctors using words like *miraculous* to describe its effects.

In the new study, two dozen MS sufferers in hospitals in Sheffield and London are, according to their doctors, basically having their immune systems rebooted. Researchers begin by administering a strong dose of chemotherapy to knock out the immune system. Then the immune system is rebuilt with stem cells harvested from the patient's own blood. After treatment, the patient's red and white blood cells begin to grow again within about two weeks. After a month, the immune system returns to normal function and the patient begins to notice amazing improvement. Confined to a wheelchair before her treatment, twenty-five-year-old Holly Drewry now finds her life transformed. "It worked wonders," she says. "I can run a little bit, I can dance. i love dancing, it is silly but I do. . . . It is a miracle but I can do it all." Experts urge caution, but many consider the results very promising. Perhaps more MS patients will one day be dancing like Drewry.

Quoted in Sarah Knapton, "'Miracle' Stem Cell Therapy Reverses Multiple Sclerosis," *Telegraph* (London), March 1, 2015. www.telegraph.co.uk.

the cell DNA untouched. The idea was to subject cells to stress by squeezing them or plunging them briefly in acid. Vacanti and Obokata based their method on a phenomenon they had observed in plants, in which severe environmental stress can turn an ordinary plant cell into an immature cell capable of producing a whole new plant. The team's discovery was dubbed STAP cells, for stimulus-triggered acquisition of pluripotency cells. Vacanti, Obokata, and their team published an article in the journal *Nature* on STAP cells and the ease of producing them.

As soon as they read the article, excited microbiologists rushed to create their own STAP cells. "Hundreds of postdocs and graduate students have tried to do this in their labs because it was supposed to be so easy," says Jeanne Loring, a stem cell researcher at the Scripps Research Institute in La Jolla, California. "They have had zero success."[38] The early excitement quickly turned to skepticism. Vacanti and Obokata have admitted to errors in their work, and an investigation by the Riken Center in Japan uncovered evidence of plagiarism and data manipulation. In December 2014 the Riken Center reported that what the researchers claimed were STAP cells were actually embryonic stem cells that had contaminated the lab dishes. In other words, STAP cells almost certainly don't exist. The fact remains that there are no known shortcuts for developing pluripotent stem cells. Many scientists now worry that the STAP fiasco will taint the public's view of stem cell research. "The rush for patents and funding can cause researchers to forget the basics of science," says Isao Katsura, director of Japan's National Institute of Genetics. "There are social responsibilities. If we look away from that, terrible things can happen."[39]

Using Stem Cells to Replace Liver Tissue

Despite setbacks like the STAP cell episode, cell biologists remain hopeful that programming stem cells to replace damaged or diseased human tissues will one day be standard procedure. Most researchers seek areas where the need is greatest. Takanori Takebe, a cell biologist at the Department of Regenerative Medicine at Yokohama City University in Japan, noticed such a need in his own country. In Japan, the list of people waiting to receive new livers outnumbers possible donors ten to one. (Because humans have only one liver, donated livers come from deceased individuals.) Thousands more in the United States and other countries wait in limbo due to a shortage of donors. Inspired to address this problem, Takebe and his colleagues succeeded in producing liver "buds," or miniature livers, from stem cells in human skin that they reprogrammed to an embryonic condition. Each liver bud is about five millimeters long. When these primitive liver cells were mixed in a petri dish with two other types of stem cells, they began to self-organize into tiny, functioning organs, complete with blood vessels. Takebe then transplanted one of the tiny liver buds into a mouse suffering from liver failure. The liver bud thrived, and the mouse was kept alive with its new, functioning liver.

In a paper that Takebe published on the new technique, he predicted that transplanting hundreds of liver buds into a human patient could restore almost a third of the normal liver function. Takebe also believes the method could be used with other organs, such as the pancreas. Nevertheless, for all the promise of Takebe's liver buds, it will probably be ten years before the technology is ready for clinical trials on humans. Experts in the field realize that the slow pace of research can be frustrating for patients in desperate need of transplants. Dr. Timothy Nelson, director of the Regenerative Medicine Consultation Service at the Mayo Clinic, spends a lot of time explaining the genuine promise of stem cell biology to patients. He says he tries to leave them with a hopeful message, but it can be difficult when hopes are repeatedly raised then dashed. Still, he sees remarkable breakthroughs yet to come. "What we thought to be impossible when I was in training will be the expected norm in coming years," says Nelson. "So I wouldn't be pessimistic."[40]

Making Minibrains in the Laboratory

An example of what Dr. Nelson means can be found in recent experiments involving stem cells and the human brain. Neuroscientist Jürgen Knoblich and his team at Austria's Institute of Molecular Biotechnology are using stem cells to produce what they call brain organoids, or minibrains. These are formations of cells programmed to mimic some of the brain's different regions. Somewhat like Takebe, Knoblich and his colleagues began with embryonic stem cells and adult cells that were reprogrammed to an immature state. When placed in tiny droplets of gel and run through a nutrient bath, the cells organized themselves over several weeks into miniature tissue structures about one-tenth of an inch across. The cells actually formed into neurons like those found in the brain's cortex. The pea-sized minibrain achieved the same development level as that of a nine-week-old fetus. However, the organoid is incapable of thought and, lacking a blood supply, cannot grow larger.

WORDS IN CONTEXT

neurons

Cells of the nervous system that process and transmit information electrically and chemically.

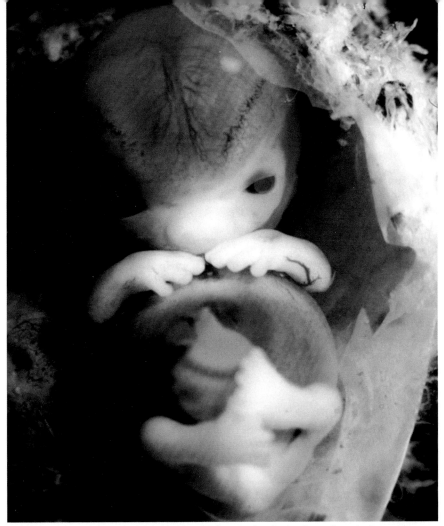

A human fetus at seven weeks old is still developing its brain and central nervous system. That kind of development is now being mimicked in the laboratory, where scientists are fashioning minibrains out of brain cells that naturally coalesce and form neural connections.

Knoblich was able to use the same method to fashion organoids mimicking other regions of the brain as well. "What our organoids are good for is to model the development of the brain and to study anything that causes a defect in development,"[41] says Knoblich. This should help researchers trace the origins of many types of brain disorder. And perhaps someday a similar technique could be used to grow specialized replacement parts for the human brain. Such a breakthrough could revolutionize the treatment of brain injuries; various forms of mental illness, including schizophrenia; and neuron-related conditions such as Parkinson's disease, Alzheimer's disease, and multiple sclerosis.

Producing brains in a laboratory might also present a whole new set of concerns for society and bioethicists. Zameel Cader, a neurologist at the John Radcliffe Hospital in Oxford, Great Britain, says no such ethical issues have arisen from the research so far. "It's a long way from [consciousness] or awareness or responding to the outside world," Cader says. "There's always the spectre of what the future might hold, but this is primitive territory."[42]

Repairing Heart Damage with Cell Therapy

While employing stem cells to replace human organs is still only a dream, using them for organ repair is much closer to reality. In September 2014, surgeons at London Chest Hospital in Great Britain used a new stem cell technique to treat a heart attack victim. When James Cross, a fifty-five-year-old landscape designer, arrived at the hospital shortly after suffering a heart attack, he agreed to submit to a new therapy that might improve his damaged heart. First, doctors took bone marrow from Cross's hip with a long needle. The next day surgeons inserted a tube into Cross's wrist artery and ran it all the way into his heart. Then they injected into the tube a syringe of Cross's own stem cells, stopping the blood to his heart momentarily so the cells would be deposited correctly. "They did this seven times with seven syringes," says Cross. "I was awake all the time, and it wasn't traumatic."[43] He was back on his feet within hours.

The hope was that the injected cells would limit the damage to Cross's heart from lack of oxygen while also helping the heart to repair itself. And results of the experimental treatment are encouraging. Immediately after his heart attack, Cross had only 21 percent of his heart muscle functioning. Months after the treatment, that figure was up to 37 percent, and Cross believes it is still improving. Cross is part of a larger study that includes three thousand heart attack victims across the European Union. The study has drawn particular attention in the UK, where cardiovascular disease is the biggest killer. Doctors speculate that the technique could end up increasing survival rates for heart

WORDS IN CONTEXT

cardiovascular

Relating to the body's circulatory system comprising the heart and blood vessels.

attack victims by one-quarter. Perhaps someday stem cell treatment will be a standard procedure in cardiac units around the world.

Despite optimistic reports, the European trial and other studies like it are already coming under fire from skeptical researchers. Questions have been raised about conflicting data and unlikely statistical results and even the supposedly random method of choosing the patients. Some cell biologists question the effectiveness of the whole approach. Christine Mummery, a cardiac stem cell researcher at Leiden

A damaged heart has suffered rupture and tissue death in the darker region. Experimental modern stem cell treatments now utilize the patient's bone marrow cells injected into the heart to stop further deterioration and assist the organ in repairing itself.

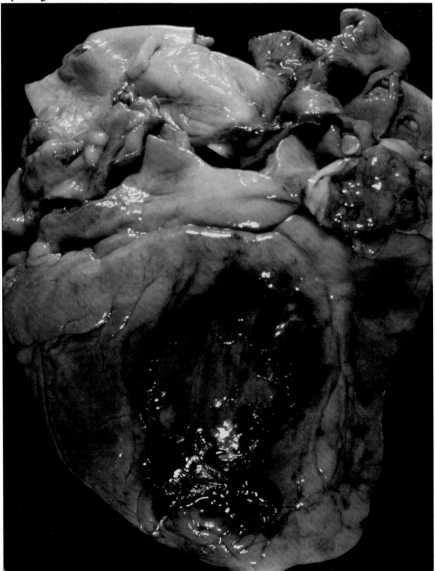

Cells and Aging

Like other parts of the human body, cells begin to wear out after years of activity. Biologists suspect that many secrets about how a person ages lie with tiny parts of chromosomes called telomeres. These protective caps on the ends of chromosomes are like the plastic tips on shoelaces, preventing the ends of chromosomes from fraying and clinging together, which might jumble or destroy the genetic information. Each time a cell divides, the telomeres shorten. Once they become too short, the cell is unable to divide, and it either stagnates or dies. This is the reason most cells do not survive in a laboratory past a few cell divisions. The shortening of telomeres in human cells is also connected to aging, cancer, and greater risk of death.

A recent breakthrough may enable scientists to extend these telomeres. "Now we have found a way to lengthen human telomeres by as much as 1,000 nucleotides, turning back the internal clock in these cells by the equivalent of many years of human life," says Helen Blau, a microbiologist at Stanford University in Palo Alto, California. The immediate goal is to increase the number of cells available for studying the effects of certain diseases. But Blau admits there might be other benefits from the technique. "This new approach paves the way toward preventing or treating diseases of aging," says Blau. In the future longer telomeres may lead to longer lives.

Quoted in Krista Conger, "Telomere Extension Turns Back Aging Clock in Cultured Human Cells, Study Finds," Stanford Medicine News Center, January 22, 2015. https://med.stanford.edu.

University Medical Center in the Netherlands, admits that injecting bone marrow cells might stimulate the creation of small blood vessels to limit immediate damage from a heart attack. "But it is not clear this helps long-term recovery of the heart," she says, "and it does not provide a mechanism for improvement in heart failure."[45]

Society's Reliance on Cell Theory

Disputes among experts on the value of stem cell therapy for cardiac patients only add to the public's confusion about cell technology. Seemingly every week the media trumpets new discoveries and new cell therapies with great fanfare, but so far much of the practical benefit for patients seems to be years away at best. Society is torn between the desire to save lives with cutting-edge cell technologies and to protect people from reckless, ineffective, unethical, or even dangerous experiments.

It is a long way from Robert Hooke's first excited glimpse of cells in a sliver of cork to today's debates over the use of stem cells in increasingly sophisticated treatments. The study of cells has produced a detailed understanding about how living organisms are structured and how they create energy, fight off disease, and reproduce themselves. Society has come to depend on insights related to cell theory in many areas of everyday life, from employing DNA profiling as a crime-fighting tool to using stem cells to treat diseases of the blood. Cell theory has not only enabled scientists to peer into the mysterious origins of life, it is also providing the means to save lives today and in the future.

SOURCE NOTES

Introduction: Cell Theory

1. Stephania Bell, "Prognosis Good on Kevin Durant's Foot," ESPN, April 8, 2015. http://espn.go.com.
2. Paul Nurse, "Cell Theory: Why Is It Important?," Biotechnology Learning Hub. http://biotechlearn.org.

Chapter One: The History of Cell Theory

3. Quoted in "Microscope History: Robert Hooke (1635–1703)," History of the Microscope. www.history-of-the-microscope.org.
4. Jonathan Lopez, "Through a Glass, Brightly," *Wall Street Journal*, March 27, 2015. www.wsj.com.
5. Quoted in "Antony van Leeuwenhoek (1632–1723)," University of California Museum of Paleontology. www.ucmp.berkeley.edu.
6. Quoted in James Southworth Steen, "A Selected Chronological Bibliography of Biology and Medicine—Part I," Delta State University: Division of Biological and Physical Sciences. http://ntweb.deltastate.edu.
7. Quoted in Richard Robinson, "History of Biology: Cell Theory and Cell Structure," Biology Reference. www.biologyreference.com.
8. "Science Quotes by Theodor Schwann," Today in Science History. http://todayinsci.com.
9. Quoted in Kate Yandell, "Sketching Out Cell Theory, Circa 1837," *Scientist*, August 1, 2013. www.the-scientist.com.
10. Jan Sapp, *Genesis: The Evolution of Biology*. New York: Oxford University Press, 2003, p. 84.
11. Quoted in Sapp, *Genesis*, p. 84.

Chapter Two: Modern Cell Theory

12. Quoted in Bruce Weber, "Lynn Margulis, Evolution Theorist, Dies at 73," *New York Times*, November 24, 2011. www.nytimes.com.

13. Neidhard Paweletz, "Walther Flemming: Pioneer of Mitosis Research," *Nature Reviews Molecular Cell Biology* 2, 72–75. www .nature.com.
14. Quoted in Qais Al-Awqati, "Edmund Beecher Wilson: America's First Cell Biologist," Living Legacies: Great Moments and Leading Figures in the History of Columbia University. www.colum bia.edu.
15. Edmund Beecher Wilson, *The Cell in Development and Inheritance*. New York: Macmillan, 1896, p. 10.
16. Quoted in "Theodor Boveri (1862–1915) and Walter Sutton (1877–1916) Propose That Chromosomes Bear Hereditary Factors in Accordance with Mendelian Laws," Genome News Network. www.genomenewsnetwork.org.
17. Quoted in Adam Doerr, "Three Generations of Imbeciles Are Enough," *Genomics Law Report*, June 25, 2009. www.genomics lawreport.com.
18. Peter Satir, "Keith R. Porter and the First Electron Micrograph of a Cell." www.mterasaki.us.

Chapter Three: Using Cell Research to Solve Crimes

19. Quoted in "Update: Man Pleads Guilty in Girl's 1974 Slaying," Associated Press, September 16, 2014. www.desmoinesregister .com.
20. Quoted in "Linus Pauling and the Race for DNA: A Documentary History." http://scarc.library.oregonstate.edu.
21. Quoted in Leslie A. Pray, "Discovery of DNA Structure and Function: Watson and Crick," *Nature Education* 1(1):100. www .nature.com.
22. Quoted in Howard Markel, "The Day Scientists Discovered the 'Secret of Life,'" PBS, February 28, 2013. www.pbs.org.
23. Quoted in Rose Pastore, "How 4 Nerds Discovered the DNA Helix 60 Years Ago Today," *Popular Science*, April 25, 2013. www .popsci.com.
24. Quoted in University of Leicester, "The History of Genetic Fingerprinting." www2.le.ac.uk.

25. Quoted in "The First DNA Fingerprint, Alec Jeffreys," DNA Learning Center. www.dnalc.org.

26. Quoted in University of Leicester, "The History of Genetic Fingerprinting."

27. Katie Lachter, "Science and the Law: The Implications of DNA Profiling." www.dartmouth.edu.

28. Quoted in Bootie Cosgrove-Mather, "DNA Fingerprint Privacy Concerns," CBS News, September 8, 2004. www.cbsnews.com.

Chapter Four: Cells in Medical Research and Treatment

29. Quoted in Carl Zimmer, "A Family Consents to a Medical Gift, 62 Years Later," *New York Times*, August 7, 2013. www.nytimes .com.

30. Quoted in Rachael Rettner, "Great Debate: Should Organ Donors Be Paid?," LiveScience, August 10, 2009. www.livescience .com.

31. Quoted in Nicholas J. Diamond, "Is It Time to Reconsider the National Organ Transplant Act?," Science Progress, July 16, 2012. http://scienceprogress.org.

32. Stephen Jay Gould, "What Only the Embryo Knows," *New York Times*, August 27, 2001. www.nytimes.com.

33. Quoted in Monya Baker, "James Thomson Shifts from Embryonic Stem Cells to Induced Pluripotency," *Nature*, August 14, 2008. www.nature.com.

34. US Food and Drug Administration, "FDA Warns About Stem Cell Claims," January 2012. www.fda.gov.

35. Paul Knoepfler, "Stem Cell Clinics, FDA, and Giant, Unapproved For-Profit Human Experiments," *Knoepfler Lab Stem Cell Blog*, January 27, 2015. www.ipscell.com.

Chapter Five: The Future of Cell Research

36. Quoted in Lilah Connell, "Mitochondrial Replacement Therapy: Is This the Beginning of the End?," *The Bioethics Project Blog*. http://blogs.kentplace.org.

37. Robert Klitzman, "Three Parents, One Baby? Not at All," *Wall Street Journal*, February 9, 2015. www.wsj.com.

38. Quoted in Tina Hesman Saey, "Dramatic Retraction Adds to Questions About Stem Cell Research," *ScienceNews*, July 7, 2014. www.sciencenews.org.

39. Quoted in Toko Sekiguchi, "STAP Cells 'Likely Never Existed,'" *Wall Street Journal*, December 26, 2014. www.wsj.com.

40. Quoted in Rebecca Jacobson, "Liver Buds Show Promise, but Growing New Organs Is Still a Long Way Off," PBS, July 3, 2013. www.pbs.org.

41. Quoted in Kat McGowan, "Scientists Make Progress in Growing Organs from Stem Cells," *Discover*, January 7, 2014. http://discovermagazine.com.

42. Quoted in James Gallagher, "Miniature 'Human Brain' Grown in Lab," BBC, August 28, 2013. www.bbc.com.

43. Quoted in John Naish, "Heart Attack Victim Has Experimental Surgery to Inject Stem Cells from His Hip into His Heart to Help the Organ Repair Itself," *Daily Mail* (London), September 8, 2014. www.dailymail.co.uk.

44. Quoted in Fergus Walsh, "Can Stem Cells Heal Broken Hearts?," BBC, February 20, 2014. www.bbc.com.

45. Quoted in Alison Abbott, "Doubts over Heart Stem-Cell Therapy," *Nature*, April 29, 2014. www.nature.com.

IMPORTANT PEOPLE IN THE HISTORY OF CELL THEORY

Theodor Boveri (1862–1915) was a German biologist who declared that hereditary characteristics are passed on through chromosomes.

Francis Crick (1916–2004) was a British physicist who collaborated on the 1953 discovery of the double helix structure of the DNA molecule.

Robert Hooke (1635–1703) was a self-educated English scientist who used a microscope to discover a honeycomb pattern of cells in a slice of cork. Hooke also coined the term *cell*, from the Latin for "a small compartment."

Zacharias Jansen (ca. 1580–1632) was a Dutch lens maker who worked with his father, Hans, to invent the first microscope.

Alec Jeffreys (1950–) is a British geneticist who in 1984 invented the basic procedure for DNA profiling. This technique is used to match crime scene cellular material to DNA from suspects and also to determine paternity.

Henrietta Lacks (1920–1951) was an American woman whose cancerous cells, removed from her body shortly before her death, developed into so-called HeLa cells, the most famous cell line in history and one of the most important research tools in modern medicine.

Anton van Leeuwenhoek (1632–1723) was a Dutch tradesman and scientist who made microscopes with improved lenses and used them to observe living cells, including bacteria.

Lynn Margulis (1938–2011) was an American biologist who proposed that complex cells evolved from simple one-celled bacteria through the bacteria forming symbiotic relationships.

Louis Pasteur (1822–1895) was a French chemist who performed a famous experiment to disprove the idea of spontaneous generation of cells. Pasteur also pioneered the scientific method for systematically testing a hypothesis.

Keith Porter (1912–1997) was an American biologist who used an electron microscope to produce the first image of a complete tissue cell. Porter's breakthrough in imaging united the study of cell structure and function.

Francois-Vincent Raspail (1794–1878) was a French biologist and chemist who made important discoveries about the structure and function of plant cells. He coined the Latin phrase *omnis cellula e cellula*—every cell is derived from another cell—which is a key insight in cell theory.

Robert Remak (1815–1865) was a Polish-born physician and scientist who rejected ideas about spontaneous generation of cells. Remak insisted that new cells come from cell division in already existing cells.

Ernst Ruska (1906–1988) was a German physicist who invented the electron microscope in 1931. This device enabled scientists to view cells in more detail than ever before.

Matthias Schleiden (1804–1881) was a German botanist who declared that cells are the fundamental building blocks of plants.

Theodor Schwann (1810–1882) was a German physiologist who formulated the first cell theory. He proposed that all living things are made of cells and that the cell is the basic unit of structure for living organisms.

James Thomson (1958–) is an American cell biologist who was the first to isolate cells from embryos to create embryonic stem cell lines.

James Till (1931–) is a Canadian biophysicist who, with his colleague Ernest McCulloch, was the first to identify blood stem cells in bone marrow.

Rudolf Virchow (1821–1902) was a German physiologist who affirmed that all cells come from preexisting cells, which was the third and final tenet of classical cell theory.

James Watson (1928–) is an American biologist who collaborated on the discovery of the double helix structure of the DNA molecule.

Edmund B. Wilson (1856–1939) was an American biologist and teacher who proposed that cell division is a product of both heredity and influence from surrounding cells, which is a basic idea of modern cell theory. Wilson was also an influential teacher and writer on cell biology.

FOR FURTHER RESEARCH

Books

Martin Brasier, *Secret Chambers: The Inside Story of Cells & Complex Life*. Oxford: Oxford University Press, 2012.

Christian Drapeau, *The Stem Cell Theory of Renewal: Demystifying the Most Dramatic Scientific Breakthrough of Our Time*. New York: Sutton Hart, 2009.

Franklin M. Harold, *In Search of Cell History: The Evolution of Life's Building Blocks*. Chicago: University of Chicago Press, 2014.

Alice Park, *The Stem Cell Hope: How Stem Cell Medicine Can Change Our Lives*. New York: Hudson Street Press, 2012.

Rebecca Skloot, *The Immortal Life of Henrietta Lacks*. New York: Broadway Books, 2011.

Internet Sources

Larry Husten, "Stem Cell Therapy to Fix the Heart: A House of Cards About to Fall?," *Forbes*, April 28, 2014. www.forbes.com/sites/larryhusten/2014/04/28/stem-cell-therapy-to-fix-the-heart-a-house-of-cards-about-to-fall/.

Robin McKie, "Eureka Moment That Led to the Discovery of DNA Fingerprinting," *Guardian* (Manchester, UK), May 23, 2009. www.theguardian.com/science/2009/may/24/dna-fingerprinting-alec-jeffreys.

Wynne Parry, "Controversial 'HeLa' Cells: Use Restricted Under New Plan," LiveScience, August 7, 2013. www.livescience.com/38728-hela-cells-restricted-new-nih-plan.html.

Kate Yandell, "Sketching Out Cell Theory, Circa 1837," *Scientist*, August 1, 2013. www.the-scientist.com/?articles.view/articleNo/36699/title/Sketching-out-Cell-Theory--circa-1837/.

Websites

Explore Stem Cells (www.explorestemcells.co.uk). This United Kingdom-based website presents informative articles and features on all aspects of stem cell research, including an explanation of stem cell technology, a look at stem cell controversies, and a list of sources for further information.

ScienceDaily (www.sciencedaily.com). This website provides links to articles about the world of science, including material on cell theory, stem cell research, and DNA profiling.

What Is a Cell? (www.nature.com). This website presents a detailed introduction to cells and cell structure, including diagrams of cell organelles, an explanation of cell metabolic processes, and a look at the cell cycle and cell division.

What Is DNA Profiling? (www.sciencemuseum.org.uk). This website explores DNA profiling in depth, explaining how it can solve crimes and trace suspects within large numbers of people. It also includes a section on using DNA profiling for paternity tests.

INDEX

for multiple sclerosis, 62
in production of brain organoids, 64–66
regulation of, 58
to repair liver tissue, 63–64
in repair of heart damage, 66–68

Takebe, Takanori, 63–64
telomeres, 68
Thomas, E. Donnall, 52
Till, James, 51

ultrasound, definition of, 9

Vacanti, Charles, 61, 62
Virchow, Rudolf, 20, 23
Vries, Hugo de, 30

Warfare of Science with Theology in Christendom, The (White), 23
Watson, James, 38, 39–40, **40**, 41
White, Andrew, 23
Wilson, Edmund B., 27, 29, 31

Yamanaka, Shinya, 56–57, 60–61

Zeiss, Carl, 17–18

BUYER BEWARE

Buyer Beware

by John Lutz

G. P. Putnam's Sons, New York

SBN: 399-11811-4

Library of Congress Cataloging in Publication Data

Lutz, John, 1939–
    Buyer beware.

    (Red mask mystery)
    I. Title.
PZ4.L977Bu   [PS3562.U854]   813'.5'4   76-14787

PRINTED IN THE UNITED STATES OF AMERICA

For Malzberg and Pronzini,
selfless sorts who pointed the way

Caveat emptor quia ignorare non debuit quod jus alienum emit.

Let the buyer beware because he should not be ignorant of the property that he is buying.

BUYER BEWARE

1

Summer was struggling hard at birth. Hail in artillerylike salvos battered the metal roof and sides of my forty-foot house trailer, as it had, interspersed with heavy rain, for the past two hours.

As time passes, hail striking the surface of a house trailer seems to take on more of a metallic ring. I was becoming slightly shell-shocked and vowed again to myself to move into an apartment as soon as possible.

But even as I made my vow I knew I wouldn't move. Not many apartment managers let you run a business out of your place of residence, and I had written permission from Mel Hardin, owner of Trailer Haven, to combine home and office here. Not a prestigious address, maybe, but prestige doesn't cook into much of a meal.

The pace of the hail picked up, and I rose from the sofa, went into the dollhouse bathroom and washed down two aspirin with a glass of tepid water. On my return from the bathroom I noticed an indistinct damp spot on the gold shag carpet where it met the south wall of the trailer. The damned thing leaked! I would tell Hardin about that tomorrow.

Before sitting down again on the sofa, I reached out and turned up the volume on the portable TV so I could better understand the six o'clock news, that and sometimes the ten o'clock report being the only programs I watched on television besides an occasional

11

sporting event. A wholesomely attractive girl was teasing viewers with the weather forecast just then, demonstrating with a pointer how a warm front moving in from the Southeast was causing all kinds of trouble. She seemed happy about it.

Her explanation did account for the hail, but not for the determined rasping of my door buzzer. I rose again from the sofa, almost afraid to let in somebody who was crazy enough to be outside in this kind of weather. Through the south window I saw horizontal fingers of lightning rend the sky over perfectly aligned trailer roofs and TV antennas, like something out of an updated Frankenstein movie.

The man standing beneath the metal awning that sheltered my trailer door fit right into the movie. He was moderately tall, hatless, dark-haired and full-bearded. His long black raincoat matched the black umbrella he held angled into the wind.

"Hey," he said, spoiling the theatrical effect, "you Mr. Nudger?"

I nodded, stepping back to let him inside, noticing the four- or five-year-old compact sedan he must have got out of parked near the rack of mailboxes that served this side of the graveled street.

He was about six feet tall, a shade over my height, and now that he was inside and his face wasn't contorted to the violent weather, I saw that he had even, pleasant features and straight-ahead brown eyes. His umbrella was still in good shape after protecting him from the hail, and he folded it carefully and leaned it against the wall by the door.

As I motioned him farther inside so he could sit down, I speculated on whether he was an insurance salesman, evangelist or client. He carried no briefcase, and he hadn't yet smiled. Could be a client. Maybe he was desperate, after trying all the other confidential investigators in the directory. Not much to choose from

12

there. It's a precarious way to make a living. You need a specialty.

"I'm Gordon Clark," he said, "and I'm here on business."

Good. I liked the ones who got to the point. I took his wet raincoat and draped it over the wooden back of a chair. Beneath his coat he was wearing dark slacks and a light-tan leisure jacket, and there was a tight muscularity about the forward set of his shoulders. He sat down as if he'd been standing too long. He was troubled.

"You are Mr. Nudger, of Nudger Investigations, aren't you?"

"The same, Mr. Clark. Alo Nudger." I bent to shake hands with him and continued standing, slipping my hands into my pockets.

"Alo?"

"Short for Aloysious, long for Al, as I used to tell the ladies."

"Sure. I want to hire you."

"You must want to hire me badly to come out in this kind of weather."

"I don't let the weather interfere with what I have to do, Mr. Nudger."

I looked at him more closely. I had gauged him wrong. He was in his late twenties, and his dark beard, no longer matted with rivulets of rainwater, was precisely trimmed in the manner of a stylish up-and-comer rather than in the natural, free-swinging style of youth. His jacket was slightly worn, but it appeared expensively tailored, though possibly for someone else.

"Did you choose my name from the telephone directory?"

He shook his head. "You were recommended by an acquaintance who was once involved in one of your cases—a Mrs. Gloria Fallering."

I sat on the sofa opposite Clark's chair. "I remember

13

her—a four-year-old son. She should hate my guts."

"She does. That's what recommended you to me."

I had to laugh. The hail had stopped suddenly, and the TV I'd forgotten was on was blaring an important message about irregularity. I reached over and switched it off.

"You used to be Mr. Happy on television, didn't you?" Clark said.

"That was me," I admitted. "The clown cop who introduced safety cartoons for the kiddies."

"It must have paid good, being Mr. Happy."

"But it wasn't police work. I like kids, but three years of Mr. Happy was enough." The real reason I was no longer Mr. Happy was none of his concern.

"So that's how you got into kidnapping."

"More or less. Is that why you want to hire me?"

"Yes." Clark crossed his arms and leaned back, setting himself to do some talking. "My wife, Joan, and I were married eight years ago. . . ."

"Begin at the end," I told him.

Clark smiled for the first time, though not a smile to light up the room. "A little over a year ago we got our divorce. Irreconcilable differences. They say some couples can be better friends, if not lovers, after a divorce. That wasn't true in our case. Looking back on it, though, I guess Melissa was the one thing we really fought about."

"Melissa?"

"Our seven-year-old daughter. At first Joan didn't seem to resent me using my visitation rights to see her, but about six months ago her attitude changed. I think there was another man."

"From before or after the divorce?"

"After, I'm sure," Clark said without hesitation.

"Do you know where your ex-wife and the child are now?"

"I received reliable information that they're in Layton, Florida. Joan's near her father, Dale Carlon, president of Carlon Plastics."

"A very big corporation."

"Which is why I can't take the long and arduous route of retrieving Melissa through the courts. Carlon can hire top lawyers and pay off the right people so the matter is tangled up in litigation for years."

"I take it Melissa was not to be removed from the state without the court's permission."

Clark nodded.

"I can't do anything unless you get a court order mandating custody of the child to you. That gives you legal custody even though it's subject to appeal. I don't work without proof that you *do* have legal custody."

"Sure. I waited until my lawyer told me we had a court order before coming here. I understand the risks you'd be taking."

"I want to be positive you do. The FBI and most states don't recognize that a parent can steal his own child, but if I snatch Melissa and you don't have legal custody, I might wind up in prison for kidnapping."

"And with Carlon's lawyers on me, so might I." Clark's complexion paled and his dark beard appeared darker.

"I charge twenty-five hundred dollars plus expenses," I said, "five hundred in advance."

Clark agreed to that with a curt nod. A fusillade of hail swept his side of the trailer, but he didn't seem to hear. "There won't be any . . . trouble, will there?"

"Not if I can prevent it," I said, and I meant that. "Do you have Joan's address in Layton?"

"Certainly."

"And a photograph. Recent. And a photograph of Melissa."

"I can supply those, too."

"Then when you show up here with the court order, Mr. Clark, I go to work."

15

Clark smiled for the second time, making it a bit better than the first.

There was a lull in the storm as well as in our conversation and no reason not to take the opportunity to leave.

Clark stood and slipped into his black rain gear. He would need the umbrella again. Though the hail had stopped, a perfectly vertical light rain fell with a gray, foreboding steadiness.

"I should be back tomorrow or the day after with the court order," Clark said as he stepped down from the trailer's threshold and opened his umbrella.

I motioned for him to wait, ducked back inside for a moment and gave him one of my cards. "Give me a call, make sure I'm here."

"Good idea," he said, tucking the card into a side pocket of his raincoat. He turned and walked to his car with an unhurried pace, refusing to make any more concessions to mere rain.

I closed the metal door, went back to the sofa and sat down. Already I could feel the heavy pulsing in my stomach that I felt every time I took a new case. Clark had asked if there might be trouble. There might always be trouble in the taking of a child from its natural mother. I didn't allow myself to dwell on the kinds of trouble that were possible.

Once I accepted Clark's money, I was committed to deal with that trouble. And I needed Clark's money.

2

He was back the next day with his court order.

I saw Clark's aging compact slow near my trailer, heard the crunch of tires on gravel and caught a glimpse of red glowing brake lights before the car passed out of my line of vision. I was doing my exercises on the concrete patio in what passes for my backyard. Having just finished my third set of deep knee bends, I was standing with my hands on my hips, waiting for my legs to stop trembling. It's not that I'm so much the physical culture type, but I'm at an age. Every day on the sports page I read about some athlete or other, washed up at thirty-six or -seven—even the great ones. That bothers me.

Gordon Clark was wearing a tailored gray suit this time, with a vest and a blood-red tucked-in tie. He was carrying an attaché case. I felt a bit shoddy in my T-shirt and sweat pants.

He smiled at me, a superior smile that said he was the superior specimen. Not that I'd argue with him. I'm big enough, and not fat, but I'm not exactly whipcord muscle. I suspected that beneath the neat gray suit, Clark was.

"You don't look so tough," he said.

"Mr. Happy's not supposed to be tough."

"I got the court order. I was near here so I thought I'd drop it by." He opened the attache case, an expensive model with chrome trim, and handed me a piece of paper with a familiar heading.

"Okay," I said, "I'll have it copied and return it to you."

He reached into the open attaché case again, like a magician reaching into his bag of tricks, and handed me out the next surprise. It was a check for five hundred dollars, closely followed by some photographs.

I walked out of the shade of the trailer to study the color snapshots. The first was of a woman, Joan Clark, leaning against what looked like a colonial pillar on a porch. She had a nifty upturned nose, close-set but large dark eyes and a small, too-curvaceous-to-be-wiry figure, one of those women who would look young even in late middle age, until the looker got close enough to notice the touches of time. The next photo was of Joan Clark and her daughter standing on the bank of a very blue lake. The daughter, Melissa, looked much like her mother, except that she was blond. And the daughter had the same innate tininess about her, the same tilt to her nose. I wondered if her mother was really blond. The third snapshot was of Melissa seated on a corner of a sofa with that characteristic knees-together, legs-straight-out pose of a seven-year-old. She had her father's smile, but with more candlepower.

"That last one of Melissa is the most recent I could find," Clark said. "It's about four months old."

I set the photos, check and court order on the metal table by my webbed lawn chair, weighting them with the heavy glass holder that contained a yellow candle that was supposed to keep mosquitoes away in the evenings.

"What's their address in Layton?" I said.

"It's three fifty-five Star Lane, on the south side of Layton. They've been there about a month. Do you want me to write it down?"

"I'll remember it, if I have to."

Clark cocked his head to the left. "What do you mean by that?"

"I mean it would be best if you flew down to Layton with me. It's the way I usually operate if I can."

He shook his head like a bull trying to shake loose a barb in the bullring. "I can't."

18

"It would be easier for the child. We wait for the right time when she's alone and simply take her with us, as if the mother knows about us."

"But I hired you so I wouldn't have to do this myself. You're supposed to be an expert. . . ." Clark shrugged helplessly, pleading to be understood. "Look, I'd like to, really. But I just can't. My job. . . . You understand. If it isn't absolutely necessary. . . ."

"As long as I have that court order and your signature on one of my contracts," I told him, "it's not necessary."

"Then I'll have to pass."

I nodded, went inside for a minute and got one of my standard contract forms and a pen. Clark read the short contract quickly and bent over the metal patio table to sign it.

"Is there any way your ex-wife could find out you hired me?" I asked.

"None at all. I haven't discussed this with anyone."

"Follow that policy," I advised him. "Surprise is important. I'll leave for Layton tomorrow, unless you have some reason for suggesting a better time."

"Tomorrow's all right with me. The sooner this thing's done, the better."

"Where can you be reached?" I asked him. "I might need to contact you, and I'll have to know where to bring Melissa when we return."

"I'm with Standard Implement." Clark reached into a gray pocket and held out an embossed white business card that proclaimed him to be a sales manager. Then he hastily drew the card back, took a pen from another pocket and scribbled his home address and phone number on the back of the card before handing it to me. His address was in a fairly expensive apartment development on the west side of the city, where expensive "executive" apartment developments were stacked on top of one another. Clark seemed to play his role as best he could with what he had.

19

"Can you tell me anything about your ex-wife that might be helpful?" I asked. "Habits, favorite activities, that sort of thing."

Clark ran his fingertips an eighth of an inch beyond the contours of his neat dark beard. "I can't think of any habits that might be helpful. Joan used to love to play tennis, though. Spent a lot of time on the court."

"Any good?"

"Good? No, but she wears down her opponents. Joan is competitive in almost everything. Aggressive. If she suspects what you're up to, your job won't be without problems."

"I'll know how to handle the situation, Mr. Clark."

He looked me up and down, as if trying to reassure himself that I could. When he turned to leave, he took two slow steps and turned back. "One thing I don't want, Nudger, is for Melissa to be hurt. Can you guarantee that she won't be?"

"I can guarantee I'll do everything to prevent it. I consider it the most important part of my job."

He stood still for a moment, then nodded, as if he'd decided I was a thorough enough professional. Then he walked toward his car.

I felt sorry for him just then. He hadn't anticipated any of this when he'd walked down the aisle and uttered his vows.

After a few more deep knee bends, I gathered up everything Clark had left with me and went inside. I phoned the airline reservation desk for space on a morning flight to Orlando. From there I would have to rent a car and drive the rest of the way to Layton.

All that remained for me to do except pack was to drive over to the post office and use their pay copier to make duplicates of the court order and the photographs Clark had given me. The original court order I would return to Clark; one copy I would place in my safe-deposit box; one copy I would take to Florida,

along with Clark's signature on a copy of my contract.
In a way I was glad Clark had refused to accompany
me. The father's presence didn't always make it easier
on the child. Sometimes the mother put up a fuss, and
the husband, out of habit or rekindled responsibility,
sided with her. When that happened, I sometimes got
my lumps from both of them; and usually I was re-
hired to accomplish the same task, now made more
difficult, a few days later. Or the woman might physically resist both of us, and she and the man would fight
over the child, yanking it back and forth like so much
merchandise. I had seen a few children injured seriously that way. Physically and otherwise.

The trailer's air conditioner clicked on and began to
hum. The sun was asserting itself outside. I got up
from where I'd been sitting, by the phone, walked into
the kitchen and mixed myself a bourbon and water.
My stomach didn't suit my profession. It was fluttering
again with precase jitters.

I wasn't in my business because I had the nerves for
it. After four years as a civilian employee of the city police department and three years as a patrolman, my superiors had come to that same unflattering conclusion.
Thus began my three-year reign as local TV's Mister
Happy—we dropped the "Officer" so the children
would realize that policemen were much like everyone
else when they weren't working—and I was the smiling cop who projected the image of Good Guy to the
kids. I had always got on with the kids; just the duty
for me, the higher-ups had decided. And they were
right. It wasn't exactly what I'd had in mind when I
joined the force, but even after three years I wasn't
about to leave before I had to.

Police work was what I was trained in, and I had my
contacts; so when I left the department, my choice of
occupation seemed logical. At the time, anyway.

But maybe I had no right to bitch. My much ma-

21

ligned and misunderstood profession kept the food and liquor coming in and a tin roof over my head.

Just as the diluted bourbon was achieving its soothing influence on my nerves, the girl at the airline reservation desk phoned back and said that she'd made a mistake and asked whether I would consider a later flight that laid over in Atlanta for an hour.

I agreed to that and took an antacid tablet.

3

My flight to Orlando, via Atlanta, took off on time into a sky resembling lovingly polished fine crystal. The ground that fell away lost movement, then detail, and became a well defined, multicolored quiltwork of neat, if sometimes unsymmetrical, patterns. It was all simple from up there, where I sat behind the wing. Too bad everything didn't fall into such simple, neat patterns. Or maybe everything did, from a distance.

I settled back in the comfortable padded seat and semislept, my scant knowledge of aerodynamics balancing out my natural queasiness at flying.

Two drinks and a sampling of Southern dialect was it for the Atlanta layover, then back on the 747 and it was Georgia's red clay falling away beneath the wing. They seemed always to be constructing something in Georgia, as if only for an excuse to lay bare acres of red earth.

The plane rolled slightly to the left, altering the stark pattern of sunlight on the wing, and we headed south, proceeding toward Orlando at what seemed to be a much higher altitude.

After landing at Orlando's sun-drenched airport, I collected my baggage and made my way to a Hertz desk, where I rented a shiny new green compact. The little car was good of its kind, but there was just enough room for me and my luggage, and I had to be on the alert for pebbles and bottlecaps on the road.

I took Interstate Four out of Orlando, turned south on Twenty-seven, then drove for a while and angled west on Thirty-two, toward the Gulf Coast. Layton was twenty-five or thirty miles inland, southeast of Tampa Bay. I made the ENTERING LAYTON—POP. 3,605 sign a few minutes before five o'clock.

There was a good fishing and boating lake nearby, and Layton was close enough to the coast to have some tourist appeal. The main street was lined with motels. But off to the left I could see what had to be Layton's main industry—a huge complex of low, dark buildings set near the crest of a hill, with half a dozen tall smokestacks looming over the town like guard towers.

Disregarding the garish signs near the street, I decided one motel looked about in a league with the other, so I pulled into the lot of one called the Clover Inn, which advertised FIFTEEN DOLLARS AND UP in sun-paled flashing neon.

"Up" turned out to be twenty-two dollars, but I stretched cramped muscles and signed the register anyway. The Clover Inn had several little flat-roofed cabins spaced far enough apart to guarantee quiet at night, and it featured a clean-looking, if plain, restaurant, the Clover Grill. Besides, I couldn't face the idea of climbing back into the little green compact with the big name.

I told the man at the desk, an old guy named Eddie, that I'd be staying a few days and paid in advance. He handed me a key chained to a plastic clover engraved with a numeral. Leaving the car where it was parked, I got my luggage and carried it to Number 5.

Cool air hit me when I opened the door to the boxy stucco cabin, and it felt good. I stepped inside, kicked the door shut behind me and my three-suiter, and looked around.

Nice. Restful. Light green walls, dark furniture and a bed with a thick mattress. I was satisfied with my choice.

After tossing the suitcase onto the bed, I began to unpack what I wanted to hang the wrinkles out of—a pair of slacks, pale blue shirt and a tan sport coat. I glanced at the alarm clock on the nightstand by the bed. Still plenty of daylight left, enough to take a quick shower, get something to eat at the Clover Grill and look into things. I was tired but I was working.

As I was walking across the parking lot, toward the motel restaurant, I decided to drop into the office and talk to Eddie. I could see through the window that he was alone, slouched in a leather chair near the desk, reading a magazine.

"Evening," I said as I entered the tiny paneled office.

Eddie looked up from his magazine and nodded, waiting for me to get to what I really wanted to say. He was a dehydrated old bird with a narrow face, wispy gray hair and blue eyes containing a quiet humor that life hadn't broken.

"Layton's a bigger town than I imagined," I said.

"You must not have much of an imagination. Thought you might want towels."

"Nope. Plenty of towels. How's the food in the restaurant?"

"Make you deathly ill. Don't tell 'em I said so."

"Sure." I saw that he was reading one of those factual detective magazines, with a cover featuring a bound girl in panties and bra, begging to be spared while the

24

determined type who stood over her with a ripsaw seemed to be listening to distant sirens.

"'Bout the Michigan Mutilator," he said, noticing that I'd scanned the cover. "You remember him?"

"Vaguely."

"Killed six."

"What's that big cluster of buildings east of town?" I asked.

"Used a chain saw, though. Black and Decker. That's Carlon Plastics you're talkin' about. Employs nearly half the town."

It was what I'd been afraid of. And now that I knew for sure how big Carlon Plastics was in Layton, my stomach arranged itself into a knot that would have done a scoutmaster proud. If anything did go wrong, I knew how the authorities would deal with me. Roughly and on the edge of the rules.

"What do they make up there?" I asked.

"Different things, from plastic cups for vending machines to some kind of parts for the government. There's nine more Carlon plants spread around the country, but this one was the first. Worked for 'em myself up to six years ago, in the molding section. Then I inhaled enough fumes to mess up my lungs. Had to quit, take my disability pay."

"Worth a lot to a town, an operation like that."

"Wouldn't be no town without it."

"Is there still a Carlon in the business?"

"Better believe it! Dale Carlon himself. Lives up near the plant in a ritzy place you wouldn't believe. He's the son. Father's dead."

"Carlon live alone in a place like that?"

"Yeah. Wife died nearly five years ago. No live-in servants. Got two daughters somewhere, though." He tilted his head slightly, much like the Michigan Mutilator on the magazine cover. "You here for the fishin'?"

"I wish I was. Business."

25

"Too bad. They're bitin', they say."

"Would you happen to know where Star Lane is?"

Eddie tapped the magazine on his bony knee for a while. "Not exactly," he said at last, "but I'm sure it'd be over on the south side, where there's a bunch of streets named after space stuff. You take Layton Avenue down to Palm Road, 'bout a mile from here goin' west, then you make a left an' you'll drive for a while till you see a big radio tower. You'll be in the area then. Ask somebody, they'll tell you where Star is."

The telephone rang, and with agility left over from his youth he rose and scooped up the receiver on the second ring. "No trouble," he said. "Be right there." He hung up the phone and said, "Family in Three needs towels."

"Thanks for the story on the restaurant," I told him as he came out from behind the desk and went through a folding door into another room.

I stepped back outside, into the parking lot. A huge cypress behind one of the cabins cast a dappled shadow that must have covered half the block. There was only so much daylight left. I decided to try the Clover Grill anyway.

I didn't think the food was all that bad.

Half an hour later, chewing idly on a mint-flavored toothpick, I got into the rented compact to follow old Eddie's directions to Star Lane. The evening had cooled to perfect tourist weather, and I drove with the air conditioner off and the window on the driver's side rolled down. I seemed to hit every red light, but I didn't care. Thanks to the quick dinner, I had plenty of time before sundown.

By the time I reached Palm Road it was evident that the quality of the neighborhood was declining. Motels, restaurants and quaint shops had been replaced by aging stucco apartment buildings nearer the street, taverns and pawnshops and secondhand stores.

26

I made my left turn onto Palm and the scenery improved, but not much. I passed some warehouses, then crossed over a tiny concrete bridge into an area of low-priced tract houses, identical but for landscaping or color. Near the top of a hill I saw the tall radio tower Eddie had mentioned, and at the next street, Planet Drive, I pulled into a cut-rate service station and got directions to Star Lane.

Two left turns and five minutes' driving got me there. Star Lane was a cul-de-sac off Star Avenue. The houses were of the same type I'd driven past for the last mile or so, with small front yards and unpaved driveways. Number 355 was a yellow frame with drawn curtains and a front picket fence in need of paint. There was no car in the driveway. I parked on the other side of the street, in front of a house with a FOR SALE sign, and sat watching.

The neighborhood seemed unpopulated except for a teenage boy four houses down, getting frustrated with an old Buick. Number 355 was quiet and humble, a rolled up newspaper near a hedge in the front yard and what looked like a folded magazine sticking from the mailbox by the door. As dusk gradually obliterated long evening shadows, I saw that there was a lamp glowing behind the thin curtains in the front window.

I didn't like the way the game was developing. Star Lane was hardly a slum, but would the daughter of the man who virtually owned the town live here with her daughter, his granddaughter? It didn't add up for me, but I knew it might add up for somebody else, to a sum I wouldn't like.

Soon the neighbors would be wondering why I was parked there, so to avoid suspicion I left and drove around for a while, returning to pass Number 355 twice. At nine forty-five there still was no sign of occupancy, no shadow of movement behind the drawn curtains, and the paper and mail were untouched.

27

I headed the compact back toward the motel, my uneasy feeling growing claws. At a big drugstore with a flashing neon palm tree I stopped and bought some antacid stomach tablets, a spray can of dog repellent and a bottle of blended whiskey. Dog repellent is almost as effective as Mace, and the can doesn't attract nearly the attention.

The vending machine outside the office at the Clover Inn furnished me with ice, and I mixed myself a drink and sat in my cabin, thinking about Lornee, as I usually did at some point or other when I was on a job. We'd had some fine, if precarious, years, some fine children; but when Mr. Happy was found to be having an affair with the wife of a city alderman, politics entered the somewhat muddled picture. Politics and divorce.

No one would believe that the affair was one-sided and far less serious than the press had intimated. The alderman's wife was one of those bored, self-styled eccentrics with money who'd met me when I was taking part in a local charity-celebrity function, and she had talked too much and thrown herself at me more jokingly than anything else. But the press was controlled by the rival party, and when her husband had me removed from the department, he only fanned the flames—or rather, the smoke.

I didn't contest when Lornee filed for divorce, and I thought it right to give her custody of Danny and Lynn as long as I had visitation rights. Then, a year later, Lornee left the state with a man named Hogan—a close friend of mine, a tall, lonely man who drank not a lot but a bit too much—and on a Texas highway he drove into a parked car at high speed and killed himself and my ex-wife and my children.

Nobody to blame, really. Nobody deserving of blame for that much horror; nobody, dead or alive, to take it out on, to hate. And only one survivor to harbor the memory.

Now I was lonely, the way Hogan used to be, and I was drinking, not a lot but a bit too much, the way Hogan used to drink.

Some people are star-crossed.

4

In the morning I was thankful that I hadn't dreamed.

I reached out, slapped down the sharp button on the jangling alarm clock and lay for a moment in its vibrating aftermath of silence. There was a sour taste in my mouth and a numbness in my left arm where I'd lain on it in my sleep. I remembered then that I'd been on one of my alcohol-induced self-pitying binges the night before. I hated the sniveling, masochistic self-analysis to which I sometimes fell prey, hated the lethargic uselessness that often evolved from it. Every day I met people more mutilated by fate than myself. The most maudlin word in the English language is "I"—at least for me, past a certain number of drinks.

The black arrow hands on the alarm clock indicated six forty-five, the minute hand pointing toward the door in a broad hint. No time for breakfast. Just as well. As my thoughts focused on the Melissa Clark case, the familiar knot tightened in my stomach and quashed what little desire I had for food.

I managed to get my feet on the floor and commanded them to propel me to the bathroom, where I showered, shaved without nicking myself, combed my hair, and brushed my teeth with toothpaste that tasted like chalk. Gazing at my lean, somewhat lopsided features in the mirror, I wondered if my hair had started to thin. I'd be the last to know.

As soon as I was dressed I drove from the motel, in the direction of Star Lane. Halfway there I stopped at a dingy little doughnut shop built like a castle and got a cup of black coffee to go. By the time I was parked near the end of Star Lane, I'd only burned my hand twice and still had a squishy paper cup half full of coffee.

At twenty minutes to eight the first child came out, a boy of about twelve carrying a ponderous armload of books. Within a few minutes two girls, younger than the boy, emerged from the white frame house nearest my car. The girls walked to where the boy was standing, and though he carefully avoided looking at them, they stood close to him on his left. More children, mostly very young, came out of the houses on each side of the street and stood in a cluster that seemed to center around the boy with all the books.

The school bus arrived promptly at seven forty-five, big and yellow and noisy; and when it had rumbled around the corner, with more noise than speed, Star Lane was again deserted. Melissa Clark hadn't come out of the yellow house fronted by the faded picket fence.

I waited until eight o'clock. Several tired types left to go to work, and the teen-age boy I'd seen yesterday passed in his old Buick. My coffee had long since got cold. I tossed the dark liquid out the window, crumpled the cup and stuck it above the sun visor. Then I drove down the street and parked across from Number 355.

The paper was still on the lawn, the folded magazine still protruding from the mailbox. In the brightening morning there was still a faint yellow glow behind the front curtains.

I decided to be an aluminum siding salesman and

got out of the car and crossed the street. When I stepped up on the porch of Number 355 and knocked, I had the feeling I was rapping on the door of an empty house. It's an instinct anyone who's knocked on enough doors acquires.

I waited a few minutes before stepping down from the front porch and walking around to the back of the house. An old rusty swing-set frame in the far corner of the yard now supported only a bald tire suspended by a rope. The grass, where it wasn't worn away, stood about six inches high.

No one was home, I was ninety-nine percent sure, but I went up on the porch and knocked on the back door for the other one percent.

"Whad'ya want, mister?"

It was a boy of about eight, standing near the corner of the house, looking at me with the open expression of fearless curiosity possessed only by young boys and terriers.

"I'm looking for Melissa's mother. You know where she is?"

"No, sir." He was wearing a blue T-shirt about five sizes too large, and he unconsciously gripped it and stretched it down on himself almost to his knees while he stared at me.

"What's your name?" I asked in a friendly voice.

"Mick."

"How come no school today, Mick?"

"I felt bad when I woke up."

"You don't look sick."

"It's on the inside."

"How come Melissa didn't go to school?"

Mick shrugged inside his T-shirt. "Maybe she's sick, too."

"How long's it been since you've seen her?"

"Few days. She was with her mom and dad."

A scraggly-haired woman in a rumpled pink

31

housecoat stepped partway out of the back door of the house on the left. "Mick, you get back in here! If you're too sick to be in school you ain't gonna be out runnin' around!"

I smiled at her, but she didn't smile back, and I didn't like the way her hand clutched her housecoat between her breasts.

"I gotta go," Mick said.

"I would if I were you," I told him. I knocked on the back door again, loudly this time, to appear aboveboard.

That's when I saw the bullet hole.

It was from a large-caliber bullet and it was just below the doorknob, where it wasn't too noticeable. And it was neat, as if the bullet had gone through the wood from the outside.

I looked the door over and saw another neat round hole, up near the top, alongside the door frame. The bullet had made a thin groove in the frame, as if it had been fired at an angle. Stepping back on the porch, I looked over the rear of the house as if figuring a siding estimate. There was another neat bullet hole in the bottom-left corner of the window beside the back porch.

My throat went dry. I was afraid now of what might be inside the house. Squatting on the back porch, I tried to see through the lower of the two bullet holes in the door, but all I could make out was what looked like the bottom of a picture frame against the pale green of the opposite wall.

I straightened and drew a deep breath that made me light-headed for a second. Maybe the bullet holes meant nothing; maybe they'd been there for years.

Feeling a bit steadier, I went to the window and tried to peer in between the drawn curtains. They overlapped too much and it was impossible. I saw something else, though. Directly opposite the neat hole in the window pane was a neat hole in the curtain.

My breath caught in the dryness of my throat and

lumped there, and my stomach felt as if it had been stabbed with a tuning fork. There was no walking away now. It was time to have Mick's mother call the law.

They got there in five minutes and I showed them my identification and they weren't impressed. A tall man with dark hair combed like Hitler's introduced himself as Lieutenant Frank Dockard, the stocky uniformed policeman with him as Sergeant Avery. By their manner I saw within a few minutes that Avery was the silent servant and that Dockard fashioned himself the brains.

Mick and his mother watched soberly from their front porch as I told my story, and Dockard made notes in a leather-covered note pad with the diligence of a monk copying an ancient manuscript. When I was finished, he snapped the note pad shut and gave no indication of what he thought, and the professionally placid, thick features of Sergeant Avery were unchanged.

After a while Dockard rubbed a long forefinger behind his right ear, as if checking for an injury. "Let's take a look at these bullet holes," he said, and led the way toward the back of the house.

The three of us stood on the back porch while Mick and his mother looked silently on from next door. Dockard grunted when he saw the holes in the door, stepped down off the porch and grunted again when he saw the bullet hole in the window and the corresponding hole in the curtain.

"Phoned Mr. Carlon," Dockard said as Avery inserted a pencil into the bullet holes to check the angles of the shots. "He said he hasn't heard from his daughter in months but knew she wasn't in Layton."

"If he hasn't heard from her in months," I said, "how can he know where she is?"

"He can know where she isn't."

33

I decided not to rise to that bait. I got a roll of antacid tablets from my pocket and popped one of the white disks into my mouth.

"What's that for?" Dockard asked.

"Nervous stomach."

He looked me over appraisingly with small brown eyes. "Can't blame you for that."

I could feel the veiled suspicion, the catlike waiting to pounce on my first wrong move, my first indication of whatever they thought I was trying to pull off.

"Look," I said to Dockard, "I'm only doing my job. We're in the same business. . . . You ought to understand that."

"I don't understand what a Carlon and her daughter would be doing living in a little dump like this, especially here in Layton. And I don't know if I like your line of business, either. It's legalized kidnapping."

"So is what Joan Clark did. The father has as much right to the child as she does. Besides, after I make the snatch I always let the child decide."

"Decide what?"

"Whether to go or stay."

"And what do they do?"

"After we talk it out they usually pick the parent who cared enough about them to hire me."

"And if they don't?"

"I leave them and refund my client's fee. It's in the fine print of my contract."

"That's stupid business."

"It doesn't happen very often. I'm a persuasive talker."

Avery was finished fooling around with the bullet holes.

"Why don't we go in?" I asked, but I was afraid to go in and Dockard could see that.

"Better the front way," he said, and we walked around the house. We must have been driving Mick and his mother crazy.

34

The front door was locked, and at a nod from Dockard, Avery leaned his bulk against it and the latch splintered from the wood frame. My heart tried to scramble up my throat as we went in.

The inside of the tiny house was uncomfortably hot, stuffy, with the thick stillness of a place that has been closed tight for a long time. We were in the living room—red shag carpet, worn sofa, recliner chair, incongruously expensive stereo set up along one wall. The lamp on the table by the front window was still glowing.

None of us said anything. The kitchen was right off the living room; I could see a corner of the green refrigerator. As we walked toward the doorway, a peculiar odor, as of something putrescent, struck me, and my legs began to tremble. The kitchen doorway seemed farther away.

There was no one in the kitchen. One of the chrome-legged chairs was on its side near the stove. On the table a horde of gnats swarmed about the rotting remains of a carryout chicken dinner in a red and white cardboard bucket.

The wood on the inside of the door had splintered away from the bullet holes. The two bullets fired through the door had lodged in the wall above the sink; the shot fired through the window had left a bullet somewhere inside a cupboard containing a jumble of aluminum pots and pans. Silent Sergeant Avery pointed a square-tipped finger at something lying on the white porcelain surface of the ledge of the sink. It was a woman's ring, a ruby surrounded by a circle of diamonds in a gold setting. A jeweler's appraisal wasn't needed to see that its value reached the thousands.

"Keeh-rist!" Dockard said with appropriate respect for wealth. He bent closely over the ring but didn't touch it.

"It might be worth more than the house," I observed.

"I'm going to make a phone call," Dockard said, straightening. "You two wait for me outside."

Within fifteen minutes Dale Carlon arrived in a long gray Mercedes. He got out of the parked car with a minimum of effort, as if he'd rehearsed the move. As he strode toward where we stood in the front yard, I took in the perfectly styled gray hair above even, masculine features, the elegant cut of the gray suit with vest, the wet-looking shine on the expensive black shoes. He was well-groomed; he was flawless. He was the department store's distinguished mannequin struck to life.

"Is this the man?" he said to Dockard without glancing at me.

"Yes, sir," Dockard said. "Alo Nudger is his name."

"Let's see the ring."

Almost before Carlon had asked, Docker's hand shot forward, palm up, with the glinting ring catching the best of the sun.

"It's Joan's," Carlon said without hesitation. "It was a graduation gift." He looked at me now with angular gray eyes. "What do you know about my daughter?" he asked in a level voice.

"That she was living here with your granddaughter."

"I don't expect you to understand this," Carlon said, "but that's rather hard for me to believe. I'm told Gordon Clark hired you."

"Yes, sir." I found myself calling him sir, too. It irritated me. "He's the one who gave me this address."

"I don't doubt that Joan was here," Carlon said to Dockard, "or someone who knows something about Joan. I want the neighbors questioned about the occupants of this house."

"Yes, sir."

Behind Dockard a dented blue Chevy pulled into the driveway next door, and a middle-aged woman and

36

a girl of about seven got out. The woman reached awkwardly into the backseat and straightened up with a brown paper grocery bag. We had caught the girl's attention, and she slipped through the fence where one of the pickets was loose and came running across the yard toward us.

"Grampa!"

The stout middle-aged woman came around the fence and in through the gate, a curious, half-fearful expression on her heart-shaped face.

I saw the smile and the pertly uptilted nose on the little girl, who could only be Melissa Clark. She flew at Dale Carlon with perfect trust, and he bent, hugged her once and kissed her.

"I'm Mrs. Kimmel," the woman said with a nervous smile that pleaded for friendship.

"What are you doing with my granddaughter?" Carlon asked smoothly.

"Are you Joan's father?"

"I am."

Mrs. Kimmel's smile lost its nervousness and gained warmth. "Joan's husband was away for a few days, and she wanted me to baby-sit Melissa while she visited an aunt who's ill in Orlando."

I held out one of the snapshots Gordon Clark had given me. "Is this the woman who lives here?"

Mrs. Kimmel shifted her bag of groceries and looked at the photograph. "Why, yes . . . of course."

I turned to show the photograph to Carlon, but he didn't look at it. He didn't have to. Melissa and the ring constituted all the proof he needed. He was standing still, one hand unconsciously caressing the seven-year-old's slender neck as she clung to his leg. I didn't know if he looked more worried or thoughtful. When he spoke, his voice had lost its aloof assurance.

"Joan doesn't have an aunt in Orlando," he said. "Or a husband anywhere."

5

We drove toward the Layton police headquarters. I sat in the front seat of the plain tan sedan, next to the driver, Avery. Dockard sat in back, directly behind me; he was silent, but I could almost hear his brain whirring. Dale Carlon drove ahead of us in his sleek Mercedes, as if forging the way.

The headquarters building was a low, beige-brick structure with several tall antennas jutting from its flat roof. It was set on a wide green lawn, neatly landscaped with low-lying shrubbery, and I could see several parked patrol cars on a blacktopped lot behind the building. Avery held the door open for us and we entered, walked past a grandmotherly receptionist-switchboard operator and down a sterile-tiled hall to an unmarked door. A scrub-faced, somber patrolman went in with Carlon and Dockard. Avery stayed behind, held open the unmarked door for me with polite instructions to wait inside.

Alone in the tiny room, I sat in a straight-backed wooden chair by a small varnished table and slipped an antacid tablet into my mouth. I chewed the tablet frantically, realized I was getting carried away and took a few deep breaths to relax.

I looked around. The room was practically unfurnished—bare floor, single dirty window with broken venetian blinds, only the one small wooden table with three matching chairs and a dented and sloppily repainted file cabinet set against one pale green wall. I didn't like the room.

An hour passed. I knew they were making me wait on purpose, trying to wear down my nerve. They couldn't know there wasn't much need for that. An automobile horn sounded in the distance, and there were muffled voices as several people passed nearby; but all that was visible outside the streaked glass of the single window were the leafy branches of a large tree. The little room smelled of perspiration and fear, and some of it was mine.

Finally Dockard entered the room with Avery at his elbow. Both men appeared tired.

"Sorry to keep you waiting," Dockard lied.

"That's all right," I lied back. "I had fun looking out the window."

He nodded in admiration at the brave front and sat down across from me in one of the straight-backed chairs. Avery remained standing, a stoic figure.

"I'd like your complete story on tape, if you have no objections," Dockard said.

"Am I being officially held for questioning in the girl's disappearance?"

Dockard raised his eyebrows. "Of course not. We thought we had your cooperation. Aren't we in the same business?"

"The same," I said. I knew how it would be if I failed to cooperate, with the missing girl's father owning the town and the police department. Not that I minded cooperating in a straight game, but this was hardly that.

Dockard smiled and rested his hands on the varnished tabletop in a passive gesture, and Avery walked to the dented file cabinet and took a recorder from the top drawer. I had the notion to request a lawyer, but wasn't that the request of a guilty man? And if Carlon owned the law, no doubt he owned the lawyers.

Avery set the recorder, a flat Japanese model, on the table in front of me, and Dockard switched it on, then sat back in his chair expectantly, as if he'd just done something wonderful. I cleared my throat and began to talk.

39

It took me close to half an hour to explain to the recorder how I'd reached my present predicament, starting with the arrival of Gordon Clark at my house trailer and ending with the arrival of the police at 355 Star Lane. Every so often Dockard would interrupt me with questions that didn't seem very pertinent, but even so, I could almost hear the clang of my cell door.

An elderly secretary came in with three large ceramic mugs of coffee on a tray, set the tray on the table next to the humming Japanese recorder and left. Dockard slid one of the mugs across the table to me and turned off the recorder. He spooned sugar and powdered cream into his steaming cup and held up the containers in an offering gesture to me. I declined and took a sip of the strong black coffee, almost hot enough to peel the skin from my lips.

"Does this story jell with the facts?" Dockard asked me confidentially.

"I wouldn't have been so cooperative if it didn't."

He pursed his lips at that. We both knew I'd had no choice.

Avery shifted his weight to his heels and crossed his arms. I'd almost forgotten he was there.

"I'm telling you this because I feel duty bound," Dockard said, "while you still have a chance to change your story. I don't know if you're exactly aware of who Dale Carlon is, but he's the last man for miles around who you'd choose to cross."

"I don't choose to cross anybody," I said. "All I was trying to do was my job, returning Melissa Clark to her father."

"Maybe she belongs with her mother."

". . . Who happens to be Dale Carlon's daughter."

There was a narrowing of his brown eyes without change of facial expression. "It's not like anybody owns this department, Nudger."

40

It's not like it, I thought, *it is it.*

Dockard waited patiently for me to answer, then gave up.

"You mind waiting around while this is transcribed?" he asked finally, slipping the cassette from the recorder.

"Not at all."

He stood and thanked me; then he and Avery walked from the room, leaving half open the door to the hall. As a snub? A dare? I leaned back and sipped coffee that was cool enough now for human consumption.

It was easier to pass the time now that I could hear part of what was going on outside the room—the clatter of a teletype from across the hall, its rhythm broken by the occasional thumping of an electric typewriter; the voices of two men passing the time, talking shop, now and then getting into the subject of the eastern division pennant race. Neither of them knew much baseball.

"Here's something on Branly," one of them suddenly said, interrupting the other's sermon on the virtues of a good defensive shortstop. "According to neighbors, he and his wife and kid lived at the Star Lane address for a little over a month."

"Is the wife the Carlon bitch?"

"So the neighbors say."

"Think they were really married?"

"Who gives a damn anymore?"

"Marion of the Saint Louis Cardinals was the best ever."

Wagner of Pittsburgh, I thought, sitting back in my chair, *and he could hit. . . . So Branly, whoever he may be, is the other man.* I remembered now that Mick, of the saggy T-shirt, had mentioned something about seeing Melissa with her mother and father. This Branly complicated things.

41

I sat quietly, straining for more information, but all I got was baseball misinformation. *Who wanted a short-stop who couldn't hit?*

What was left of my coffee was cold when Dockard came back into the room as if he'd only stepped out a minute ago. I was surprised to see Gordon Clark behind the detective.

Clark stepped into the room and gave me a quick, humorless smile. "Mr. Nudger." He looked bedraggled, and there was slack flesh beneath his reddened eyes. His brown suit was rumpled, and his dark beard was slightly flattened on one side, as he he'd slept on it. I guessed he'd been airborne for the past several hours.

"This him, Mr. Clark?" Dockard asked.

"He's the man I hired."

"Things took an unexpected turn," I said. "I'm sorry."

"I should have come down here with you as you suggested," Clark said.

"That wouldn't have changed anything."

"Nudger's right about that, Mr. Clark," Dockard said. He floated a hand to Clark's shoulder to lead him from the room.

"I'm at the Clover Inn, on Main Drive," I said to Clark.

He nodded as he left the room. Dockard stayed behind.

"He verified your story," Dockard said.

"Then if you don't mind, I've done enough cooperating for the day."

Dockard grinned, opened the door. "Come into my office, Nudger."

It was more than a simple invitation. I got up wearily and followed him down the hall to let him hold open another door for me.

Dockard's office was large, or at least it seemed so to

me after my confinement in the tiny interrogation room. There was a nice walnut desk, pictures on the walls and a soft vinyl chair for me to sit in. The chair was best of all.

"Tired?" Dockard asked, sitting behind his desk and lighting a cigarette.

I didn't think it was a question that deserved an answer.

"Things have gotten even muckier than you think," Dockard said.

I wasn't surprised to hear him say that. The whole affair had taken on a certain inevitable feel, evoking in me the same foreboding that must brush the senses of someone gradually approaching the vortex of a whirlpool.

"Joan Clark and her daughter were living with a man named David Branly," Dockard said, attempting to blow a smoke ring and creating something closer to a mushroom. "Know anything about him?"

"Only that he's lived with Joan and Melissa Clark on Star Lane for a little over a month. I overheard that here earlier." I wondered if I'd been meant to overhear, so Dockard could observe my reaction from some hidden vantage point on the other side of one of the tiny room's walls. "Wasn't I meant to eavesdrop?"

Dockard neither confirmed nor denied. "He's dead," he said.

I considered that a hell of a way to change the subject. My stomach dropped a few notches. "You mean Branly?"

Dockard nodded, lifting a hand to brush back his Hitlerian lock of hair. "Mr. Branly was found dead yesterday in a car parked behind a Laundromat on Surf Avenue."

"And not of natural causes?"

"A twelve-gauge shotgun sawed down to less than eighteen inches was fastened with electrician's tape to

43

the steering wheel column of his car, down low near the floor, where he wouldn't see it. It was aimed up the column, straight through the center of the steering wheel, and a wire ran from the trigger to a lever attached to the accelerator pedal. When Branly stepped down on the pedal to start the car. . . ." Dockard spread his hands, palms down.

In spite of myself I imagined what Branly must have felt—the shock, perhaps the instantaneous knowledge and horror at the blast of flame and noise at his feet.

"He was struck in the stomach and groin," Dockard went on. "Killed instantly."

"Mixed up with an organization, maybe?"

Dockard shrugged. "If it was a gangland killing, this is the first time I've heard of this method being used. Generally these things follow a pattern, and generally they don't happen in Layton." Dockard drew open his flat center drawer, reached in and tossed several glossy photographs on the desk before me.

I tried to swallow my squeamishness, forced myself to pick up the photos and look.

They were Branly's death photos, but they were surprisingly undisturbing to my stomach. The pictures showed a fairly young man from the waist up who appeared to be sleeping and experiencing a bad dream. There were several front shots and two with the head turned for a profile angle. It was a classically handsome profile. Branly was still wearing a plain sport coat and loose-knotted tie, and the only indication of violence was some splatters of blood marring the pattern of the coat. I tried not to think of how the area of the body below the bottom edges of the photographs must look.

"I've never seen him before," I said, laying the photographs back on the desk.

"Neighbors of the Star Lane house have. When they saw those photographs, they identified him immedi-

44

ately as that nice young Mr. Branly. And they identified Joan Clark as Mrs. Branly. Said they were a pleasant young couple, not outgoing, though. Said they moved in just over a month ago and led a quiet life."

"What prompted you to ask the Star Lane neighbors about Branly?"

"The car he was found dead in had out-of-state registration—under Joan Clark."

I sighed, rested my palms on my knees and felt their warm moisture through the material of my pants. "Lieutenant Dockard, if I could help in any way, I would. What I am is a man trying to make a living, and I don't mind telling you I'm into something here I don't want to be into. I never heard of David Branly until today, and I don't like being involved in the investigation of his murder. All I know about any of it is what I've already told you."

Dockard ground out his cigarette stub in a glass ashtray, slowly and carefully, as if it were something alive and he savored the killing of it. The last hazy wisp of smoke had drifted up from the ashtray and dissipated before he looked at me again.

"I believe you, Nudger," he said, "but I don't disallow the fact that I might be wrong. We don't railroad people here in Layton, but you've got to understand that this is an unusual case, an important case to everyone involved." He stood to signify that it was at last time for me to leave.

"Because Carlon is a big man?"

"We both know that's why," Dockard admitted, "and we both know that's the reason certain rules and procedures might be stepped over, or on, in this investigation. If we don't come up with something within a reasonable length of time, there'll be repercussions, so everyone connected with the case wants results."

"What I want is to be out of it."

45

"Maybe you can be, Nudger. Your car's parked in the lot out back."

I stood up stiffly, almost reluctantly, from the soft vinyl chair, crossed the thick carpet to the door.

Walking from Dockard's office was pure pleasure, equaled only by the pleasure of walking from the building.

My humble motel cabin beckoned like home.

6

I steered the green compact into the Clover Inn's gravel parking lot, listening to the tiny stones pinging off the insides of the fenders. Afternoon shadows were lengthening, and I saw that the parking space in front of cabin 5 was in shade.

After I parked and switched off the ignition, the little car's engine turned over a few times on its own, as if overheated. I felt overheated myself. Today brought me closer than I wanted to get to becoming involved in a murder case. The problem with homicides was that there was always someone else involved who was a murderer. All my frayed nerves needed was the knowledge that someone might be stalking me—with my death in mind. I didn't kid myself. I knew it was better to be a dead hero than a live coward. It was just that I didn't have the stomach for it. I lived on.

I struggled out of the car and stretched, realizing abruptly that I was hungry. After a cool shower to make me alive again, I'd eat at the Clover Grill, then phone for reservations on the first flight I could board out of Orlando.

When I entered the cabin, I found Dale Carlon sitting on the bed.

"Afternoon, Mr. Nudger."

I closed the door behind me, wishing I hadn't bothered to come back for my luggage. Carlon was smiling at me—a new side of him. It was an even, handsome, definitely PR smile.

"How did you get in here?" I asked.

"It happens that indirectly I own part of this motel, Mr. Nudger." The smile turned genuine. "You'll find that few doors are locked to me here in Layton."

I was momentarily angry with myself for feeling uncomfortable, awed by his authority. "That brings us around to why you're here," I said.

"I thought you'd like to know you've accomplished your objective. Melissa is returning home with her father on the earliest direct flight. Gordon and I decided it would be better this way until things are settled."

"Maybe I can be on the same flight," I said. I considered offering him a drink, then decided my brand would probably fall below his standards. To hell with it.

"I hope not, Mr. Nudger. I want to hire you."

That took me aback, but it explained why he'd been waiting for me. "As you said, I've already accomplished my objective." I wondered if he was letting Gordon Clark take Melissa because he wanted to or because he knew he'd have to eventually anyway. Or would he have, here in Layton?

The handsome smile grew more confident. "I'm sure I can change your mind."

I knew what he was getting around to. "Why do you want to hire me, Mr. Carlon?"

"To find my daughter."

I walked to the small writing desk, half leaned, half

47

sat on it. "Your daughter is mixed up in murder, Mr. Carlon. I don't want to be. I don't extend my investigative activities that far, but I can give you the names of some top investigators who'd be interested."

"I'd like you to make an exception in my case."

"I'm afraid of murder, Mr. Carlon."

"Would fifty thousand dollars for your services make you less afraid?"

I sat down all the way on the small writing desk and looked at him. He was serious—more than that, sure of himself.

"Not less afraid," I said, "only wealthier. Why would you be willing to pay me that much when you can hire better investigators for a small fraction of the cost?"

With thumb and index finger he smoothed a crease in the leg of his elegant suit. "I have much to lose by unfavorable public exposure of any kind, Mr. Nudger. You're already into the case by accident, as it were, and you've seen some of the dirty linen that I don't wish made public. Since you've seen some, I prefer that you, rather than another unnecessary party, see whatever else must be seen. That way I have only you to trust and not you and someone else. And as your client you owe me at least a modicum of confidentiality. The fifty thousand dollars is for your secrecy as well as your services."

Fear fought greed while Carlon watched with the air of a man who'd seen the battle often.

"A good deal of money," he commented, rooting for his side.

"I'm known for my avarice, Mr. Carlon."

"I see you as practical."

I laughed inside at that, even as I cringed. I already knew what I'd decided, against every instinct but greed.

"This will have to be a handshake deal, Mr. Nudger,

48

without written records of any kind. Ten thousand now, forty thousand when Joan is located or returned to me. And of course I'll pay your expenses." Without averting his gaze he reached into an inside pocket and withdrew a thick stack of green bills, not in an envelope but rubber-banded together. A bit of psychology there. Good psychology. "I won't require a receipt, Mr. Nudger, as a gesture of our mutual trust."

That was meaningless, we both knew. Where could I hide from him if I did decide to run with the ten thousand?

I stood away from the writing desk. With my left hand I accepted the bills, with my right I shook Carlon's dry hand. I detected a very subtle change in his attitude, a confirmation in his eyes. He had judged me correctly.

"I think you'll find," he said, "that my influence can help in your investigation by opening many doors."

"I don't doubt that," I said, glancing at my own door.

"Now, Nudger, where do you intend to start?" Carlon adopted a much more familiar bearing now that he'd bought me, as if any moment he might slip off his shoes and stretch out on the bed.

"I'd like to know where Gordon Clark is."

"Gordon? Why?"

"Because I need to talk to Melissa."

I could see the hesitancy move through his body. He didn't like being probed in a soft spot, and Melissa was that. "Surely there's no need to bring her into this, not at this point."

"She spent the last several months with your daughter, Mr. Carlon. The missing months."

He stared hard at me, trying to read something in my face. "She's only seven. . . ."

"I'll know how to talk to her."

He saw in me what he wanted, and nodded.

"They're at the Dolphin Motel in Orlando. Their flight leaves at seven tonight."

Carlon gave me the motel's phone number and his own private number. Then he left, without the ten thousand he'd brought.

Seven o'clock. To get to Orlando in time to talk to Melissa, I'd have to put off eating again.

Thanks to Carlon, I wasn't hungry now anyway.

7

I was on the outskirts of Orlando by five that evening, and by five fifteen I was listening to the measured ticking of my directional signal while waiting to make a left off a wide four-lane street to park in front of the Dolphin Motel. The drive had taken longer than I'd planned. A brief late-afternoon shower had slowed highway traffic, and though the sun was out brightly again, there were still a few clear droplets and streaks of rainwater on the compact's windshield and gleaming green hood.

The Dolphin Motel was one of those neat and moderately priced family motels, two stories high and built in a wide, sweeping U around a fenced-in swimming pool. The pool was crowded now with a few adults and a proliferation of the preteen and very young, leaping and splashing with unfeigned ecstasy, as though it would never be over. Near the office I walked past a large sheet-metal dolphin that was lurching repeatedly in clumsy mimicry of that species' graceful arcs through ocean waves. There was a self-satisfied, silly grin on what passed for its face.

Gordon and Melissa Clark were in Number 27, second floor, toward the rear of the motel. I climbed metal steps to an iron-railed cement walkway, stepping aside for another flock of small children. The motel was no doubt packed with families here for the illusory adventure of Disney World. For a moment the memories began to bloom at the back of my mind, and I reminded myself of why I was here.

Gordon Clark opened the door immediately at my knock. He looked fresher than he had at police headquarters. The redness was gone from his eyes and he wore neatly creased plaid pants and a blue short-sleeved sport shirt open at the neck. He invited me in and stepped back.

The room was motel modern—two single beds, angular low furniture and a ceiling fixture that resembled a space satellite. Melissa was sitting cross-legged on the floor, near the foot of one of the beds, piecing together a small jigsaw puzzle. Good practice for her, the way her life was going.

"I'm sorry about how things turned out," I told Clark.

"It wasn't your fault. And I have Melissa." He turned toward her. "Melissa, this is Mr. Nudger."

She glanced up from the puzzle. "He has to shave."

I crossed the room and sat on the edge of the bed nearer her. "I've decided never to shave again. I'm going to grow a long beard and tuck it into my belt."

She looked at me and smiled slightly. "How long will that take?"

"Few days."

Melissa put down her puzzle piece. She was ready to argue about that. "Dave didn't shave once all weekend and his beard wasn't that long."

"Must be something wrong with his beard. Who's Dave?"

51

"Mommy's friend."

"I came here to talk to you about your mommy."

"She's gone."

"Do you know where?"

"She said she'd be back."

"Did you like living on Star Lane?"

Melissa shrugged and stared down at the half-completed puzzle, a striped kitten jumping over something not yet pieced together.

"It was bigger than your other house, wasn't it?" I asked before she could get interested again in the puzzle. But she was only staring at it for a focal point.

"No," she said, "the other house was bigger, with lots more people in it."

"Where was the other house?"

"On a street with tall houses on it. It was a 'parment."

"An apartment building?"

"Uh-huh."

"In Layton?"

"Uh-uh." She shook her head no.

"Where at?"

"On a street with other tall houses on it."

"How far away?"

"Long ways."

She picked up a puzzle piece from the carpet, held it with her little finger extended, as if she were holding toast spread with jam.

"Did you like Dave?" I asked.

"Most times. . . ." she answered absently.

"That one goes there, doesn't it?" I said, helping her fit the piece into the puzzle to complete one of the kitten's forepaws. I was given a smile of gratitude. "Did you like living at the apartment best?"

"No, there were people all the time. Mommy and Vic always had people there, talking 'stead of sleeping."

"Who's Vic?" I asked Melissa, glancing at Gordon Clark, who looked stupefied.

"You know. . . ."

"A friend of Dave's?"

She laughed, picked up another puzzle piece.

"A friend of your mom's?"

"Yes."

"What did all these people talk about when they came to your apartment and you were trying to sleep?"

"Ingerence. Other things sometimes, too."

"I don't know what ingerence is, Melissa."

"Well, that's what they talked about. Mom and Vic talked about it all the time, too."

"Did Dave?"

She laughed again. "You're silly."

"Was your mother happy on Star Lane with Dave?"

She seemed to consider, her wide eyes looking inward. "She was worried all the time."

"Did they ever argue?"

"Uh-huh. The time when Vic didn't shave."

"What did they fight about?"

"I dunno." She had about reached her limit of conversing with me and was being drawn back to the challenge of the puzzle. I leaned down again, helping her fit the pieces.

"Did your mom like Vic better than Dave?"

She giggled as she completed the red ball beneath the kitten.

"Vic and Dave are the same person, aren't they?" I said.

"Course."

"Where did you live before the apartment building?"

"Someplace the same. I'm hungry, Dad."

"We'll eat in a little while, Melissa," Gordon Clark said.

I stood up from the bed. "Thanks for talking to me, Melissa."

"I'm hungry now."

"Okay, honey," Clark said, "in just a little while."

53

He and I stepped outside on the bright cement walk-way.

"Did talking to her help you any?" he asked.

"I know more than I did."

Clark slipped his hands into his pants pockets and stood with his shoulders back, as if to expose himself to the maximum amount of sunlight. "Why do you think this Branly guy called himself Vic?"

I glanced down at the kids yelling and thrashing their way through cool water in the pool. "We'll know that when we find out why he was killed."

"And why Joan's disappeared?"

I nodded. "Why everything." I watched him half close his eyes to the sun. "Do you think Joan might come back to you?"

"No, but I'll let you know if she does." Clark smiled his curiously dreary smile, shook my hand. "I'll mail you the second part of your fee."

"That won't be necessary," I told him. "I didn't earn it." As I heard myself speak, I was amazed at the generosity rooted in my newfound wealth.

"I have Melissa back."

"You probably would have got her back without me."

He slipped the fingertips of his right hand back into his pocket. "I feel I should warn you about something, Nudger."

"Go ahead," I told him. "I have so much to worry about now, it probably won't make much difference."

"In confidence, of course."

"Of course."

"I don't think you should trust your client all the way."

I waited for him to tell me why. He chose not to, so I nodded and thanked him for the word of caution. He was Dale Carlon's son-in-law; he should know.

When Clark opened the door to go inside, Melissa

peered out from the comparative dimness of the motel room.

"Come back when you have your beard," she said.

I decided to have dinner at a western-style steak house in Orlando before driving back to Layton. As I ate the surprisingly good rib-eye and baked potato, I thought over my conversation with Melissa. She was a typically succinct and scatterbrained seven-year-old, and though our talk had brought out a few hard facts, I suspected that what she'd given me were puzzle pieces much like the ones she'd held in her hands. Why did Branly use two first names? Where was the apartment in which they'd lived? Who were the people who had visited them often? And what the hell was "ingerence"?

By the time I reached dessert I knew which way I'd have to go in the investigation. Melissa hadn't given me a starting point, so it would have to be the dead David Branly. *He* was easy enough to keep tabs on, and the Layton police should have had some background information on him by now. If I probed about in that area of time just before his death and traced his movements, I was bound to learn something of the recent activities of Joan Clark. The trouble was that Branly's murderer was also a part of that area of time, making it a dangerous area in which to be probing about.

The house on Star Lane would be the place to start, and with Dale Carlon's influence the Layton police should be completely cooperative.

I finished my ranch-house pudding and signaled a cowgirl for a refill on the coffee. It was going to be a long drive back to Layton.

8

Gaining access to the Star Lane house was no problem, involving only a phone call to Dale Carlon, who offered to meet me there the next day with the key.

In the morning, again using Carlon's influence, I phoned Dockard at the Layton police headquarters from my cabin at the Clover Inn and asked him what had been turned up on the Branly killing.

"To date, nothing much," Dockard said. "The ME tells us Branly died in his late twenties, perfectly healthy except for all those shotgun pellets. Nothing on the gun yet, either. Wiped clean of prints. You know how impossible it is to trace a shotgun. It's an Ithaca twelve-gauge semi-automatic with the stock and barrel sawed down. A fairly expensive gun, about seven years old, according to the company's check of the serial number."

"Making it all the harder to trace. Anything found in the house that might help?"

"We combed it fine; there's nothing there, but you're welcome to look for yourself if you want."

As long as Carlon's behind me, I thought. "What about Branly's fingerprints? You should be able to get some specific information about him through them."

Dockard's tone was tolerant. "His prints aren't on file. Apparently he was never in the service and hasn't got a record."

I thanked the lieutenant and hung up. The fact that Branly had no record was in itself interesting. It made the possibility of his having been killed in a gangland assassination all the more unlikely.

There was little comfort for me in that unlikelihood. The lone and unpredictable killer frightened me more than the underworld hit man. If I had to be murdered, I wanted it done by a professional. Anything to reduce the possibility of prolonged pain.

I shook my head and called myself a few derogatory but accurate names. After setting my watch by the clock on the nightstand, I left for my appointment with Carlon at the Star Lane house.

I was ten minutes early but Carlon was there, waiting in front of 355 Star Lane in his gray Mercedes. When he saw me drive up in the green compact, he got out of his car and came toward me. He was dressed in a tailor-made, very expensive navy-blue suit that was as out of place on Star Lane as was his Mercedes. I, on the other hand, fit right in.

Carlon nodded a hello to me, then handed me a house key. "You might as well keep it, Nudger."

"Okay," I said, "let's go see if it works."

I unlocked the front door and we stepped inside, onto the red shag carpet. The atmosphere was hot and stifling, and I had the same claustrophobic feeling that I'd experienced entering the house the first time, with Dockard and Avery. There was even an aftertaste of fear.

"My God!" Carlon said. "Don't they have any air conditioning?" He spotted a thermostat and went for it, pushing something that brought a click, a rattling hum and supposedly cool air.

I walked around the living room slowly, then went into the kitchen. The rotting remains of the carryout chicken dinner had been removed. The slugs had been dug from the wall, and presumably, the bullet in the cupboard had been located and removed. Everything else seemed unmoved, as if I were looking at a photograph for the second time. The chrome-legged chair still lay on its side on the linoleum, and I saw that the kitchen wastebasket still contained litter.

"The landlord's being compensated to keep hands off for a while," Carlon explained behind me.

I opened the green refrigerator, found a still-sealed quart of milk, a few condiment jars and some bologna going bad on the top shelf. The refrigerator clicked on to add its hum to the air conditioner's, and I closed the door.

"Do you really expect to find something here that the police missed?" Carlon asked.

"Not necessarily, but I might interpret something differently."

He faded back into the living room. After checking out the kitchen, looking inside cupboards and drawers, under shelf paper, behind the stove and then through the litter in the wastebasket, I joined him.

"Find anything?" he asked.

"Only what you'd expect after somebody moved out on a few hours' notice." I went to check the bedrooms.

The first bedroom must have been Melissa's. There were a few toys lying about, some brightly covered books and some threadbare dresses in the closet. The dresser drawers contained only the usual assortment of underclothes and some blankets. Decals of cartoon characters covered the wall behind the bed, and their happy, zany expressions seemed out of place in the otherwise drab room.

The other bedroom had been Branly and Joan's, a pale blue room furnished cheaply and sparsely. There was little sign of Joan there—a pink hairbrush on the dresser top with a few dark hairs caught in its bristles, an empty perfume bottle and a pair of high-heeled shoes with one of the heels broken. There were more of Branly's effects in the bedroom, but they were curiously impersonal. A suit and three shirts in the closet—pockets empty—and some socks and underwear in one of the dresser drawers. I could almost imagine Joan Clark removing anything that might pertain to his identity before she left. Sadly enough, she seemed to have forgotten nothing.

I checked empty drawers, the tops of closet shelves; I even peered under the bed. With no results. On the floor, near the bed, were a couple paperback books—a Gothic romance and a self-help book on salesmanship, both worn and dog-eared. I turned the books binding-up and thumbed through the pages in the hope of finding something wedged there, but nothing fell out. Maybe Branly had been a salesman, or maybe the books had been left in the house by a previous tenant. I walked back into the living room, disgusted with my lack of progress, my stomach churning just from being in the small and depressing house.

"It seems to me you're wasting valuable time here, Nudger," Carlon said, standing with his hands locked behind him as he stared out the front window.

"There was only one way to know for sure," I said, reaching for my roll of antacid tablets. I fumbled, trying to pry the top disk loose from the silver foil, and the roll of tablets squirted from my fingers and bounced across the carpet, not getting very far in the thick red shag. When I bent to pick up the roll, I saw something that made me forget my immediate need for a tablet.

The house had apparently been decorated just before Branly and Joan had moved in; the woodwork was freshly enameled. But near the kitchen doorway, where the telephone sat on a small table, I saw a set of numerals scratched on the underside of the flawlessly enameled molding that ran along the wall, four feet above the floor. I moved nearer and examined the phone number more closely.

"This number mean anything to you?" I asked Carlon, then read off the numerals.

But he hadn't heard me. He was staring, as if fascinated, at a newspaper on the sofa. I walked over and saw that the paper was folded to the story and photo of a man named Robert Manners, a Los Angeles business executive who had committed suicide due to the pressures of his job. He'd jumped from the high roof of his office building, and a photographer had caught his image on the way down, arms and legs outspread, tie trailing like an aviator's scarf, coattails of an expensive dark suit—one like Carlon's—standing straight out in the rushing wind. I wondered how much contentment Carlon's money had really bought him. Then I recited the phone number again and he gave a little start and focused his attention on me.

"I'm unfamiliar with the number," he said. "Where did you find it?"

"It was freshly scratched on the woodwork near the phone. There's a writing pad and pencil by the phone, so it could be that whoever scratched this number considered it very important. A piece of paper can get lost a lot easier than a piece of woodwork."

"That makes obvious sense, to a point," Carlon said. "How could the police have overlooked it?" There was an edge to his voice, the voice of a man uncompromising toward incompetence.

"It wasn't meant to be found. I'd have missed it myself but for the good fortune of being clumsy." Why was I sticking up for Dockard?

"I don't see any reasonable excuse," Carlon said. "The number was in the house; it should have been found."

He was right, but it was a waste of time to quibble. I went to the phone, started to lift the receiver, then replaced it. A call might only serve to put someone on his guard. "The phone company should have a cross directory that will give us the address that corresponds with this number. Why don't I give the number to Dockard and let him check it through them?"

"The police overlooked the number," Carlon said. "I see no reason to give it to them now."

I stood, dumbfounded, and stared at him. "You want your daughter found, don't you?"

"Of course! That's why I hired you. But perhaps we should take the incompetence of the Layton police as a measure of luck. As far as I'm concerned, Mr. Nudger, the police are involved in this case only because I have no choice."

I stood in the stale air of the living room, waiting for him to continue. The rattling air conditioner had made little headway, and a bead of perspiration sought its way like a drop of cold mercury down the contours of my ribs.

"What I don't want," Carlon said, "is for the police to be delving into my daughter's private life. There's more at stake here than just the solution to a murder, to which Joan happens to be merely coincidental. Ruthless as it may sound to you, I have my career to consider. And beyond that, certain political possibilities that might surprise you."

"And your daughter's behavior reflects on you, is that it?"

"Not only that. For her own sake I don't want Joan's reputation blackened by aspersions."

"Or facts?"

"Or facts, damn it!"

"We're not only talking about poor judgment here, Mr. Carlon. Withholding evidence in a murder case is illegal. Even a hint of it and I can have my investigator's license revoked and lose my livelihood."

"You'd have me behind you, Nudger. And how long would it take you to earn fifty thousand dollars?"

I put my fists on my hips, started to pace on the red shag. I didn't like what he was suggesting, not only because it was illegal but because it was dangerous. I'd counted on the police involvement to give me at least some protection if and when I crossed paths with Branly's killer, and there was a factor in this case that made that crossing of paths even more likely than Car-

61

lon thought. I wondered if he'd considered that the death trap that had killed Branly might have been meant for Joan Clark. After all, it was her car, and going to the Laundromat was still basically a woman's chore.

"I'm not suggesting that we automatically withhold from the police everything you turn up," Carlon said with a note of exasperation. "Whenever you learn something of importance, we can determine whether the police should share in the information. Remember—you're searching for Joan, they're searching for Branly's murderer."

"What about this phone number?"

Carlon smiled. "I'll have it checked for an address, confidentially. I'll phone you later today with the information." He walked over, rested his arm on my shoulder in a grand gesture of camaraderie. "After all, it might not be anything important. This might be the phone number of a dry cleaner or delicatessen. . . ."

"Or Laundromat."

The smile stayed but the arm went. "That might be, Mr. Nudger. We'll just have to determine the facts."

We left 355 Star Lane together. I sat in my car for a minute, fixing into my key case the house key Carlon had given me. As I looked up, I saw Carlon lift a manicured hand from his steering wheel in a parting wave as he passed me in his Mercedes. He'd bought a lot for his fifty thousand. That "let the buyer beware" adage is backward.

But Carlon was good for his word on the phone number. He called me that afternoon at the Clover Inn and gave me a name and address on Dade Avenue, and he asked me to phone him as soon as I'd checked it out.

Daisy Rogers was the name. I was hoping the number wouldn't belong to a woman. What if Branly had been seeing Daisy Rogers on the sly? That would explain the concealed phone number, and whatever information it might lead to about Branly would be just what he'd chosen to let her know about himself. Probably very little.

I got directions to Dade Avenue from Eddie at the motel office and found that the street was only three blocks east of the motel, though the 2200 address I wanted was some distance south.

The 2200 block of Dade turned out to be a palm-lined street of inexpensive stucco houses set almost at the curb, as if the wide avenue had eroded the front lawns like the sea. The address Carlon had given me was on the corner, a small house painted a pale flamingo pink. A screened-in porch ran across the front of the house, and in the front yard was an old wheelbarrow, also painted pink, used as a planter and exploding with a colorful display of flowers. When I got near the porch, I saw that the screening was old and rusty, paint peeling about the framework.

After five rings of the bell the door was opened by a very old woman with lank gray hair hanging down onto her forehead. She was thin to the point of being emaciated, and age had bent her and humped her narrow back.

I caught myself staring at her. "Daisy Rogers?"

"That's me," she said brightly.

"The Branlys wanted me to let you know they'd be out of town for a few days." I knew I'd be safe in telling her that, since Carlon had kept David Branly's death out of the Layton papers.

She peered at me with lusterless eyes and cocked her head. "The who?"

"The Branlys—David Branly. He gave me your address and phone number. I was going to call you but was near here anyway on business, so I thought I'd relay the message personally."

Daisy Rogers shook her head slowly. She might have been seventy or ninety. "Don't know any Branlys."

I endeavored to look as puzzled as I felt. "Are you sure? . . . This is your address and phone number, isn't it?" I handed her a piece of paper with the information.

She placed an ancient pair of rimless spectacles, somebody's future heirloom, on the bridge of her nose, moved out closer to the sunlight and concentrated on the paper for almost a full minute. A musty scent wafted out of the house behind her. "Yep. You're at the right place. Maybe these Branlys know my boy Mark."

"Is he home?"

"Should be soon. Why don't you come in? Or you can sit there and wait on the shady end of the porch if you want. Cooler than inside."

I'd decided to wait on the wooden glider suspended on rusty chains from the porch ceiling when Daisy Rogers looked past me and white eyebrows raised on her speckled forehead.

"There's Mark now."

I turned to see a tall, stooped man, bald with a fringe of gray, shuffling toward the porch steps. He was carrying a paper bag, and he looked, if anything, older than his mother.

"Mark, this is Mister. . . ."

"I came with a message from the Branlys," I told him.

"Damn young punk bastards!" he said, wobbling his head as if he hadn't heard.

"The Branlys?" I asked.

"All of 'em! I don't mind their fashions and their alley cat morals, but I don't like to be cheated without 'em botherin' to try to fool me!"

I stood patiently and let him talk, knowing I hadn't made contact.

"Took this new shirt back"—he held up the wrinkled bag—"'cause it ripped under the arms when I put it on. Young clerk said he couldn't take it back 'cause it

64

was torn. Told him that was why I brung it back! He said he knew the material was weak; that's why the shirt was on sale. Turned his back on me!"

"Keep yourself calm, Mark," his mother put in.

"Did you ever!" he said.

"I ever," I told him. "Do you know Branly?"

He stared at me as if I'd dropped from the porch ceiling. "Don't know any Branlys, didn't I tell you?"

"No, sir."

"Offer you a cold beer?"

I declined with thanks.

As I left, he was trying clumsily to light a pipe while discoursing on the advantages of wooden matches over the new paper ones.

In the sun-heated compact I sat for a minute and looked around at the other houses. I had come to the address Carlon had given me, and Daisy Rogers had confirmed the telephone number. It was possible I'd misread one of the numerals scratched in the woodwork by the Star Lane phone. I started the car and drove farther south on Dade Avenue, until it intersected Palm Road.

The air conditioner Carlon had turned on yesterday was still humming its rattling tune, and the air inside the Star Lane house was almost breathable. I shut the door behind me and went directly to the phone and examined the numbers scratched on the underside of the woodwork. They were as clearly legible as I remembered.

A phone directory rested on the crosspiece of the telephone table's wooden leg braces. I reached down for the directory, opened the front cover, then tossed the book onto the red shag carpet. Picking up the telephone by the hand-hold behind the receiver cradle, I brought it down with me as I settled onto the carpet, next to the directory, and leaned my back against the wall. I opened the directory and began going down the line, dialing long-distance area codes, then the number scratched into the woodwork.

As each distant telephone was answered, I would ask for David Branly, then Vic Branly, and I would try to gauge the reaction of whoever was on the other end of the line. What I most often got was a vague puzzlement, sometimes annoyance.

I was beginning to perspire, and my back was aching from leaning against the hardness of the wall. Then finally, after dialing area code 312 and the phone number that was now etched in my memory as deeply as it was in the woodwork, I got the sort of reaction I'd been seeking.

"Dave? . . ." came the puzzled voice after I'd spoken. "There is no David Branly here . . ." It was a man's voice, nasal and uncertain.

"What about Vic?" I asked.

"Who is this?"

"A friend of Dave's."

A click and a buzz greeted that statement.

I replaced the receiver in its cradle and waited, watching a fly crawl laboriously up the opposite wall. As if the altitude had become too much for it, the fly began to veer to the right as it neared the ceiling. Something was making a hissing sound in the quiet room—my breathing.

The telephone rang.

On the third ring I picked up the receiver and pressed it to my ear, said nothing.

"Hello, Dave? . . ." came the same voice that had been on the line a few minutes before. "Vic? . . ."

Gently I replaced the receiver, picked it up again for a dial tone. Dale Carlon's secretary followed her instructions and rushed through my call to him.

"How long would it take you to get me a name and address for the Daisy Rogers number with a 312 area code?" I asked Carlon. "Probably in Chicago."

"You mean it's not a local number?"

"Not for our purposes. A very old woman and her son live at the Dade address."

"What about the son?"

"He seems older than the mother and has rips in his shirt."

There was little time in Carlon's day for digression. His telephone voice was terse. "I should be able to have that corresponding name and address for you within an hour."

"I'll be waiting at the Star Lane phone," I told him and got off the line so he could get busy.

Sitting on the carpet with my arms crossed on my knees, I wondered if Carlon could do it, if his influence carried that far from Layton.

I got up, stretched, and walked around the cramped, oppressive living room to work the stiffness from my aging bones. The air seemed to get staler, the walls closer together.

An hour and ten minutes had passed when Carlon called back.

The phone number belonged to a man named Roger Horvell, 67 Sirilla Street, in Chicago. I thanked Carlon, then punched and freed the cradle button to get a dial tone. After talking to Eastern Airlines in Orlando, I drove to the Clover Inn to pack.

This time Lieutenant Dockard was waiting for me.

9

Dockard was standing with his foot propped on the dusty front bumper of his unmarked car, parked in front of my cabin. He smiled as I parked next to him, looking over my rented compact as if pondering whether to get one for himself.

I got out of the car, nodded to him and walked over to where he was standing.

"You and I need to talk," Dockard told me, squinting into the sun behind me but holding his friendly smile.

"We talked a lot yesterday," I said.

Dockard didn't move from his relaxed position, but I could see he was waiting for me to invite him inside, out of the heat. I decided to let the sun work for me and keep the conversation short.

"We need to understand a few things about your working for Dale Carlon," Dockard said, seeing that our talk was going to be brief and getting to the point. "Mr. Carlon has . . . let's say a habit of stepping outside the rules sometimes and doing things in his own fashion."

"You were careful to explain that to me yesterday."

Dockard picked at an imaginary wart on his palm. "I understand the confidence you owe Mr. Carlon," he said, weighing each word for its potential to boomerang, "but you also have some responsibility to the law. Mr. Carlon means well, but he's not a professional like we are. He might get some mistaken notions. . . ."

"Any particular notion in mind?" I asked.

A large mosquito droned in unpredictable circles around Dockard's head, sizing him up. Dockard swatted the air where the mosquito had been. "What I mean, Nudger, is that the more people we have work-

68

ing on this case, the sooner it's likely to be solved. I wouldn't want you to think it would be best to with-hold anything from the Layton police. And of course we'll share whatever we know with you."

There was a something-for-nothing offer. Dockard wouldn't dare withhold anything pertinent from me now that I represented Dale Carlon.

"I'm aware of my obligation to the law," I said.

"I'm sure. It's just that Mr. Carlon, well-meaning as he is, might instruct you to operate, sometimes, with us still in the dark. And I think, considering the circum-stances of the case, that I owe you a certain confidence if you keep me informed."

"Without Carlon's knowledge?"

"I'm only asking you to obey the law, Nudger." He flicked a hand again at the phantom mosquito.

What Dockard was saying was that whenever Carlon instructed me to keep something from the Layton po-lice, I could tell Dockard without fear of Carlon's finding out. It was less serious to betray a client's trust than to withhold evidence in a murder investigation, and Dockard was giving me the opportunity to ex-change one transgression for the other. I remembered his words of yesterday, about Carlon being the one man not to cross; and today he was asking me to do just that.

"You're telling me I can have it both ways," I said.

"If that's how you want to think of it. Either way I'd like you to keep this talk confidential."

"You've got that."

"At least my way, if Mr. Carlon does have some wrong suggestions, you've got an out."

At the risk of fifty thousand dollars, I thought, not to mention the possibility of Carlon's revenge. I doubted if Dockard knew the stakes were that high. People like Carlon confused things.

"If the situation comes up," I said to Dockard, "I'll think about it."

69

There was something in his face that made me feel he knew the situation already had come up. He nodded, removed his foot from the dusty chrome bumper. "It's something for you to consider."

Now the mosquito began droning about me. I'd thought it was my friend. Dockard walked around to the driver's side of the car and opened the door.

"I remember Joan Clark," he said before he got in. "She's not going to be found easily if she doesn't want to be."

I stood and watched Dockard drive off the lot. He yielded to an overloaded station wagon making a left to get to the Clover Inn's office, then his plain car, with its square-tipped shortwave antenna, merged with the light traffic on Main Drive.

Dockard had given me something to think about. Was his proposition made out of a genuine concern to solve Branly's murder and find Joan Clark as soon as possible? Or was he trying to make sure that the Layton police department and Lieutenant Dockard accomplished whatever was needed and received full credit from Carlon? I didn't doubt that the latter might be his motive. A man like Carlon could do a lot for a police lieutenant like Dockard in a town like Layton.

I swatted at the mosquito.

There was another very strong possibility I couldn't overlook. Was Carlon aware of Dockard's visit? After our conversation at the Star Lane house, had he asked the lieutenant to put the proposition to me to test me?

That possibility was reason fifty thousand and one for me to play the game straight with Carlon and to not mention to Lieutenant Dockard that I was going to Chicago.

10

My flight arrived at Chicago's O'Hare International on time to the minute. After making my way through the crowd that was bustling to the incomprehensible rhythm of the public address speakers, I claimed my luggage and took a Continental limo into the city.

At one of the big hotels on North Michigan, I got out and left my luggage in the check room. There was no point in registering anywhere yet; I had no way of knowing if my stay in Chicago would last for days or for hours. Outside the hotel I got into one of the cabs parked in single waiting line at the curb and gave the driver Roger Horvell's address.

After a drive through the hippiness-mellowing-to-campiness of Old Town, the taxi entered an area of recent renovation and pulled to the curb in front of a fairly new tall building with a glassed-in lobby that gave off a silvery mirrored effect. I paid the driver, left the cab, then watched my image ascend the concrete steps and reach for the push plate on one of the wide glass double doors.

The lobby featured a small, bubbling Florentine fountain that on close inspection appeared to be constructed entirely of plastic. I walked around the fountain and crossed the scuffed tile floor to a bank of metal mailboxes by an ornate wrought iron gate that blocked access to the elevators. I pressed the pearled plastic button beneath Horvell's mail slot.

He was home. I identified myself over the intercom and told him I wanted to see him regarding David Branly. His nasal voice betrayed confusion and maybe a little fright as he invited me to come up. I understood how he felt; my own gut was beginning to tighten with apprehension. A buzzer sounded, and I passed through the wrought iron gateway and rode the elevator to the fifth floor.

Roger Horvell was a small man in his late twenties, balding prematurely, with thick glasses and a large nose a bit too bulbous to be charitably called hawklike. He was wearing window-check pants and a loose-fitting brown knit pullover shirt with an alligator sewn above the pocket. His casual attire didn't fit his nervousness.

"What is it about David?" he asked, pacing to a large window that afforded a view of the building across the street. It was a taller building than the one we were in, with draped and private windows.

Horvell's nervousness made me feel more confident. I sat on a modern, uncomfortable and obviously inexpensive sofa, noticing that the plush blue carpeting in the new apartment was already beginning to wear. "I need some information about Branly," I said, "and unfortunately he's in no position to help me."

Horvell turned to face me, scratched a scrawny arm as if he had poison ivy. "Is Dave in some kind of trouble?"

"It could be put that way," I said.

He nodded jerkily, sighed, as if he'd expected to hear that news. "You said you were a private detective. What has that to do with David?"

"Nothing directly. Where do you know Branly from?"

Horvell hesitated, then the apprehensive, magnified eyes behind the thick lenses seemed to register the expression of a man waist deep in cold water who has decided to submerge the rest of himself. "We worked together, for the same company."

"What company?"

"David hasn't done anything, has he?"

"No," I said, and waited silently for the answer to my question.

Horvell ran a hand over his balding head as if he still had a mop of hair. "High Grade Hardware," he said in a resigned, nasal tone. "I still work there."

"How long has Branly been gone?"

"Almost a year."

"Fired or quit?"

"Neither," Horvell said hastily. "He was a good company man, one of the best at High Grade, but his job of secondary cost analyst became obsolete."

"If he was so competent, why didn't the company keep him and work him into some other job?" I asked, wondering just what a secondary cost analyst was.

Horvell smiled bitterly. "Things are tight at High Grade, as they are now in most businesses. But blood is still thick, and as in most businesses, there's a certain amount of nepotism at High Grade. David's job was primarily a backup position in a system of double checks that the company felt they could eliminate. I know for sure they didn't want to let him go, but a favored nephew was 'working his way up' in the organization, and since David had no marketing experience. . . ."

"How long had Branly worked there?"

"About five years—the same as me. We were brought here to the main office at the same time, got to be good friends. I frankly admired him for his shrewdness and ambition."

I sat there with the feeling that all this information wouldn't get me anywhere, or Horvell wouldn't be giving it to me.

"Where did Branly go after he left High Grade?" I asked.

Horvell's mouth opened and closed and he shrugged his thin shoulders.

"I have certain restrictions on what I can tell you without my client's consent, Mr. Horvell, but I *can* tell you that you're not helping Branly anymore by keeping his secrets."

"You called here this morning, didn't you?"

I nodded.

He peeled off his glasses, wiped them on his shirt and looked at me myopically. "Who is your client, Mr. Nudger?"

I had a good idea of what button to press to get Horvell's cooperation. "Have you heard of Carlon Plastics?"

"Of course."

"My client is Dale Carlon, president and chairman of the board."

"Christ!"

"Almost."

Horvell paced back and looked out the wide window. That seemed to be a favorite move of his to gather his thoughts. I saw his shoulders square, and he turned to face me again and replaced his glasses on his oversize nose.

"You're investigating something criminal?"

"Yes, and I advise you strongly not to implicate yourself by lying to me. I understand your loyalty, Mr. Horvell, and I do give you my word that nothing you tell me can be used to harm Branly."

"He lived here for a while," Horvell said, "after he was let go at High Grade. It was a matter of economics. The company wasn't able to give him much severance pay. I was glad to help him."

"How long did he live here?"

"Until about three months ago. Then he got some money from somewhere, moved into an apartment with a girl he was going with."

"An apartment where?"

"He never would tell me, and that's the truth."

"Did you ever meet the girl?"

Horvell nodded. "A few times. Joan Clark was her name."

"This her?" I showed him one of the photographs Gordon Clark had given me.

74

"Yes, that's the same girl," Horvell said. There was something else he wanted to say. I waited patiently for him to get it out. "You'll be doing more checking, won't you? Asking questions at High Grade Hardware?"

"I plan to."

"Then there's . . . something else," Horvell admitted. "David Branly never worked there. There is no David Branly. His real name is Victor Talbert."

"Why did he change it?"

"He never said. He changed it after he moved out. I asked him once but he was evasive." Horvell stuttered a nervous, nasal laugh. "I really don't know much; that's why I don't so much mind trying to answer your questions."

I believed him there. He saw that he'd been drawn into something with the potential to pull him all the way under. I was in a perfect position to sympathize.

"What other friends of Victor Talbert's did you meet?" I asked.

"None," Horvell said quickly. "The only friends we really had in common were from the office, and Vic seemed to lose interest in them entirely after he was let go. He formed new friendships somewhere. I don't know what he did while I was working; one reason we shared the apartment was because of my long working hours. We knew we'd seldom get in each other's way."

"You remember him or this Joan Clark mentioning any names?"

Horvell bit his lower lip and thought hard. I expected him to pace to the window, but he didn't. "One," he said finally. "Somebody or something named Congram. I remember because Vic mentioned the name once and Joan seemed to get angry."

"That's all—Congram?"

"That's all he said. I don't even remember in what context."

75

"All the time he was living with you, was Talbert trying to land another job?"

The stuttering laugh came again. "At first he was. Executives like Vic can't, or won't, take just any job. And as scarce as middle management positions are, his back was to the wall. Oh, he had some menial jobs offered to him, but it isn't in Vic's nature to take a step backward."

"How did you come to have Talbert's phone number, Mr. Horvell?"

"About a month ago Vic dropped by here. He said he was going away—wouldn't say where. But he left me his number for a sort of touchstone. He told me he was going to live under the name of David Branly, and he might phone me if he needed anyone, in case of trouble."

"What kind of trouble?"

"I tried to get him to tell me, but he wouldn't. He was frightened, though. I could tell that. It was the first time I'd ever seen him scared. Vic Talbert is the sort of man who exudes confidence."

"What about the girl?" I asked in a throwaway voice.

"Vic said Joan Clark would be with him. And he mentioned something about her little girl."

"Have you talked to him since then?"

"No. When I asked him what I was supposed to do if he phoned, he said 'maybe nothing,' that he'd let me know if the time came."

Horvell walked over to a small portable bar set up in a corner.

"Can I get you something?" he asked.

I told him no thanks and watched him pour himself two fingers of good Scotch. His hands trembled slightly, and the neck of the bottle clinked on the glass and seemed to embarrass him. He knocked down half the drink in one loud gulp. I couldn't be sure that he was uncomfortable because he was hiding something; he was a human nerve.

76

"I'd like to ask a favor of you, Nudger," he said in an unsteady nasal whine. "When you go to High Grade Hardware, try to leave my name out of it. I just can't afford to be messed up in my career."

"I don't know if that will be possible, Mr. Horvell. Victor Talbert is dead."

I thought he was actually going to drop the glass. It slipped an abrupt inch in his hand, and he staggered to a chair and sat down. "Dead? . . . How did it happen? Was it the trouble Vic talked about? . . ."

"Maybe. He was murdered, Mr. Horvell."

"Murdered! Christ! Is that what you're investigating?"

"No, the police are investigating that, and when they get around to you, I advise you to tell them what you told me. Unless you have something to add."

He shook his head absently. "Murdered . . ." he said unbelievingly to himself.

I thanked him for talking to me and stood to leave. Instead of showing me out he continued sitting and tossed down the rest of his drink. His myopic eyes were desperate. I could almost see his agitated brain writhing like a mass of worms.

"Nudger!" The imploring nasal voice stopped me when my hand touched the doorknob.

I turned and waited for Horvell to wring out whatever he had to say. His mouth worked before any sound came out, as if the air in the apartment had suddenly become too thin to carry sound.

"Do you promise to leave my name out of it, if possible, at High Grade?"

"If possible," I told him.

He stared hard at me and seemed to find me trustworthy, but then, he wanted to so badly.

"Vic was seeing another woman at the same time as Joan Clark," he said, as if we'd struck a deal. "Her name was Belle Dee."

"Do you know where I can find her?"

"I have her address. Vic had me pick him up there one evening." He got up and walked to a small desk near the entrance to the dining room. With a bit of rummaging about in one of the drawers, he found what he was looking for, copied it on another piece of paper and handed it to me.

"Remember about leaving me out of it," he said.

"I'll do what I can," I told him, opening the door.

"Vic, dead . . ." he murmured again unbelievingly, running his hand through his imaginary hair.

"Dead . . . dead . . . dead . . ." I repeated to myself, walking down the long carpeted hall to the elevator, as if that would help to exorcise the growing, twisting sensation of fear in my chest and stomach.

It didn't help.

11

After leaving Horvell's apartment I took a cab to claim my luggage. Then I rented a car—knowing I'd be in town for a while—this time a full-size sedan.

I checked in at the TraveLodge Motel, on South Michigan Avenue, not too far from the headquarters of High Grade Hardware. I made a few phone calls, had dinner and a few drinks to untie my knots, and slept almost as deeply as Victor Talbert.

High Grade Hardware's corporate headquarters turned out to be a tall, square building of what looked to be burnished copper glinting in the bright morning sun. Outside the imposing entrance was a tall aluminum flagpole, and beneath the American flag flew the company's smaller flag, a black crossed hammer and wrench insignia on a field of white.

The reception area inside the entrance was also done up in black and white. I walked over to an astoundingly beautiful blonde seated behind a wide, bare desk and told her who I was and that I had an appointment with T. J. Harper, the personnel manager.

Harper saw me immediately, which surprised the blonde. She didn't know that after a Dale Carlon phone call the president of High Grade Hardware had passed down the word to cooperate with me. I was beginning to experience occasional exhilarating delusions of power, but I knew that I'd still bleed.

T. J. Harper's office continued the black and white motif, with a large plaque with High Grade's hammer and wrench insignia mounted on the wall behind his desk. An affable-looking man with an air of efficiency, Harper was wearing a blue pinstriped suit and a semimilitary haircut that was gray wire at the temples. He smiled a nice smile and motioned for me to sit down, then sat down himself and laced his fingers on his desk top. I felt somewhat like a job applicant.

I told him I appreciated his taking the time to see me and that I wanted information about a former employee at High Grade. He didn't seem surprised when I told him the name of that former employee.

"Victor Talbert was a fine young man," he said, "an ideal employee. It was regrettable that we no longer had a niche in which to fit him. Under present conditions it simply doesn't pay to do some of the things you'd like to do."

"Did Talbert get along all right with the other employees?"

"Certainly," Harper said, as if I'd been indelicate to ask. "He had no enemies here except within the framework of honest competition. If it were possible for Victor Talbert to walk in here today, and an opening suited his qualifications, I'd rehire him without a qualm. He was strictly the victim of declining sales, and job training that became obsolete practically overnight. That sort of thing happens frequently."

"How did he take his dismissal?"

Harper unlaced his fingers and dropped his hands out of sight beneath the desk. There were faint damp spots on the polished wood where his hands had rested. "He was disappointed," Harper said, "but I explained the situation and he understood. At least he said he did."

"Did he mention what he planned to do when he left High Grade? Or have any of his prospective employers contacted you for a reference?"

Harper stood and walked to a file cabinet. He pulled open a long drawer and withdrew a thick file folder as if he'd known exactly where to reach. Seated back at his desk, he flipped the folder open and leafed through the contents.

"It's a fine record," he said. "High scores on every sort of test, several commendations from superiors. Here's what I want—yes, a bank, First Security Trust, called on the thirteenth of last month in regard to a loan application Victor Talbert had submitted to them. They learned nothing here that would discourage them from granting him the loan."

"Loan for what?"

"That I couldn't tell you. Banks don't go into detail on such matters." Teeth flashed in a confidential smile. "Usually we here at High Grade don't reveal anything we might consider personal about present or past employees. If it weren't for the extenuating circumstances in Victor's case, you wouldn't have gotten in to see me."

I'd been put in my place. Outside Harper's window I could see the corner of the white company flag cracking in the breeze.

"Of course, you found that out earlier," Harper said, still smiling.

The office was suddenly cold. "Earlier?"

Now the smile faded. "Yes, didn't you phone yesterday morning for an appointment?"

"This appointment was arranged for me."

"But I thought. . . . Well, someone called here yesterday and requested to see me regarding Victor Talbert. The caller was informed that High Grade Hardware has a policy that forbids giving out any unauthorized personnel information."

"Did the caller leave a name?"

"No, that's why I thought you'd called." The intercom buzzed and a female voice informed Harper that someone named Mr. Sathers wanted to see him at his earliest convenience. That seemed to put Harper on edge. "Mr. Sathers is the top man," he explained.

I took my cue to get to the essentials. "Mr. Harper, did you know anything about Victor Talbert's social life, what he did after hours?"

He drummed his fingertips, thinking. "No . . . not really. He attended all the company functions, handled himself quite well. He was well mannered, didn't drink to excess and possessed an admirable sense of tact. I'd be very surprised if there was anything . . . irregular about Victor."

"He was earmarked for bigger things here, wasn't he, until the presence of a favorite nephew eased him out?"

Harper's expression didn't change but his color darkened and a vein throbbed briefly at his graying temple. "I don't know who you've been talking to," he said, "but that's hardly an accurate way of describing the situation. Sheer economics dictated that someone had to go. Victor's job specialty was no longer needed, and to utilize his talents anywhere else would have meant a costly retraining and breaking-in period."

"And the nephew had this training?"

"Precisely." He leaned back, laced his fingers again. "Mr. Nudger, at Victor Talbert's level, potential isn't enough."

I nodded. Harper couldn't tell me flatly that Talbert had potentially been the superior of the two employees.

"Not that it matters now," he said.

"It might matter," I told him, "only not to Victor Talbert."

"I understand he's been murdered. Any ideas as to who and why?"

Carlon must have had to divulge the fact of Talbert's murder to get my appointment with Harper. "None here," I said. "That's more in the police department's line."

Harper shifted in his chair and licked his lips. I could see he wanted to say more but knew he shouldn't.

"Do you have any past or present employees named Congram?" I asked.

Harper pressed his intercom button and repeated my question to his secretary in the outer office.

Within a minute she buzzed him back with a negative answer.

It had been a blind stab anyway. "What's the nephew's name?" I asked.

"Paul Madden."

"Is he in the building now?"

"Probably."

"I'd like to talk to him. And I'd like to talk to whoever was Victor Talbert's direct supervisor."

"They're busy," Harper said, "but I'll arrange it." He punched a button on his desk phone for an inside line and cleared the way for me. I thanked him, shook hands with him and left his black and white office.

After getting myself lost several times in the building's labyrinth of halls, I managed to talk to both Madden and Victor Talbert's old supervisor, a tall, stern man named Graham Winkler. Madden had seemed a decent, sympathetic sort, somehow too lethargic for his surroundings. He told me he'd felt bad about Talbert's dismissal but that Talbert had taken it well and they'd remained friends, even to the point of having an after work drink together on Talbert's last day at High Grade.

Winkler substantiated what both Harper and Madden had told me. Victor Talbert had been highly thought of, considered an ideal company man. He was keenly intelligent, remarkably ambitious, and above all, a realist. I thought I detected a touch of resentment in Winkler over Talbert's dismissal, and I didn't blame him, if the man had been such a whiz. He'd have made any supervisor look good.

Talbert's past, as I uncovered it, wasn't exactly shaping him up to be the fugitive murder victim he'd become. Ambitious, hard working, a young man who inspired admiration and loyalty, he'd been the type a father would want his daughter to marry, the type Dale Carlon might have chosen for his own daughter Joan. Then had come the break in the pattern—the fear Horvell had described—and the blast of a rigged shotgun in a parked car in Florida. I needed to know the reason and was almost afraid to discover it.

The things a man will do for money. . . . You think the temptation doesn't apply to you, that you're too solid and sensible to bend, until the time arrives and temptation becomes opportunity.

One thing I knew was that I didn't belong in a place like this, with its contrived pressures, strict written and unwritten rules that had to be obeyed if you wanted to survive, much less advance, in the pecking order. That advancement was the important thing, the thing that drove the Talberts of the world.

I found my way out of High Grade's headquarters,

passing in the hall several dignified-looking types with gold hammer-and-wrench insignia pins on their lapels. As I walked toward my car, I could hear the snap of the flags and the dull metallic thumping of rope against the tall aluminum flagpole. I wondered idly if High Grade employees held a ceremony each morning as they raised the flags, and I wondered which flag they saluted.

Before starting the car I reached into my shirt pocket and pulled out the slip of paper that Horvell had given me with Belle Dee's address written on it. I laid the paper beside me on the front seat and unfolded a Chicago and surrounding area street map. Without much difficulty I located the street I wanted and used a ballpoint pen to circle it.

12

I drove from High Grade headquarters directly to Belle Dee's address.

She lived in one of a line of old four-story brick apartment buildings on Lampan Street, in a neighborhood in the gray area of urban decay. Several small businesses were hanging on in the block—a men's clothing store, a jeweler, a secondhand shop, and on the corner a little Italian restaurant with an unappetizing, mottled red sign that was supposed to represent a pizza. There were a few clusters of the young and denim-clad on the sidewalks and an old couple walking a big, fine German shepherd.

Belle Dee lived on the third floor, up steep and newly painted creaking stairs. The still-drying paint overpowered some of the normal apartment scents of cooking, and lingering disinfectant. I found the door with Belle Dee's number on it and knocked, experiencing my "nobody home" feeling.

No answer.

When I knocked again, louder, the door across the hall opened and a stocky man with a bushy head of hair and a large brown mustache looked out at me. Aside from the fact that he was barefoot, he was fully dressed in tan slacks and a silky shirt with swirling orange designs all over it.

"You looking for Belle Dee?" he asked, smiling.

I told him I was.

The smile got wider. He was justifiably proud of his teeth. "You're not a process server or anything, are you?"

"No, I was told to look her up by a mutual friend." I let him make what he wanted of that. He decided he wanted to believe me.

"She's probably working at the Poptop Club," he said, stroking his brown mustache, "about four blocks east on Delorel. Easy to find."

He was right about the Poptop Club's being easy to find. It dominated the block of seedy buildings with a tall sign that proclaimed it to be the home of "the biggest and the best."

There was no sign of either of those as I entered and looked around. I was in a long room, bar to the right, tables and chairs to the left and booths along one wall. At the end opposite the door was a raised stage with a purple-curtained backdrop and some speakers aimed out over the tables so that no one could escape the sound. There was another platform, about eight feet off the floor, behind the bar and supported from the raised ceiling by heavy silver-colored chains.

The Poptop must not have had much day trade. It was peopled only by a bearded, purple-shirted bartender and two customers morosely sipping beer in one of the booths. I walked to the bar and ordered a bourbon and water, which I needed.

"I was told I could find Belle Dee here," I said to the bartender when he set my drink on its coaster.

"You can, but it'll have to be after five."

"She wait tables here?"

"That and dances," the bartender said. "All the girls here double up."

"I checked her apartment. Any idea where I can find her now? It's important to her."

"She might be at the beach. Spends a lot of warm days there."

"Which part of the beach?"

"Why? You going to look for her?"

"Probably." I sipped my drink, which was on the weak side.

"Wish I was going with you," he said.

While I finished my drink, he described Belle Dee as a tall, blue-eyed blonde with dark eyebrows and long hair, and he gave me easily understood if overstated directions to her favorite strip of beach.

"You can't miss her," he said, as I got down off my bar stool to leave. "She's got . . . you know." He cupped both hands about six inches from his chest. "Outstanding!" he added.

I nodded knowingly.

It was a warm day and there were a lot of outstanding "you knows" at the beach. I stood for a while and watched but could not determine which belonged to Belle Dee.

I gave up trying to figure it out, bought myself a hamburger and Coke for lunch and sat watching a young boy trying vainly to bury his overweight father in the sand. The boy was about the age my own son would be. I pushed away the maudlin mood that threatened to envelope me, leaned back and watched wisps of white cloud over the sparkling lake water.

The breeze off the lake was a soothing massage, and the shouts and laughter of the bathers were pleasantly muted by vastness. I could understand why Belle Dee liked it here. I stayed longer than I should have.

It cost me a two-dollar cover charge when I returned to the Poptop Club that evening. The personality of the club seemed to have changed with the setting sun. Now it was crowded, the only light coming from candles on each table and flickering purple flashes of brilliance in time to the frenzied music bursting from the band on the rear stage. Dancers writhed about the small, crowded dance floor between tables and bar, and several fantastically built waitresses in skimpy but unimaginative costumes wove among the tables with trays of drinks. I took a table near the booths, and one of the waitresses appeared immediately to take my order.

When she returned with my bourbon and water I told her I wanted to talk to Belle Dee, repeating it several times so she could read my lips.

"You'll have to wait!" she shouted through the din. ". . . dances next!" She pointed toward the suspended platform behind the bar.

I sipped my weak drink and waited, and within a few minutes there was a blast of music, the suspended platform was spotlighted and Belle Dee danced.

She was tall, and her long blonde hair swaying in rhythm to the music made her seem more graceful than she was. Her spectacular, gyrating body was probably the siliconed product of science, and the amazing thing was that she managed to keep everything from going in the same direction at once, maybe for fear the building would shift.

She finished her dance to loud, enthusiastic applause punctuated by shouts, whistles and a few remarks she pretended not to hear. Ten minutes later she appeared at my table in street clothes, a surprisingly plain blue dress with a sash belt and flat shoes. "I don't know you," she said.

"You know Victor Talbert. I'd like to talk to you about him." I waved a hand for her to sit down.

"Police?"

"No." I caught the attention of a waitress and bought Belle Dee a drink—one I'd never seen before, tall and tropical and made with gin. "My name's Alo Nudger," I said. "I'm a private detective, and I promise that nothing you tell me will be used to harm Victor."

"He's not married, is he?"

"No. He's involved indirectly in what I'm working on. How long's it been since you've seen him?"

She trained almond-shaped blue eyes on me as if she'd just noticed me across the table; there was an emptiness in them; they were doll's eyes. I didn't think she was going to answer, but she did. "It's been . . . three, four months, maybe."

"You were seriously involved with him, weren't you?"

"We had it going between us, but we weren't serious."

I thought about asking her what the hell that meant, but decided against it. She must have seen the puzzlement in my eyes.

"Vic wasn't serious about me," she said, "and he knew I wasn't about him. I was interested in fun and he was interested in what interests all men."

I nodded. "An honest arrangement. Did Talbert have any enemies you can remember?"

She laughed—a musical laugh, but it was the blues. "Vic was too much of a square head to have any enemies. He played life right out of the rule book, an up-standing, ambitious citizen. If you cut him he'd bleed apple pie."

"Then he wasn't into drugs, that sort of thing?"

"Too straight for that, straight but nice. He didn't even drink heavy."

"How'd you meet him?"

"Oh, something like the way I met you. He came in here one night, wanted to talk to me. Next night he was back. I liked him, but I saw he was gonna get hurt. He was too afraid of failing at anything—he wanted to be a success so bad it burned. The hell with that kind of stuff."

I smiled at her. "He doesn't sound like your type."

When she smiled back I could understand what Talbert had seen in her. She had that bony symmetry beneath velvet skin that inspires casting directors. "Don't get the idea Vic doesn't know how to have a good time," she said. "I think he has to cut loose now and then, uptight as he is."

"Did he come in here often?"

"Quite a bit. But not in the last few months."

"Didn't you wonder where he was?"

"I didn't care. That was our arrangement."

I felt almost a cruel desire to shock her, to instill some feeling into her beauty. "Talbert is dead. He was murdered."

Immediately I regretted the bluntness of my words, but I honestly didn't know if I'd reached her or not. She lowered her head so I couldn't see her eyes, and a tightness crept into her features. Then she raised her head and looked directly at me. "No kidding!"

"Any idea who killed him?" I asked.

"None. He must have been mistaken for somebody else."

I ordered us each another drink. "Did you know any of his friends?"

She shook her head no. "It was just me and Vic."

"Did he ever mention Joan Clark?"

"Not that I can recall."

"What about the name Congram?"

Something like recognition came into her eyes. "That's right, yeah. Vic knew somebody named Congram; really thought he was important, from what I gathered. But he only mentioned the name a few times. I didn't pry." She drained half of her fresh drink. "Dead, huh?" I wasn't sure, but I thought her eyes glistened with more than their usual moisture. Or the light might have done her a favor.

The band, which had been taking a break since Belle Dee's dance, blasted out with another discordant specialty.

"They're lousy," Belle Dee said, "but lousy with a beat. Listen, I've got some of Vic's stuff at my apartment. What am I gonna do with it?"

I swirled the ice in my glass to appear disinterested. "What kind of stuff?"

"Clothes, mostly. Just stuff he left there."

"Mind letting me look it over?"

"I don't know if I should."

"I'll bet you do a lot you shouldn't."

She laughed her blues laugh. "You're right; it doesn't make any difference to me. I can let you look at the stuff when I get off at midnight." She finished her drink and stood, attracting eyes. "I gotta get back to work."

I told her I'd see her at twelve.

She smiled and turned toward the crowded dance floor, disappearing in a blast of flashing blue light and drums.

I made my drink last another twenty minutes and left.

The hours remaining before it was time to meet Belle Dee I spent in my motel room, lying on my back in bed and trying to figure out where events were taking me.

How was it going to set with the law when they found out I'd withheld the information that Branly was actually Victor Talbert, that I'd gone through some of his effects? I knew that eventually it would all have to come out; I didn't think even Carlon could keep that from happening. I hoped he could; I hoped I wasn't being cynical enough.

I thought about Belle Dee and then Lornee. The coldness grew in my stomach, and blood pulsed in my ears. I concentrated on the fifty thousand dollars.

At ten thirty I phoned Dale Carlon and filled him in on my activities, and I asked him if he could smooth the way for me to talk to someone at First Security Trust about Talbert's loan application. Carlon told me he'd see what he could do and then call me in the morning.

It was almost twelve thirty when Belle Dee fished a glittering jeweled key ring from her purse and let us into her apartment on Lampan Street.

We were in a small living room, furnished glass-topped and chrome modern. A jaggedly designed tapestry hung on one wall above a long black-vinyl sofa that couldn't have been more than six inches off the floor. Beneath the clear glass top of a coffee table before the sofa was a plastic flower arrangement.

Belle Dee tossed her purse onto a chair and went into the kitchen. She returned in less than a minute with two glasses containing generous measures of bourbon on the rocks and held out one of the drinks for me. I accepted that and her offer to sit on the low black couch.

"Vic's things are in the other room," she said. "I'll be right back."

I sat and watched her walk into what I assumed was

the bedroom. The low sofa was more comfortable than it looked, and there was a pleasant, faintly perfumed quietness about the apartment that was relaxing.

Belle Dee returned carrying some folded clothes, an attaché case and a pair of shiny black wing-tip shoes. "This is all Vic left, Mr . . . Nudger?"

"Call me Alo."

"That sounds foreign."

"Sometimes I think it is."

She handed Talbert's possessions down to me then sat next to me on the sofa while I examined them. I was disappointed to find that the attaché case, a metal-trimmed, expensive model, was empty but for a black knit tie. The clothing promised little more—a wrinkled pair of slacks, neatly folded undershirt and a white windbreaker. The pants pockets were empty, but when I felt inside the jacket pockets my fingers touched a thin, stiff rectangle of cardboard. I withdrew my hand without it, set the folded clothes aside and finished my drink.

"Mind?" I asked, holding out the glass.

Belle Dee checked her own near-empty glass. "I could use a refill myself."

When she'd disappeared into the kitchen, I drew the business card from the jacket pocket and examined it before slipping it into my own pocket. It was a plain white card engraved only with GRATUITY INSURANCE. No address, no phone number. On the back of the card a name was penciled in angled, hasty print: Robert Manners. Another Victor Talbert AKA?

Belle Dee returned with the drinks and sat next to me again on the sofa. "Did anything of Vic's help you?"

"Hard to say. It was worth a look."

"You can take it all with you if you'd like."

"I'd keep it if I were you. Eventually the police might want it."

She made an expression as if she hadn't thought of that and raised her glass to her lips. There was a softness in her eyes, maybe from the bourbon, and I fancied I could feel the heat from the closeness of her lushly perfect body.

"Ever get tired of living alone?" I asked.

"Everybody does sometimes."

I reached out and traced the line of her pale cheek with the backs of my fingers. She drew away, more with the change in her eyes than any motion of her head.

"I'm not lonely tonight," she said, "only sometimes." A smile to show me she regarded the effort as a compliment.

I returned the smile with a futile one of my own and stood.

"Thanks for showing me Talbert's effects," I told her. I let her know where I was staying and asked her to contact me if anything else about Talbert came to mind.

"If you have any more questions," Belle Dee said, "come around to the club."

We both knew the answer to the current question was no, so I said good-night and left.

13

The jangling telephone by my bed yanked me out of sleep at nine the next morning.

It was Carlon, as promised. He told me that arranging for me to get what information I needed from First Security Trust had been difficult, but that he'd managed it. The bank was one of an affiliation of Midwestern banks with which three of the Carlon plants did business. He told me to ask for a man named Tom McGregor, the loan officer who'd processed Talbert's application.

I thanked Carlon and asked him if he'd heard of Gratuity Insurance. He hadn't. And he said the name Robert Manners meant nothing to him.

When Carlon hung up I placed a call to Lieutenant Frank Dockard in Layton. When he answered the phone, he seemed not at all surprised to hear from me. By now he'd know I left Layton. I assumed he knew I was calling from Chicago.

"I'd like you to check on a Robert Manners for me," I told him.

"Who's he?"

"I don't know. That's why I phoned you. Anything new in Layton?"

"The bullets taken from the Star Lane house were thirty-eight caliber, from the same gun, if that helps you any."

"You never can tell."

"Anything I should know, Nudger?"

"I don't think so."

"What number are you calling from? So I can phone and let you know if there's anything on Manners."

"I'll call you, Lieutenant. Sometime this afternoon. And thanks." Before he could reply I hung up.

I dressed, had a quick buckwheat pancake breakfast and headed for First Security Trust. The extent of Carlon's influence amazed me. His nationwide corporation seemed to touch everywhere in the business community. What he could accomplish with his index finger on the telephone was to me the most startling revelation of the case. He'd mentioned political prospects that might surprise me. Maybe that was part of it; maybe it was known that Carlon might soon be in a position to do some important people important favors. I wondered, how many Carlons were there, how many men with that kind of encompassing influence on other lives?

First Security Trust was one of Chicago's older banks. There was more polished wood and marble in the lobby than formica. Half a dozen female tellers were at their windows, and the bank was active with customers either waiting in short lines or standing and writing at long, elbow-high tables.

I identified myself and asked a young girl at the information desk for Mr. McGregor. She spoke for a moment on the phone, and soon after she hung up, McGregor came into the lobby to greet me.

He was a middle-aged man, short and overweight, with a seamed, smiling face and a broken-veined drinker's nose. Not at all the banker type. After a firm handshake he led me behind the tellers' cages to one of a series of small, frosted-glass cubicles, each containing a desk and chair. He moved behind the desk and motioned toward the chair with a smile, waiting for me to be seated before he sat down. I sensed his deference to someone authorized to receive normally confidential information.

"I understand you're the bank officer who processed a loan application by Victor Talbert," I began. When he nodded, I asked him how much Talbert had wanted to borrow, and why.

McGregor unlocked a top desk drawer and pulled out some forms stapled together. He laid them on the desk and bowed his head to stare at them, the fingertips of his left hand touching his temple near his eye. He spoke without looking up, as if the forms intrigued him.

"Victor Talbert requested a loan of sixty thousand

95

dollars for capital to form a hardware distribution firm."

"Collateral?" I asked.

"The loan was to be granted in phases, secured by inventory."

"What made you decide against granting the loan?"

McGregor raised graying eyebrows in surprise. "But we didn't decide against. Talbert had an impeccable record, and his previous employer vouched for his integrity and ability. And my own personal assessment of Talbert was favorable. He was an impressive young man."

"Speaking as a nonbanker," I said, "it sounds risky."

"The phasing of the loan minimized the risk. In actuality we'd have been loaning the second half after the first had been paid. It was to be amortized over a ten-year period."

"Did he actually receive any money?"

"No, that's the strange thing about it. Talbert was contacted and told the directors had approved the loan. I talked to him myself. But on the date he was to come here to finalize the loan, he didn't show up."

"What day was that?"

McGregor traced a steady finger over the form before him. "The fifteenth of last month."

"What address did Talbert give you?"

The finger shot diagonally to the lower left corner of the form. "Five seventy Oakner, apartment seven."

I drew a folded slip of paper from my breast pocket and scribbled the information down. McGregor rotated the forms on the desk for my perusal in an exaggerated gesture of cooperation. I thumbed through them but saw nothing else useful. Talbert had listed himself as twenty-eight and single at the Oakner address. He'd had several employers before High Grade, but his experience was almost entirely in the hardware wholesaling business.

When I was finished, McGregor solicitously showed me out.

From First Security Trust I drove to the Oakner address Talbert had listed on his application, a tall brownstone apartment building set back on a narrow lot. Ivy was taking over the building's southeast corner, as if trying to bring the tall structure to earth.

I discovered what I'd expected. The apartment manager told me that Talbert had lived there for three months with a woman and young child, and when I showed him a photo of Joan Clark he identified her as the woman. They had moved out just over a month ago, without notice, but they had left behind an envelope containing the remainder of their rent money.

When I got back to the TraveLodge, I phoned Dockard and also got what information I expected from him. There were four men with major criminal records who used the name Robert Manners, either as their genuine name or an AKA—two in prison, one out of the country and the other eighty years old in a home in Iowa.

I replaced the receiver and stretched out on the bed, my shoes off, thinking about the day's main development. Keen, likable, admirable and ambitious Victor Talbert had run out on a sixty-thousand-dollar loan that would have enabled him to start his own business.

I found that remarkable.

14

I'd left word at the desk for a wake-up call at eight in the morning. When the phone rang it wasn't eight o'clock; it was three A.M. But it definitely woke me.

"Somebody's hurt me! . . ."

At first I didn't recognize the hysterical female voice.

"They beat me! . . ."

It was Belle Dee. "Belle, where are you?"

"Home . . . just got here. . . . They told me not to call the police. Said they'd kill me if I did. They kept asking about Vic. . . . I couldn't tell them any more than I told you!"

"I'll call a doctor."

"No! Please! A doctor might tell the police." The voice was still high, agonized, but she was gaining control.

I was responsible. I'd led somebody to her. "How badly hurt are you?"

"Don't know."

"I'll be there."

"Please, Alto! . . ."

"It's Alo," I said and hung up.

I was sitting on the edge of the bed, trembling, telling myself it was because the room was too cool. But I was scared. I reached for my pants.

The drive to Belle Dee's apartment was a skip in time, one of those chores performed automatically and precisely with the best part of the subconscious mind while the conscious boiled.

They'd done a job on her. She took a long time to answer my knock and reassurances, and when she inched open the door, she flinched in fright at the crack of light from the hall.

In the dimness of Belle Dee's apartment I could see that her upper lip was grotesquely swollen, and there was a slender track of blood down her neck, behind her right ear. She clung to me for a moment when I entered; then she slumped to the floor and sat against the wall, pressing the back of her head against the plaster, her eyes closed.

I switched on the softest light I could find, but she didn't like it. I didn't either. When I looked closely at the blood on her neck and the delicate splatter marks on her face, my stomach threatened and the room suddenly became an elevator going down.

"You all right?" she asked.

"I think so. Got any bandages?"

"Bathroom."

I found my way into the tile bathroom and opened the mirrored medicine chest. There was a bandage box, empty. But I found a roll of adhesive tape, some cotton, and on the vanity shelf beneath the washbasin an aerosol can of spray antiseptic.

Belle Dee was watching me, frantic-eyed, when I returned. "That stuff burns!"

"We'll use soap and water as much as possible," I said, helping her to her feet, then into a chair. Fighting off my dizziness, I went back to the bathroom and got some damp washrags and soap. Then I came back and did the best I could for her.

By the time I was finished, Belle Dee was leaning back in the chair, peering out at me from beneath a strip of tape over her right eyebrow. The eye was beginning to blacken. I got her some brandy, but it stung the cuts in her mouth, so she settled for ice water. I drank the brandy.

"How many were there?" I asked.

"Two. They were waiting for me when I came home. I shut the door, turned around and there they were."

"Do you know who they were?"

Belle Dee shook her head no. Her left hand was un-

99

consciously clutching her stomach. She said they had kicked her. I was ashamed for being more frightened than angry.

"What did they say? What kind of questions did they ask you about Talbert?"

"They asked me how well I'd known him, if I had any idea who'd killed him, why Vic had left town. I told them I didn't know the answers. That got them mad, made them mean. They warned me not to answer any questions about Vic, from anyone, or they'd be back."

I poured another glass of brandy. "Could you identify them?"

"No, they wore something over their faces, like gauze."

"Nylon stockings?"

"Maybe. All I can tell you is, one of them had terrible breath." For an instant some inner pain etched twenty more years on her face. "Jesus! . . ."

"Sure you don't want a doctor?"

"I'd rather be hurt than dead."

There was my kind of logic. "Can you think of anybody who knew both you and Vic?" I asked.

"Nobody who'd do this. Just some of the people at the club, the other waitresses. They know him from when he'd come in to see me."

"Do you think Congram might be involved?"

"I only heard the name a few times, never met him. What's that?"

"Antacid tablet, for my stomach. Is there anybody who knew both Talbert and Congram?"

Her pain-filled eyes brightened. "Yeah, Vic once mentioned that Smit was involved with this Congram. That's been a while ago."

My heart picked up a beat. "Smit?"

"He's just a guy who comes into the club now and then—not so often anymore. Maybe once a week. A run-down looking guy who pops some kind of pills with his beer."

"How about a first name?"

Belle Dee licked her swollen lip and shook her head. "Smit's all I ever heard him called. One of the other waitresses used to go out with him, though. She might know his full name."

"And his address?"

"She might know. Unless he moved."

I finished the brandy, washing down the taste of the antacid tablet and gritting my teeth at the combination. "Can you find out for me tomorrow?"

She looked at me with her hurt doll's eyes and nodded. "I'll try."

I ran my fingertips over my stubbled chin and sighed. I was tired, and there was a knot of dread in my stomach. Joan Clark and Talbert had been mixed up with Congram, who knew Smit, who might lead me to trouble. Apparently Joan and Talbert had lived in the Oakner apartment before leaving unexpectedly for Florida. That must have been the apartment Melissa had described. I smiled as I remembered something else Melissa had said.

"Ever hear of Robert Manners?" I asked Belle Dee.

"No, why?"

"It probably isn't important. What about Gratuity Insurance?"

"Not that I can remember."

I walked into the kitchen and returned with one of the wooden chairs that had been at the table. "Wedge this under your doorknob when I leave," I told Belle Dee. "Then sometime tomorrow buy a chain lock."

She raised her head as if at a sudden sound. "You don't think they'll be back, do you?"

"No, I don t. They did their job. But you should have a chain lock anyway."

And Belle Dee's assailants had done their job

101

smoothly, probably slipping the apartment door lock with a credit card, then working swiftly and ruthlessly. There was no sign of a struggle.

I glanced at my watch and stood wearily before Belle Dee, waiting for her to invite me to spend the night. She didn't. So I cautioned her again to seal herself in, and left.

Back at my motel I wedged a chair under my own doorknob and had little success at sleeping. I had that uncomfortable feeling of being drawn into something I couldn't handle, and even thinking about the fifty thousand dollars didn't help.

I picked up the receiver on the first ring when Belle Dee called, a little after ten the same morning.

She told me where Smit lived and described him as a skinny, pinch-faced man in his thirties. She also warned mc that Smit was involved in some kind of drug operation and had been arrested several times but never convicted.

That last part took away the possibility of breakfast. People involved in drug operations see life as being cheap.

15

The stench was the first thing that hit me. Stale sweat and the fetidness of something rotting.

Behind the half-open door a young girl stood staring blank-faced at me, unaware of the stench. She had narrow, bare and bony shoulders above a red halter that covered child's breasts. Her patched jeans appeared to be stained with grease. Behind her I could see a few pale faces in the dimness, some litter banked against one wall as if it had been swept there. The building was one of the few still occupied in a block of aged brick buildings that mercifully were due to be torn down.

"I'm looking for Smit," I told her. "There's money in it for him."

She laughed, spoke almost without moving her narrow lips. "What's he gotta do?"

"I'll talk to Smit about that."

"He ain't here anyway." The door closed.

I turned to walk down the graffiti-scrawled hall to the exit. A round peace symbol in fresh red paint had been brushed awkwardly over the door by somebody who hadn't heard we'd pulled out.

"You, Mister!"

My head jerked around to look behind me. A skinny, pinch-faced man in dark pants and a too-small sweater stood just outside the door the girl had closed. I waited and he walked toward me with that skinny man's ginger lightness in his step. He had protuberant dark eyes, curious despite fear.

"I'm Smit," he said.

"Nudger." I held out my hand and he shook it.

"So what do you want to talk to me about?"

As he spoke he was walking ahead of me, his head half turned, like a dog leading its master. He stopped when we were in the vestibule, where there was sunlight, cracked plaster and complete privacy.

"Congram," I said. "I'm not police and I'll pay."

I watched him think about it. The flesh of his slender face was mottled as he moved in a nervous little dance in the dust-swirled sunlight. From certain angles he was thirty-five, from others, fifty.

"Why do you want the information?" he asked and gnawed his lower lip as if he had something against it.

"Private matter."

Smit grinned and shook his head. I was aware of his gaunt hands, unafraid of him because of his slightness—as long as he didn't reach for a weapon.

"We're talking about a hundred dollars," I said.

The grin stretched, giving his face a cadaverous look. "Haven't you heard of the code of the underworld?"

"Two hundred dollars," I said, knowing Carlon would consider that cheap.

Smit's yellow grin contracted to a thin line, and he fondled a dimple on the point of his chin with a dirty forefinger.

"I can always say you talked anyway," I told him.

His face contorted as if he'd been stabbed. "Hey, Nudger, you wouldn't do that!" He began his nervous shuffle again.

"No," I said, "I wouldn't."

His nervous body was still. He'd come to a decision. "All right. It don't matter by now."

I placed a pair of hundred dollar bills in his skeletal, stained hands.

"How do I know this'll spend?" he asked, holding up the bills to the sunlight.

"How do I know you're going to tell me the truth?"

"Because I'm not going to tell you anything you can hang on Jerry. I don't know of anything."

Smit had already supplied me with a first name. I stood and waited for what else he had to say.

He nervously twisted the two bills into a cigarette-size roll and slipped them into his pocket. "I met Jerry at the Poptop Club, right after I got off on a possession charge. I guess that's how he found out about me and wanted to use me for an in on his business deal."

"Business deal?"

"This was over a year ago, understand. It can't do no

104

harm to tell now, or I wouldn t be telling it. Jerry wanted to buy into the middle of a connection; I don't exactly understand how. I think he was going to supply the capital to buy from the big dealer for a percentage of everything right down the line."

"How about some names?"

His eyes seem to contract in their sockets. "That I don't tell you, for any price. What I will say is that the operation no longer exists. It hasn't for almost a year. The law made some key busts and somebody knew when to quit. At least that's what I was told."

"Did you set it up for Congram to talk to the people involved?"

"Sure," Smit said with a hint of pride, "that I could do. But they turned Jerry down."

"For what reason?"

"They had no way to trust him. And it didn't help him being so clean-cut straight-city, hair above his ears and all that."

I waited for Smit to continue, there in the syrupy sunlight of the vestibule. A few cars passed outside, beyond the door's cracked glass, and in the distance a truck's air horn sounded three long notes. Smit crossed his arms over his sunken chest, squeezing in on himself nervously. He saw I wasn't satisfied.

"I was told you could be trusted," I said. He wondered who might have told me, and I wasn't about to tell him.

"Jerry tried to talk them into a deal," Smit said, "but they refused, and he finally gave up and forgot the idea. I ain't seen him since—almost a year. . . ."

"You brought Congram to the operation's attention," I said. "Didn't they ever ask you about him?"

"Sure. I told them what I told you. It was good enough."

I breathed out, loudly. "I'd have wanted to know more if I'd been them."

He uncrossed his arms and flexed his fingers, but he

didn't go into his dance. "Okay," he said, "they wanted to know where he lived, so once they had me follow him when he left the Poptop."

"Where did he lead you?"

"Hey, I don't remember the address! It's been a year!"

I drew another hundred of Carlon's money from my wallet.

"I'll have to take you there," Smit said, snapping the bill from my hand. "Money *is* the root of all evil, you know?"

"I'm not in any position to argue with you."

I drove the rental while Smit gave me directions, pointing the way with a lean and dirty-nailed finger. He sat leaning forward, pulled by his eagerness to be done with the unpleasantness of our agreement.

We didn't have to travel far, only out of the depressing, blighted area of the city and through the marginal neighborhoods that marked the boundary. I pulled to the curb where Smit told me to, and he pointed to a tall apartment building that had had a recent face-lift, up to the third floor only. EXECUTIVE TOWERS, a blocklettered sign proclaimed, a bit too grandly for the condition of the building.

"Which apartment?" I asked.

"I don't know," Smit said with almost desperate sincerity. "Only the building. . . . They had me follow him to the building, is all."

"What does Congram look like?" I asked.

"Hard to describe. Average height, build, nice-looking, nothing unusual about him except he's a great dresser. But there's something to him that tells you he's sharp."

"What color eyes?"

"Blue. His hair's dark and curly, cut short."

When there was a break in the traffic, I made a U-turn and drove Smit back to his own neighborhood

106

and whatever his three hundred would buy. As he got out of the car, I assured him that our conversation would be kept confidential, but he knew there was no such thing and had the money in his pocket to prove it. He would worry for weeks, maybe months, in the shabby room where he lived with the thin, sad girl and whoever else slept there. Maybe he'd worry about our conversation for the rest of his life, as part of his collective worry. Some world.

I drove back to the Executive Towers.

The lobby of the face-lifted apartment building had also been remodeled recently. The walls seemed to be freshly painted, and the few cigarette butts and scuff marks were like a sacrilege on the gleaming red-and-white tile floor. I walked to the bank of brass mailboxes and scanned the name plates. No Congram. I pressed the button lettered MANAGER.

After a short wait I head a door open around a corner, and I walked toward the sound.

The manager's name was Toggins. He was a barrel-chested man wearing a leisure jacket and shirt open at the collar to reveal reddish hair that seemed to grope to reach his neck. He could have used that much hair on his head, bald but for some reddish strands combed sideways, like pencil lines, over his crown.

"I'm looking for Jerry Congram," I said. "I couldn't find his name on the mailboxes."

"No Congram lives here."

"Do you recall when he did?"

"Don't have to think hard to remember him," Toggins said. "Curly-haired young guy, nifty dresser. World by the tail."

"That's him."

"Moved out about four months ago without a forwarding address. And he still owes me three months on his lease." The barrel chest puffed out in resentment.

107

"Did he live here alone?"

"Ha! Signed the lease alone, but he always had company." Toggins smoothed the front of his shirt with an outspread hand, as if sensitive about his paunch. "Not the sort of company to cause trouble, though. Upstanding-looking young people, like from good homes. Course, Jerry Congram seemed that way, too, and he vamoosed without paying his rent."

"How many of these people would visit him at a time?"

"Sometimes seemed like a dozen, men and women. Never had any complaints, though. They were quiet types, like I said." He narrowed pink-rimmed eyes at me. "You ain't no friend of his, are you?"

"I'd like to find him, just like you."

"He owe you money?"

"You might say that." I reached into my wallet and got out a photo of Joan Clark. "This one of the young women who visited Congram?"

Toggins gave the snapshot his same narrow-eyed glare. "Yeah, sure is! She was in to see him all the time, like the rest of them. Hey, they didn't have anything goin' up there, did they?"

"Like what?"

"I don't know. You ain't a cop, are you?"

"No, a private detective."

Toggins backed up a step. "You puttin' me on? I never met one of you guys."

"There aren't many of us."

"If you find this Congram, will you let me know? Because of the rent."

"Sure. Did he keep pretty regular hours while he lived here?"

Toggins scratched the freckles on his forehead. "Well, that's pretty hard to say for sure, but he seemed to. Like I said, a typical clean-cut young guy, like you'd want your daughter to take up with. If I had what he does, I'd be doin' somethin' with it."

"How long had Congram lived here?"

"Nine months of a one-year lease." Toggins clamped a long cigar in his teeth and fired it up with a silver lighter. I wished he hadn't. The thick gray smoke that clouded the air around us gave off a pungent, sickening odor.

"Cherry-scented," he told me. "I smoke these and my wife don't bitch."

"Do you have any idea what Congram did for a living?" I asked him.

He did a George Burns with his cigar. "I couldn't say. He left here every day with his sharp suit and little briefcase. We got a lot of 'em here, captains of industry, if you know what I mean. I shouldn't be surprised when they skip out on their rent."

I told Toggins I appreciated his cooperation and got away from his cigar's fallout.

It had begun to rain, an insincere sort of drizzle from a half-blue sky. I stood for a while beneath the awning outside the Executive Towers, waiting for the rain to stop. The sidewalks were clear of people, and the tires of passing cars hissed on wet pavement. After Toggins' cigar, the rain-freshened air seemed especially sweet.

The deeper I delved into Talbert's murder and Joan Clark's disappearance, the more Congram emerged as a catalyst. I had no idea yet as to how he was involved, but I was almost certain of his involvement. Be it awe, envy or fear, the man had made an impression on everyone I'd talked to who'd known him.

The rain stopped as if it had been turned off, and I jogged across the bright, puddled street to my car.

I turned the ignition key and pulled out behind an old Ford full of teenagers. Most of the paint had been sanded from the Ford, giving it the appearance of a camouflaged military vehicle. I turned on my wipers to clear the windshield of raindrops and stopped behind the old Ford at a red light. Even a car-length behind I could hear the deep bass rhythm of the Ford's radio at high volume. A miniature figure with outstretched arms and legs dangled by a thread or rubber band from the rearview mirror, like an obscene crucifix.

The traffic light flashed to green, and the Ford's tires whirred on wet cement. I didn't know why the driver was in such a hurry; there was a stop sign a block away.

The Ford braked to a nose-diving halt at the stop sign and had just stopped rocking when I pulled up behind it. Cross traffic had the intersection blocked for a few minutes, and I sat staring at the silhouetted, gently bobbing, spread-armed figure suspended from the Ford's rearview mirror. The dangling figure loosened something on the edge of my memory, and suddenly that something illuminated into image in my mind—the image of a newspaper photograph, a man in a dark business suit, plummeting to his death, limbs outstretched and body arced as if in a last desperate and maniacal attempt to soar. A man the photo's caption had identified as Robert Manners.

Dale Carlon had been examining the newspaper in the Star Lane house, but he'd been concerned mainly with the idea of a top business executive's pressures driving him to suicide, relating the story to his own problems. So he hadn't remembered the man's name, as I hadn't until my memory had been flicked by the sight of the dangling rearview mirror ornament. And Robert Manners was the name penciled on the back of a business card lettered GRATUITY INSURANCE. "Ingerence," as Melissa Clark had mispronounced it.

I tried to remember some details of the story. Manners had been a Los Angeles business executive, member of a long list of boards and committees. Had he been depressed over something specific? Had he left any family? I couldn't remember.

I stopped at a service station and got directions to the Chicago Public Library, at Michigan and Washington.

110

The Chicago papers had carried the Robert Manners story on the same date as the Layton paper. The library had it on microfilm. Manners had been district manager of a big firm called Witlow Cable, the exact business of which wasn't stated. He had leaped to his death from the roof of Witlow Cable's twelve story office building. Business associates said he had been unusually tense lately, though the business was going well. And Manners' widow reported that he had seemed depressed lately, but not to the point of suicide. No note had been found, but Manners' personal effects had been removed from his pockets and arranged neatly on a corner of his desk. Police had no reason to suspect foul play but were investigating.

I leaned back from the microfilm viewer. I knew how the police investigated that sort of case. How much time and manpower did they have to waste on a violent death that was almost certainly a suicide? Not all of the troubled who choose their own time to leave this world are considerate enough to leave behind notes of explanation.

Back at my motel, I looked in the Chicago telephone directory for a Gratuity Insurance. There was none listed. I phoned a few national insurance organizations for information about Gratuity, but as far as they could determine there was no such company.

The direction I had to take was clear. West to Los Angeles, the City of Angels. I didn't like that allusion to an afterlife.

I got in touch with Dale Carlon and brought him up to date on developments. He said that at the Star Lane house he'd been interested in the Layton paper's photo and news account of Manners' death because of the business-pressure angle, the presumed motive for suicide. Everyone involved in high level decision-making had felt that pressure, Carlon told me, including himself. The prospect of suicide was considered, if only fleetingly, by many who shouldered such responsibility. It was difficult for me to imagine someone as wealthy and self-serving as Carlon contemplating suicide, but bearing in mind the fifty thousand dollars, I didn't tell him that.

He did agree with me that it was now hard to believe the newspaper's being folded to that page at the Star Lane house was coincidental. Either the paper was deliberately left arranged that way or, more likely, someone had been reading the account of Manners' death with interest and had put down the paper still folded to the story.

Carlon also agreed that the answers to some of our questions were in Los Angeles and that I should travel there immediately. He would spare no expense to find his daughter. He would spare no one.

16

The weather wasn't good in Los Angeles. The city was in the midst of a heat wave combined with a thick layer of smog.

By one o'clock, when I arrived at Witlow Cable in downtown L.A. for the appointment Carlon had set up for me, the sun had burned away most of the smog, but the heat remained. Witlow Cable's headquarters were frigidly air-conditioned, though, and I was only inside the building for about five minutes before I found myself almost longing to be back out on the street.

A pertly sweet secretary informed me that I could see Mr. Brian Cheevers, and she ushered me into an office that was nothing if not sumptuous. A royal-blue carpet I found myself wading in stretched to mirrored walls and thick, paler blue ceiling-to-floor drapes. A white sofa with blue throw pillows sat against the wall on my right, and there were matching white chairs before an enormous desk of bleached wood trimmed in blue.

Behind the desk Mr. Brian Cheevers, a squat, swarthy man with a lumpy face and hungry eyes, stood to shake my hand. His appearance was civilized somewhat by the elegant suit disguising the powerful bulk of his shoulders.

He motioned me into one of the exquisite, soft white chairs in front of his desk, and I sat with the feeling that I was deflowering a virgin.

"You want to talk about Bob Manners," he said, as if planting the thought in my mind.

"I won't take much of your time, Mr. Cheevers. I want to know primarily about the time leading up to Manners' death."

"I notice you didn't say suicide."

"I try to keep an open mind. Do you have any opinion on whether or not it was suicide?"

"No, I don't worry about it. It's passed. Manners is dead. I leave that sort of speculation to the proper authorities."

The no-nonsense mind in action, I thought. Too busy to be curious about the death of an associate. On the other hand, Cheevers might have an hour each day scheduled for curiosity. I cautioned myself against judging too harshly.

"Did you know Manners well?" I asked.

"He was my immediate superior for five years," Cheevers said with vaguely military overtones.

"According to the newspapers, fellow employees said that business pressures had upset Manners for several weeks before his death. Can you tell me what sort of pressures?"

Cheevers picked up a gold pen and held it gently, as if it were a royal scepter. "There are always great pressures being brought to bear in this job, Mr. Nudger, as there were in the period immediately preceding Bob Manners' death. I will say he seemed unusually tense at the time, but if that tenseness was the result of business pressure, it had to have been accumulative."

"What about pressures from his home life?"

Cheevers' lumpy face twisted into a slight grin. "Not with that wife of his. Elizabeth is the perfectly trained executive's wife. I don't think I'm maligning the man by saying that Manners would never have attained his position without her."

"Didn't Manners ever talk to you . . . on a personal basis?"

"Not often. He never gave me any idea what was causing his apprehension, and I didn't consider it my business."

"Was there anyone here he might have confided in?"

"I doubt it. Bob Manners was all business. He didn't believe in confiding his personal problems to his subordinates, and everyone here was a subordinate."

"Do you know of anyone else, outside the business, he might have talked to about his problems?"

Cheevers shook his head. "Manners' career was his life. On this level, that's the way it has to be." He pretended to sneak a glance at his watch.

I hung on. "Has Witlow Cable ever done business with Gratuity Insurance?"

"No." Cheevers' answer was immediate and confident.

"What about when Manners was in charge?"

"I'd have known about it." Cheevers' manner was as cool and unruffled as the office decor. Behind him the sun beat futilely on the tall window. "I'm a bit pressed for time, Mr. Nudger. Is there anything else?"

"Yes, I'd like to talk to Manners' secretary."

114

He seemed to consider the reasonableness of that for a moment. "All right," he said. "Her name's Alice Kramer. She's in accounting now." He picked up the white receiver from the phone on his desk and punched one of a row of buttons. "Bernie, Cheevers. A man named Nudger is coming down to talk to Alice about Bob Manners. Tell her to cooperate." Cheevers hung up the phone, apparently without waiting for a reply.

I stood and shook hands with him again and slow-bounded over the deep carpet toward the door.

"By the way," I said as I was going out, "what exactly does Witlow Cable produce "

"Industrial cable, petroleum storage tanks and carpet," he said. I shouldn't have been surprised.

The secretary who had ushered me into Cheevers' office gave me directions to accounting, on the second floor. I took an elevator down and followed a long hall to a wooden door with ACCOUNTING lettered on it in neat black print. The door was locked. I turned left with the hall, glanced into a large empty employee's cafeteria, then came to another door, open. I stepped inside to see a small gray-haired woman savagely putting an electric typewriter through its paces.

"Accounting?" I asked.

She nodded without breaking rhythm.

"Alice Kramer?"

"She's waiting for you in there," the mad typist said, jerking her head toward a door on her left as the typewriter's margin bell chimed.

I walked through the door and was in a small green-walled room with two chairs and a low table with a lamp on it. It was the sort of room used only for heart-to-hearts, and I could sense that it was haunted by many a departed accountant. In one of the chairs sat a neatly dressed, attractive woman in her mid-forties. Her dark brown hair was short and disciplined; her smile was pleasant but harried. After introductions, we got to the subject of her ex-boss.

"I've been told Manners was the all-business type," I said to her, slipping into the other chair, "so as his secretary you were probably closer to him than anyone else in the company."

She nodded briskly, conceding the truth in that.

"Did you notice any tenseness, any apprehension in him before his death?"

"Everyone did," she said in a carefully modulated but warm voice. "Not that he behaved in such a way that it would sound extravagant, or even unusual, if described; but it was the contrast. Before that time Mr. Manners was one of the most even-tempered men you could meet, always considerate and genuinely concerned with other people. Then suddenly he became . . . grim, constantly drawn into himself."

"And he never told you why?"

"No. You were right in assuming Mr. Manners put more trust in me than in anyone else here, but our relationship was still one of employer to employee. He kept his personal problems to himself."

"How long before his death did you first notice the change in him?"

She crossed her long legs primly, folded her arms. "I'm sure I was the one who first noticed a change, about two months . . . before. Then other people began to notice that he always seemed preoccupied, which wasn't at all like Mr. Manners. Approximately a week before . . . it happened he became increasingly agitated, depressed." Her eyes took on the sheen of suppressed tears. "I asked him what was bothering him, if I could help, but he said not to worry about him, that things would work out."

I didn't like wringing her, but I had to. I was getting a lump in my own throat. "Were you here at work when he died?"

116

Alice relinquished just enough self-control to brush at her eyes with a long-nailed forefinger. "I was at my desk. Mr. Manners came out of his office and walked past me without speaking, but he seemed quite normal. He must have gone directly to take the service elevator to the roof. Ten minutes later I was told that he'd fallen."

"Fallen?"

"Suicide wasn't considered at the time. The police put that theory together later."

"But you don't believe it?"

Her entire body seemed to stir in a weary shrug. "I don't know. Something *was* disturbing him. . . ."

"What do you think of Mrs. Manners?"

"I like her. At first I didn't; I thought she was too . . . pushy. Then I came to realize that she was totally dedicated to her husband's career. I saw her make many sacrifices over the past several years."

"Were you friends with her?"

"Not exactly. I think she knew her husband might not want that."

The low hum of an air conditioner or ventilator fan, which I don't think either of us was aware of, suddenly stopped, leaving a somehow louder silence in the tiny room. Alice Kramer spoke again, quickly, as if to keep the silence from engulfing us.

"Are you investigating his death?"

"Only indirectly."

"Then why? . . ."

"I'm investigating a disappearance, Miss Kramer. Have you ever heard the name Victor Talbert?"

"I don't think so."

"Jerry Congram?"

"No."

"Gratuity Insurance?"

She hesitated. "No . . . not that I can recall."

I watched her reach into her purse, which leaned

117

against the leg of her chair, and draw out a pack of cigarettes. She offered me one and I declined. Her lean fingers trembled as she held a dainty gold lighter's flame to the tobacco.

"Do you think Mrs. Manners would talk to me?" I asked. "You could phone, tell her who I am."

"I'm sure she'd see you," Alice said, drawing on her cigarette as if trying to collapse it. I could see she smoked for medicinal purposes.

I stood and held the door open for her, then sat back down and watched through the still-open door as she used the phone on the typist's desk to call Mrs. Manners. I couldn't hear what she was saying, didn't particularly want to. Now and then she'd glance over at me as she talked.

After a few minutes Alice hung up the phone and walked to the doorway. "She can see you at four o'clock today."

I stood and thanked her. The expression on her face told me no thanks were necessary. She was still loyal, doing a last service for her ex-boss.

The four o'clock appointment with Mrs. Manners left me some spare time, but not much. I decided to have a late lunch in the employee's automatic cafeteria I'd noticed down the hall, then drive directly to see Elizabeth Manners.

The cafeteria was still empty. The center of the room was filled with small round tables and metal-legged plastic chairs, and the walls were lined with vending machines that dispensed soup, sandwiches and desserts. Next to a coffee machine, in a corner, was a small microwave oven on a table under a sign that read KEEP OUR LUNCH ROOM CLEAN.

After only a moderate struggle, I managed to coax one of the sandwich machines to accept my money and part with a ham and cheese sandwich. But the soda machine worked with clicking, whirring perfection

118

and winked at me as I withdrew the cup. I sat at a table near a corner and peeled the cellophane from my sandwich. After a few bites I noticed the piped-in music, as bland as the food.

When I'd finished eating, I dutifully threw my debris into one of the trash containers placed about the cafeteria; then I got a cup of black coffee from the machine near the microwave oven and sat back down to try to relax.

The coffee wasn't bad for machine coffee, and I lingered over it. Two young office girls came in and regarded me as just another machine while they traded dimes for chewing gum, then left. Other than that I drank my coffee alone; then I leaned back in my chair and idly rotated the empty plastic cup on the tabletop.

"I did it just the opposite," a female voice said behind me. "I saw Mrs. Manners first."

A statement like that in a room I'd thought empty wasn't the sort of surprise I liked.

I turned in my chair.

17

She was a tall, auburn-haired woman in her early thirties, clear-complexioned, leanly well built and with carefully penciled, arched eyebrows that gave her a sharp eyed, inquisitive expression. "I'm Alison Day of *Business View*," she said, "and you're Alan Nudger."

"Alo," I corrected her, "but how did you come so close?"

She smiled an all-knowing, sharkish smile that had a curious sexual appeal to it. Her features were of a sharpness that would have been unattractive but for their chiseled perfection. "I'm a feature writer for my magazine, researching for a series of articles on the pressures and unexplained suicides and accidental deaths of top business executives across the country. You came here to Witlow Cable and now plan to go interview Mrs. Elizabeth Manners; I did things the opposite. I've talked to Robert Manners' widow, and now, here I am at Witlow. I was just getting ready to leave Mrs. Manners when her husband's secretary phoned. I asked about the call and Elizabeth Manners told me about your appointment. Though I thought you might be gone from here, I decided to check anyway. And here we are."

"Why?"

She appeared surprised. "What?"

"Why are we here? Why did you want to see me?"

"Oh, I wanted to find out about your involvement in this, of course." She spotted my empty cup, then the coffee machine. There was a boldness in her lean-legged stride as she crossed the cafeteria to the vending machine. She reached into her purse and pulled out some change. "Can I buy you another coffee?"

"Thanks, no. I don't want to make a pig of myself, and a chauvinistic one at that."

She gave me the knowing, eyes-sideways smile to show I hadn't rattled her. I took an antacid tablet.

"We can help each other, I think . . . Aldo, is it?"

"Alo."

"Call me Alison. You're a private detective. That's really fascinating."

"It's all in the eye of the fascinatee. What did Mrs. Manners tell you, Alison?"

"She said that her husband had seemed worried about something for months before his death, but that he never told her exactly about what. When she pressed him on the subject, he would simply categorize his worries as business pressures. I find this recent trend curious because the suicide rate among top executives is well below the national average. Statistically, six-point-six percent—"

"Alison," I interrupted her, holding up my palm in the universal stop signal, "I am not a believer in statistics."

"Really?" She sipped the coffee she'd bought and strode back to my table. "I should think you would be, being in a sense a policeman. Given sufficient and accurate data, statistics are an invaluable tool, in the business world especially. More sales are generated—"

I held up my hand again. "I'm not interested in sales being generated," I told her. "I've got too much on my mind as it is. Is that all that Manners' widow told you?"

She stared down at me with amused eyes that were a cattish pale green. "Essentially, yes." She smiled. "What did Brian Cheevers tell you?"

"So we can cross check their stories?"

She nodded, still smiling. She had a good idea. I gave her most of what Cheevers had told me.

"There is one thing," I said as she sat across from me, mentally digesting what I'd told her. "I can't promise to tell you everything; I have certain obligations you don't."

"Sure, I understand that. I never thought you trusted me completely, either. Who are you working for?"

I had a vision, then, of her descending on Dale Carlon, using my name, spouting her *Business View* facts and figures at him in her crisp, confident tone. Then the questions. I guessed Alison Day might be the last representative of the press Carlon would want to know about his missing daughter.

"I have to keep that confidential for the time being," I said to her.

She appeared disappointed but not surprised. I was

becoming more wary of her by the minute. I said, "You mentioned something about the deaths of several top executives across the country. . . ."

"Yes," Alison said, "counting Manners, six, nationwide, in a very short period of time."

"I wasn't aware of the trend."

"One would have to be in a position to see the entire cloth to discern the pattern."

"And your magazine thinks there is a pattern?"

She lowered her coffee cup from her lips. "That's partly what I've been assigned to discover."

I wadded my own cup and tossed it neatly into a trash container. I didn't like the idea of becoming mixed up with a reporter, but at this point there was little to lose. She had no idea who or what I was actually investigating, and I could keep it on those terms.

"Have you ever heard of the Gratuity Insurance Company?" I asked her.

"No, why?"

"I wondered if anyone you've questioned in connection with the other deaths mentioned them."

"No, but on the other hand, I didn't ask. I can check back, though."

I smiled at her. "That's what I was really asking."

Alison pulled a notebook from her purse. "Gratuity Insurance," she said, jotting it down as she pronounced it.

"How about the name Jerry Congram?" I asked while she had her notebook out. The pencil darted again while Alison spelled the name aloud to me.

She looked at me expectantly for a moment saw nothing else was forthcoming and snapped the notebook shut. "I'm at the Clairbank Hotel," she said, "room four oh seven. That's an invitation only to exchange information after you've talked to Elizabeth Manners and I've talked to Brian Cheevers."

"I thought you might want to show me your stock market graphs," I said innocently.

She looked at me with something like genuine disgust. "Can you be there about seven?"

"I'll try. We can discuss things over dinner, but only because I'll be hungry."

We left the lunchroom to keep our respective appointments, walking together to the elevator.

As I passed from the cool lobby into fierce heat outside I was trying to decide whether the advent of Alison Day would prove a hindrance or a help. Then I realized there was no way to make that decision until I determined that there actually was a connection between the deaths of Robert Manners and Victor Talbert.

If no connection existed, Alison Day wouldn't matter, and I'd have to try to pick up the thread of the investigation in Chicago.

18

Elizabeth Manners lived in a sun-faded but stately neo-Spanish home not far off the Ventura Freeway. Azaleas were thriving along the wide front of the pastel yellow house, and as I rang the doorbell I could see a curved garden path flanked by rhododendrons, some of them still displaying rosy-purple blooms.

Mrs. Manners answered the door almost immediately. When I identified myself, she smiled at me and held the door open wider. She was a very thin, graceful woman, somewhere in her sixties, with the sort of beauty that retains its gentle magnetism far into old age. Her face was lined but taut, and her thin frame was draped in a simple but expensive purple dress. If one word were needed to describe her, it would be "gracious."

She endured my clumsy expressions of sympathy, then led me to a room of pinks and blues that had been blessed by a decorator's touch. After I'd declined her offer of something to drink, we sat to talk.

"Have you any idea what was bothering your husband?" I asked her.

Her folded hands, strangely older than the rest of her, lay, withered yet elegant, in her lap. "No, Mr. Nudger, Robert didn't share that problem with me, which was uncharacteristic."

"Why do you think he chose not to confide in you?"

"I don't know. One of the reasons I agreed to talk to you and the young lady is my curiosity about that matter. Robert and I were close; we worked together for his career."

"But you agree with the consensus that he was depressed."

"I would describe it more as anxious, apprehensive." She frowned as she sifted for explanations. "Perhaps he was afraid for me to know why."

"Do you think it was something connected with his work?"

"I doubt it. As I said, we worked together for his career." The withered hands in her lap shifted, briefly separated, as if seeking some purpose, then folded back into each other.

"Do you think, in the week or so before your husband's death, that his apprehension grew, reached a peak?"

"To the point of driving him to suicide?"

She was trying to make my tact unnecessary. "Well, yes."

"I think that's apparent, Mr. Nudger."

"Then you believe it was suicide?"

"I know it." Something in her pale eyes turned inward for a second, surveying her thoughts. "I'm going to tell you something I chose not to tell the young lady and I'd like you to keep it confidential unless you absolutely must reveal it. Only under those terms will I tell you, and then I'll tell you only because you are the only representative of the law still investigating my husband's death, and I'd like to know why he elected to die. Miss Day is a magazine writer, and I do not want my husband to become a case in point in some article, an example."

"I can understand that," I told her, "and I can promise you."

She looked at me for a long moment, her hands still. Then she stood and walked to a dainty walnut secretary desk near the white-curtained window. She drew an envelope from one of the flat drawers and handed it to me.

"My husband's suicide note," she said in a voice detached from emotion. "It was delivered in the mail the day after he died."

I accepted the white envelope, examined the postmark. "Do the police know about this?"

"No one has known about it but me, and now you."

Elizabeth Manners sat back down as I drew the neatly typed, folded paper from the envelope and read.

Dearest Elizabeth:

I die by my own hand because I know this to be my wisest alternative—indeed my duty. I have never balked at responsibility, nor would you want me to even now if you could know the circumstances.

I am grateful for all that you have been to me, saddened to cause you this necessary pain.

Your loving husband forever,
Robert

125

The letter was signed beneath a typed signature, a distinctive black-inked scrawl.

"Is this your husband's signature?" I asked.

Elizabeth Manners nodded. "I have no doubt of that, Mr. Nudger."

I replaced the letter in its envelope and handed it back to her. "Why haven't you given this to the police?"

She leaned forward in her chair with a strangely graceful, compelling intensity. "I knew if the police learned my husband had definitely killed himself they would stop investigating his death. And I wanted to know *why* he committed suicide." She leaned back, smiled a sadly resigned smile. "I see now that it made no difference; the police are no longer concerned with the case anyway. They've accepted the theory of Robert's suicide, like everyone else."

"And it would be pointless to tell them about the letter now," I said.

"Exactly. You are a private detective, Mr. Nudger. Would you consider undertaking to find the reason for my husband's death? Obviously you already have some interest in doing this or you wouldn't have talked to Brian Cheevers and Alice. So I would like to hire you."

I shook my head. "That won't be necessary, Mrs. Manners. What you want coincides with what I'm presently investigating, and if I find out anything I'll be glad to let you know."

"I insist on paying."

"We'll talk about that if the time comes," I told her. "In the meantime, maybe you can help. Did your husband ever mention the Gratuity Insurance Company?"

"No, I never heard of them."

"The names Jerry Congram or Victor Talbert?"

"Neither of them are familiar."

An evenly spaced, relentless thudding and scraping

126

sound came from outside the window, a sound that seemed to violate the quietly tasteful and orderly room.

"My gardener," Mrs. Manners explained.

I recognized then the sound of a hoe being worked in soft earth. "Do you know who, at Witlow Cable, profited the most from your husband's death?"

"Brian Cheevers, although I doubt that at the time he knew he would profit."

Unless he'd known something Mrs. Manners hadn't. Cheevers was definitely the close-to-the-vest type. I didn't want to think that Manners' death might be unrelated to whatever his connection was with Gratuity Insurance, but it was a possibility. The problem was that there were a number of unrelated possibilities.

"Who was your husband's doctor, Mrs. Manners?"

"Steiner, on Hobart Avenue. I asked him about my husband. He said Robert had been in perfect health except for high blood pressure that could easily have been remedied."

I sat back, crossed my outstretched legs at the ankles and thought about Robert Manners—a man in good health, near the top of his profession, and with a dedicated wife whom he obviously loved. When a man like that committed suicide, it was usually brought on by something outside his normal sphere of existence, something often impossible to discover. I didn't envy Elizabeth Manners her quest, and I couldn't look with optimism on my own task.

Outside the gardener continued his toil, each *chunk* of the hoe like something breaking off and lost forever. Elizabeth Manners seemed impervious to the sound.

I assured her I could find my own way out and left her there.

From the Manners home I went to see Dr. Steiner, on Hobart Avenue.

His office was in one of those quasi-hospital medical

127

centers equipped to do everything but bury the patient. It was a white-brick building with few windows and an arrowed sign explaining that the emergency entrance was around the back.

Happy to use the front entrance, I walked across a large reception area lined with red-vinyl sofas and low tables spread with dog-eared magazines. Everything but the magazines seemed new, slickly and professionally done, and there was a toy-and-game-equipped alcove off the reception area for the children to play in as they waited.

Half a dozen people were seated about the room, ignoring each other—two elderly men and four women. One of the women had on a low-cut dress she could have worn anywhere, another a heavy, jeweled necklace that soaked up most of the light in the room.

Behind a long, curved counter several white-uniformed women were moving about with smooth efficiency, and as I approached, one of them, a severe-looking young darkhaired girl, asked if she could help me.

I told her I'd like to talk to Dr. Steiner.

"Do you have an appointment?"

"No," I said, "it has to do with one of his patients."

"The doctor's very busy right now."

"I can wait for a while."

"He has a full schedule today."

The nurse, or whatever her title was, was beginning to annoy me. No doubt part of her job was to protect Dr. Steiner from pesty private detectives and medical supply salesmen, but I did wish she'd let him know I was there.

"I only need a few minutes of the doctor's time," I told her, careful to hide my growing irritation. "My name is Nudger, Alo Nudger. Would you tell him I'm here?"

She neither moved nor dropped her professionally detached manner. "If you'd tell me the nature of your business. . . ."

'It's private."

"Concerning which patient?"

"Mr. Robert Manners."

She pardoned herself and turned her back on me to riffle through a long, slender drawer of indexed three-by-five cards. There was something about her squarish hips and broad waist. Even from behind she looked intractable.

"I can find no Robert Manners," she said, sliding the long file drawer shut as she turned again to face me.

"Who am I talking to?" I asked.

"Nurse Malloy."

"Nurse Malloy, will you do me a favor and tell Dr. Steiner I'm here, and that it concerns Robert Manners and that it's important."

She glared at me with cool disinterest, as if she'd tired of toying with me and had more important things to do. "I checked. I'm sure the doctor has no such patient, Mr. Nudger."

"Manners is dead," I told her, my voice taking on ice. "And I'm sure Dr. Steiner wouldn't like it if he knew you were preventing me from talking to him about that unpleasant fact."

She stared at me as I were inanimate yet thought-provoking. "I'll inform the doctor," she said with distaste. "You should realize I'm only performing my duties. If everyone who came in here wanting to see one of the doctors was allowed to go in without first establishing a good reason, there'd be little time to care for the patients."

I didn't like the implication that I and people like me were somehow a threat to the proper medical care of the ill, but I said nothing as Nurse Malloy turned and disappeared through a doorway behind the curved counter. The two other women behind the counter continued their work and ignored me.

Almost five minutes passed before the nurse returned.

"Dr. Steiner can give you a few minutes," she said. Then her face brightened as if the sun had struck it, and she looked past me. "Mrs. Nesmith!" she said in a pleased voice. "You're here to pick up your medicine." The very old woman who was Mrs. Nesmith shuffled forward and basked in Nurse Malloy's good cheer. I saw that it helped to be a paying customer.

Dr. Steiner invited me into a small, antiseptic room with a sterile white washbasin and a leather-upholstered table covered with something resembling butcher paper.

Steiner looked like an expensive doctor—stocky, middle-aged, with heavy-lidded, serious eyes and a brush mustache. It was easy to imagine him in a laboratory somewhere, a microscope-glance away from some major medical breakthrough.

"Nurse Malloy tells me you're interested in Robert Manners," he said. "I am busy, Mr. Nudger. . . ."

"What I'm interested in, Doctor, is the state of Manners' health preceding his suicide."

"I see." A cautious note had entered his voice. "Who do you represent?

"No one directly connected with Robert Manners. The information I'm seeking is only incidental to the case I'm on."

I could see he didn't believe me. "I'm sorry," he said with a smile. "Professional ethics forbid me to divulge a patient's medical history without permission."

"I'm not exactly asking you to do that, Doctor. Can you just tell me if Manners' medical state prior to his death might have caused him to commit suicide?"

Dr. Steiner gave my question a lot of thought, thick

eyebrows lowered in a superb bedside frown. Maybe he was worried about a malpractice suit.

"I've already talked to Mrs. Manners," was all he said.

"So have I."

"Then I assume you know the answer to your question." He gave me a good-bye smile. "As you saw in the reception area, we have several patients to be served."

And in the income bracket not to be kept waiting, I thought as he stepped smoothly aside to let me exit first.

I left Dr. Steiner's hoping my health would last forever.

Outside the medical center I made a few phone calls from a public booth, trying to get in touch with an old friend of mine, Lieutenant Sam Hiller, of the Los Angeles police.

Hiller was off duty, but I contacted him at his home, and he told me to drive in to see him and gave me directions.

It would be good to see Hiller, I thought, getting back into my car. We'd worked together for a while, until he decided to go with the Los Angeles Police Department because it had the reputation of being the best and most demanding of its officers. That was the sort of situation Hiller craved.

Then, six years ago, Hiller was shot while attempting to quiet a family disturbance, and five months of hospitalization and three operations changed him. He eased up somewhat, on himself and everyone around him. I'd gotten along with the old Hiller, but the new Hiller was much more pleasant company.

He lived in a condominium unit in one of those sprawling low projects that look like luxury military barracks. The slant-roofed two-story buildings were lined along a wide cement walkway punctuated by potted trees and ornate lampposts. A young boy was repeatedly running at one of the metal posts, gripping it and letting his momentum swing him in circles.

My knock on Hiller's door was answered by a call to come in.

The room was neatly and symmetrically arranged, clean, without clutter—books lined precisely on their shelves, lamp shades and pictures as straight as if they'd been adjusted with levels. Hiller himself was sitting with his stockinged feet propped on a hassock, watching the Dodger game on television. I was struck, as I had been before, by how he maintained his uncompromising perfectionist's attitude toward things but not toward people.

He stood and shook my hand, got us each a beer and told me to have a seat on the couch.

"They don't bunt," he said, settling back into his chair. "Ballplayers nowadays can't bunt." He looked older than when I'd last seen him, had less hair and more loose flesh beneath his jutting jaw.

Together we watched an attempted sacrifice bunt result in a sickly pop fly to the third baseman. Hiller shook his head in disgust.

"What are you onto, Nudger?" he asked.

"I need to know something about a suicide here," I said without directly answering his question, knowing he wouldn't push. "A big businessman named Robert Manners."

Hiller sat still for a while, eyes fixed on the TV. "I recall it, but I don't know much about it."

I sipped my cold beer. "There probably isn't much to know, but Manners' doctor was no help. I thought I might be able to check the autopsy report and whatever else is available through you."

"Sure."

The third out was a near home run. Hiller groaned, excused himself and left the room. I heard him talking on the telephone in the hall. He was on the phone for a long time. When he came back to the living room, he was carrying two more cans of the very cold beer.

"What happened, Nudger?"

"Strikeout, walk, double play," I said, accepting the chilled wet can. "What happened where you were?"

"Probably a strikeout there, too. The autopsy report on Manners says he was in good health until he hit the sidewalk. And a subsequent investigation turned up nothing to suggest his death was anything but suicide."

I nodded, took a pull on my beer in disappointment.

"There is one thing, though," Hiller said. "I talked to the officer who handled the investigation. For what it's worth, he says a suicide finding didn't sit quite right with him, but it was only a feeling. The facts said suicide."

I understood what Hiller was saying, but I also knew how often hunches were wrong. "Is the case still being actively investigated?"

Hiller stared at me "You know better than that. Time, money and manpower come into it. They don't let us go looking for crime when there's no live victim and there are far to many live victims walking around out there today."

Hiller had a point I couldn't contradict.

"Stick around for a while," he invited. "Watch the ball game. It's a genuine pitchers' duel."

"For an inning or so," I said. "I've got an appointment later at a hotel with a beautiful girl."

Hiller laughed. "As long as no money changes hands." He propped his feet on the hassock again.

When I left him to drive to the Clairbank, the Dodgers had just scored three runs on a triple, and he was happy.

The Clairbank was one of L.A.'s older hotels, spacious and accommodating, the sort that still offers top service at moderate rates. I crossed the carpeted lobby, took a smooth but slow elevator to the fourth floor and knocked on the door of 407.

"You're late," Alison said as she opened the door.

"And hungry," I told her, glancing at my watch to see that it was five after seven. "Why don't we talk things over while we're having dinner downstairs?"

Alison must not have eaten, either, because she agreed, stepped into the hall and closed the door behind her. She was wearing a pale-green outfit with a loose-fitting skirt and chunky, thick-soled shoes, which, despite the work of a deranged fashion designer, failed to rob her ankles of their grace.

The Clairbank had a comfortable restaurant with good food and a varied menu. Over chicken oreganata specials, we discussed.

"What did Elizabeth Manners tell you?" Alison asked, sipping her wine.

"That her husband committed suicide," I said truthfully, but stopped short of mentioning the letter. "He'd been apprehensive for some time, then especially so just before his death."

"Do you think she really believes it was suicide?"

"I'm sure she does. And I'm sure she'll never get over it."

"You might be right. This sauce is terrific."

I watched her use her knife and fork enthusiastically on her chicken breast. She bothered me. She was one of the few women whom I felt I should dislike but who greatly appealed to me. I considered trying to work out a way to spend the night in the Clairbank, in room 407. Maybe it was something in the sauce.

"Okay," she said, "let's compare notes on Mr. Brian Cheevers."

Cheevers had told her, almost word for word, what he'd told me. Alison had also gotten a duplicate story from Manners' secretary, Alice Kramer. Not much on the West Coast had panned out.

"So we learned nothing," Alison said, with some dejection, to her half-consumed chicken breast. "There was nothing unusual or business-related about Manners' suicide."

For some reason I felt I had to console her. "Either that or everyone has his story memorized to perfection."

She looked up at me. "Do you suppose that's possible, some sort of conspiracy?"

I understood why she was a reporter. Some of the juiciest news is wished into being.

"You know anything's possible," I told her.

Alison waited until we'd got to the rice pudding before saying, "Oh, incidentally, I found something on your Gratuity Insurance. I phoned the secretary of Craig Blount, a high-level executive killed in a hit-and-run accident a few weeks ago in Seattle. She told me she remembered that some time ago a man from Gratuity had called at the office and seemed to upset her boss tremendously."

"Upset him how?"

"Made him edgy and bad-tempered," Alison said, "which wasn't like him."

Good as the food was, my fluttering stomach would accept no more. I set my fork down and sat back in my chair.

"What's the matter?" she asked.

"The thing about Gratuity Insurance," I told Alison, "is that there is no such company."

19

The next day I knocked again on Elizabeth Manners' door. When I got no answer I looked about and found her in the garden, with a pruning shears, working on an espaliered lemon tree. She turned, startled, as she heard my footsteps on the path.

"Mr. Nudger!" she said with what seemed to be genuine pleasure. "I hope you've returned because you've discovered something."

"Maybe a crack of light, Mrs. Manners." It was peaceful in the garden, pleasantly shaded. I hated to pull Elizabeth Manners into the subject of her husband's death.

"Gardening pacifies the soul," she said, working the red-handled shears expertly; but I could see her tenseness as she waited for what I had to say.

"Was your husband acquainted with any of these business executives?" I asked, feeling somewhat like the serpent in the garden. I read her the list of five names given to me by Alison.

Mrs. Manners continued to work the shears for a while before answering. Then she lowered them to her side and faced me. "Craig Blount. I don't think they were acquainted, but I remember the morning Robert and I were having breakfast and he read about this Blount's death in the newspaper. It seemed to disturb him, so much so that he couldn't finish his breakfast."

"Did he say what it was about Blount's death that upset him?"

"No, he tried to pretend that he wasn't upset, but I could see that he'd been thoroughly shaken. After he'd left for the office, I picked up the newspaper and read the piece on Craig Blount, but I couldn't find anything that warranted Robert's reaction."

"How long before his death was this?"

She laid the shears on the cement bench, as if they'd suddenly taken on weight. "Only about a week," she said. "That's why I remembered. Many things seemed to upset Robert during that period, but that newspaper story did particularly."

"May I use your telephone?" I asked her.

"Certainly. The door's unlocked." She bent gracefully to pick up the shears, to displace her grief again in the garden.

I phoned Alice Kramer, Manners' secretary, at Witlow Cable and asked her if she'd heard of Craig Blount. She hadn't, and she couldn't remember Manners' mentioning even a similar name in her presence.

I left Elizabeth Manners' home with an idea, about which I had more than a few doubts. But it was the only idea I had, so I clung to it.

At a large drugstore that sold everything from cough syrup to furniture, I got a handful of change from a schoolgirlish blonde cashier behind one of the registers and made my way to the phone booths.

The booths were in a secluded spot behind men's outerwear, and I was glad for the privacy. I fed change to the hungry telephone until it was glutted, then managed to get in touch with Dale Carlon.

"What have you learned?" Carlon asked immediately in his crisp business voice.

"I've got a connection between Talbert and Gratuity and the Robert Manners who killed himself, Manners and Gratuity and somebody named Craig Blount, who was killed in a hit-and-run accident in Seattle a few weeks ago."

"There is no Gratuity Insurance, Nudger. I checked."

"So did I. That's what interests me."

"Whoever or whatever they are, do you think my daughter is mixed up with them?"

137

"I'm reasonably sure of it."

Carlon's exasperated outlet of breath was amplified to a drawn-out rasping in the receiver. "You're keeping things quiet, aren't you, Nudger?"

"Too quiet. The police should know what I know, Mr. Carlon. If they did, you might see an extensive and effective investigation."

"We'll decide when and what to tell the police, Nudger."

What he meant by that was *he* would decide, and he had fifty thousand good arguments in his favor.

"Ever heard of *Business View?*" I asked him. "It's a magazine."

"I have. Used to subscribe to it."

"Then I take it it's a reputable publication."

"Very much so. I think it's published in Chicago. It's one of those financial monthlies that reports on the stock market and analyzes and predicts trends."

"There's a female reporter here who works for the magazine, gathering information about Manners' death. Her name's Alison Day."

"Alison?" He sounded surprised. "I know her well, Nudger. She's dedicated and, despite her comparative youth, widely respected in her profession. I've known Alison both professionally and as a friend of the family, for years. She recommended Joan to her college sorority."

"Then you vouch for her?"

"Completely. She's a thorough professional in her field. That's not to say, Nudger, that you should confide in her. She is a reporter."

"She doesn't know who I'm working for or why," I assured Carlon.

"I think you should go to Seattle," Carlon said after a pause.

"I don't think it's necessary at this point," I told him. "If I decide to, I'll let you know."

Gently I replaced the receiver, before he could insist. I had worked for Dale Carlons before; their egos demanded that they be better than everyone at everything.

On the way out of the drugstore, I stopped at the pharmaceutical counter and bought a fresh roll of antacid tablets. My next stop was going to be the Clairbank Hotel.

20

Alison's room at the Clairbank was large and comfortable. It lacked the careful color and style coordination of chain hotel rooms. The long triple dresser didn't quite match the smaller dresser on the opposite wall, two overstuffed wing chairs looked more like they belonged in an English men's club than a hotel room, and the flowered spread on the double bed matched neither beige carpet nor heavy drapes. The overall effect was one almost of hominess.

I could see a gleam in Alison's shrewd eyes as I told her what Craig Blount's name has evoked from Elizabeth Manners. Alison began to realize then, I think, that I was holding back a great deal from her.

"You're right about Gratuity Insurance," she said. "No such company is listed with—"

"I know," I told her, "it's been checked and double-checked."

She was wearing a tailored pinstriped outfit that couldn't subdue the curves of her lean body, and I found myself wondering if she would approach sex with her usual brisk and cool efficiency. The feline something in her eyes and the generous arc of her lower lip told me that wasn't likely.

"Where did you get the name of a fictitious insurance company?" she asked, pausing before the window in fetching silhouette.

"It's cropped up throughout my investigation. Now it's a link between Manners and Blount, two men who don't seem to be linked in any other way."

"Nudger," she said, "could you tell me what, precisely, you're investigating?"

I smiled and shook my head. "We agreed from the beginning there'd be some things I wouldn't tell you."

She narrowed an eye but didn't argue. "What do we do now?" she asked.

I was glad she said "we," because right now I needed her. "Can you draw up a list of the business establishment's top executives, nationwide?"

The suggestion didn't throw her. "How many names?"

"How about the top fifty? Not the obvious multimillionaires—the corporation men."

Alison walked to the writing desk, drummed longnailed fingers on smooth polished wood. "What do you intend to do with the list?"

"I want you to use your professional status to contact the secretaries or other satellite personalities who surround these men. Let them know that you want to be notified immediately if they hear of a Gratuity Insurance appointment. Can you do it?"

"Not as easily as you make it sound." She caressed her chin in thought. "How about my drawing up a list of the top people with whom I have connections, or with whose satellite personalities I have connections? I can't guarantee they'll be in the top fifty, but I feel safe to say they could all make the top hundred or two."

"That should help."

"And I can talk to the heads of some secretarial organizations," Alison said, picking up enthusiasm. "They can get the word out to their members to phone if they hear anything about Gratuity."

That was something I hadn't thought of, and it put the plan well into the realm of workability. "That's good," I told her. "The list doesn't have to read like a who's who. I want the names of executives in the same league as the men who died."

"Big league, but not the superstars," Alison said. She took a well-worn portable electric typewriter from the closet and set it on the desk. Then she dug through her luggage and came out with an expandable cardboard file and several flat leather-bound books. "This is going to take a long time," she said.

"Most everything worthwhile does," I told her sagely, myself doubting the wisdom of that pronouncement. "I'll look in on you later."

"Where are you going?"

"To see about some stocks."

As I closed the door behind me, I heard the ratchety sound of paper being rolled into the typewriter.

At the Gilford and Hollis brokerage firm, I talked to a broker's representative and got a prospectus on each of the five companies that had employed the dead executives whose names had been given to me by Alison, plus a prospectus on Witlow Cable.

I sat in a chair behind a low wooden railing, among several stricken-looking gentlemen who stared at the constantly sideways-traveling ribbon of the big board's lighted numerals, those numerals depicting the rise and fall of stock prices and men's fortunes in eighths of dollars. Now and then one of the men would seem to break the mesmeric spell of the lighted board, get up and walk over to check a teletype or speak in soft tones to one of the busy representatives at a row of desks beyond the railing. I was sure no one would disturb me as I settled back to examine the first prospectus, telling me in accountant's language all about a company called Avec-Stern.

A great deal of time, concentration and occasional help from one of the broker's representatives revealed no common denominator among the six companies for which the dead men had toiled. The main businesses of the companies were diverse: industrial cable, shoe manufacturing, heavy drilling equipment, bottling, trucking, and importing. Except for the bottling firm and heavy drilling equipment manufacturer, business was down the past several quarters for each company—at least on paper. And there had been no recent dramatic movement in the prices of their stocks. The broker's rep advised against my buying into any of them—except, possibly, the bottling firm.

Using a pay phone, I called Brian Cheevers and asked him if Witlow Cable had ever done business with any of the other companies. He promised to check, but his answer was a tentative no.

Outside the brokerage house I sat on a bench and tried to piece something together from what I'd learned inside. The weather was clear, and it wasn't so hot today. The sun felt good on my face and shoulders. I leaned back with my eyes half closed, watching through a haze the bright, multicolored stream of traffic, wondering if anything would ever fit together again for me.

Lornee was gone; and the children, gone, not just from me but from the world in which I lived. Life had taken a sudden, unpredictable direction, and now things seemed either too real or unreal, by turns. What was I doing here, on a curbside bench in Los Angeles, the sun on my face and a cold weight in my heart, full of fear and uncertainty as I goaded for greed the possibility of my violent death? What was anybody doing anywhere? I needed a drink.

142

But I knew better. I stood and moved away from the sun-warmed bench and the debilitating melancholy that I both courted and hated. As the traffic light changed and I crossed the concrete street in the sanctuary between parallel lines, I felt like an unreal man in an unreal city. The L.A. syndrome. This wasn't the place for me.

When I got back to the Clairbank, Alison had just finished telephoning, running up an enormous bill. I told her not to worry about the cost, that it came out of expenses.

"Maybe we can collect on it twice," she said, "me from my magazine and you from your client."

It occurred to me that I might want to sleep with her so I could reform her, but that didn't sound reasonable.

She leaned back from the phone, stiffly flexing the fingers of her right hand. Then she took her half-smoked cigarette from the ashtray, drew on it, and released thick smoke from her mouth sensuously, as if that were some exotic power she alone possessed and the cigarette had nothing to do with it.

"Getting cooperation?" I asked.

Alison laughed. "Of course. They're all afraid I'll write something nasty about their company and they'll lose their jobs."

"Did anyone you talked to know anything about Gratuity?"

"No. I thought they might, too. It would have saved us the trouble of waiting for a call."

"Maybe we won't have to wait long," I said. "Gratuity is pretty active for a nonexistent company." I tried not to show my disappointment at hearing that none of the people Alison had phoned knew anything about Gratuity. Maybe I expected too much. Interlocked and overlapping as the business world was, it was a vast world nonetheless.

143

Alison's telephone would have to be answerable at all times, so I offered to take a room at the Clairbank to spell her if she wanted to get out of the hotel. But she assured me that wasn't necessary, that she had volumes of work to do and would be glad to stay cooped up in her hotel room to do it while waiting for the phone call that might not come. Television would supply the entertainment; room service, the food.

I took a room at the Clairbank anyway.

During the next few days I got better acquainted with Alison, though not to the degree I had in mind. Maybe there was something to the "opposites attract" theory, because we seemed to hold opposite opinions on almost every subject. Or maybe Alison intrigued me because I didn't know how much of her was an act and how much was genuine. Sometimes she would say things in a certain tone, with a certain unguarded expression, and I would glimpse, beneath her surface, something like the fear that knotted my insides. Her facts and figures and cold logic, then, seemed a device to hold off a world that puzzled and frightened her.

On the third day, Alison's phone rang and I picked up the receiver. The call was from Chicago, and it was for Alison. I handed her the receiver and watched her cool and perfect features as she listened. As she replaced the receiver, she smiled a smile from one of those Italian Renaissance paintings.

"Somebody representing Gratuity Insurance has a nine o'clock appointment tomorrow morning in St. Louis with Tad Osborne, divisional manager of Heath Industries."

"What do you know about Osborne?"

"He's in his late forties, worked his way up through the sales division of Gayton Equipment, left them about five years ago to take over at Heath, an electronics component manufacturer with a lot of government contract work."

144

"How would you say Osborne ranks in the scheme of things with the six who died? In prestige, income, responsibility?"

Alison twisted a turquoise ring on her finger as she thought. "Generally they're in the same league, VIPs, but not the top men." She stood, looking at me expectantly, wondering, now, how we were going to act on the information we'd come up with.

"We should be able to get a flight to St. Louis today," I said.

"That's no problem," Alison said. "I have the airline schedules. The problem, as I see it, is getting Tad Osborne's cooperation."

"Leave that to me," I told her with some pleasure, watching her cock her head with inquisitive surprise.

Alison's lips parted, and I thought she was going to ask me how I was going to handle Osborne, but she said, "I'll get reservations on the next available flight."

We had two hours until flight time. I left Alison to her packing and went to my room and phoned Dale Carlon.

21

Los Angeles had been hot, but St. Louis had it beat. This was the damp, sticky kind of heat that followed you indoors, made you perspire even when you were still, and melted the body from the fabric of your clothes so that they clung limply to you.

I waited for our luggage to come around on the metal

carousel while Alison made her way through the milling throng of travelers and greeters to rent a car. A woman rattled off flight numbers over the public address speakers as if she were calling a bingo game. No one seemed to be listening.

Our luggage came up fast, and Alison was just completing arrangements for the car when I met her at the Avis desk. The terminal's cocktail lounge looked dim and cool as we walked past, and I could have used a drink but thought better of it. It was almost midnight, and tomorrow morning I might have to be sharper than I'd ever been.

Alison drove the rented Chevy too fast to the Ramada Inn near the airport. We took adjoining rooms, an unnecessary expense in my estimation but not in hers.

I stretched out on the bed and expected to lie awake for a long time, but when I blinked, it was seven A.M. and time to get moving to make Heath Industries before nine. A cold shower focused my mind on my fear, and I dressed more slowly than I should have. But nothing I did slowed the minute hand on my watch.

Alison was downstairs, waiting for me. We had a quick breakfast of Danish rolls and coffee, then walked out onto the already-warm blacktopped parking lot and got into the rented Chevy. I drove, knowing I'd be less nervous if I kept myself occupied.

Heath Industries was in Westport, a new and sprawling industrial development, west of the city, that was either the downtown or the slum of the future. The morning rush hour traffic was a study in heat and frustration, and it was eight-thirty when we finally parked in the lot of Heath's regional headquarters in an impressive, recently built, tall structure fronted by an artificial lake from which rose a graceful, gull-winged cement sculpture. The Heath building was the tallest in the area and commanded a view of a teeming four-lane highway that dwindled to a sun-shimmering ribbon on the horizon.

We topped the cement steps and entered the lobby—high-ceilinged, decorous and cool. A gold-framed directory told us that Tad Osborne's office was on the top floor. The elevator was a smooth rocket that didn't help my stomach.

A blond Nordic type with too much bulky jewelry sat at a desk in the plush outer office. She smiled at us when we entered and told her who we were, and she seemed to know Alison. Osborne must have instructed her to send us right in when she buzzed him, because she immediately jangled over to the main office and opened the door for us.

Tad Osborne's office was cool and ordered, and beyond a huge window the ribbon of teeming highway stretched to an even more distant horizon. Osborne himself was a medium-sized, balding man with broad, pleasant features, seated behind a very wide desk on which sat only the basics—pen set, ashtray, "out" basket, telephone, and on one corner the mandatory framed family photographs.

"What is it about Mr. Bender that interests you?" Osborne asked after we'd been seated.

Alison arched an eyebrow beautifully. "Mr. Bender?"

"Why, yes . . . Frank Bender, the Gratuity Insurance agent."

"There's really not much we can tell you, Mr. Osborne," I said, "because we don't have hard information. Why did Bender want to see you?"

Osborne rotated back and forth slightly in his swivel chair, but his gray eyes stayed trained on me. "He called and said there'd been a series of insurance company mergers and he needed my signature to transfer some of my policies. He assured me it would mean a savings without loss of coverage."

"Whatever he tells you, Mr. Osborne, I'm afraid you're on your own. We don't know enough to predict exactly what he'll really have in mind, but there's sufficient reason for us to believe it won't be insurance."

"I'm sure there is, or Dale Carlon wouldn't have vouched for you." He looked at his digital watch. "It's quarter to nine. How is this thing going to unfold?"

I didn't tell him that that question was ruining my health. "Just pretend we're not here. Listen to what Bender has to say, tell him what you think best, and when he leaves, I'll follow him. If it's all right, I'll wait in the file room off your secretary's office so I can see him enter and leave."

"Fine," Osborne said. "I'll tell Mary to cooperate with you."

"Miss Day will be waiting with me, and when I've left she'll want to talk to you to get all the details of your conversation with Bender while they're fresh in your mind."

"Suppose I record our conversation without his knowledge?"

"I wouldn't advise it. Bender might have one of a number of devices to detect an operating recorder."

"Our talk should only take a few minutes," Alison said through her best interviewer's smile. "I'm with *Business View*, but I promise you nothing you tell me will be used without your permission."

I thought she was putting herself in a corner there, but I kept quiet.

"I've read some of your articles with interest, Miss Day," Osborne said, spreading thick honey. "You do fine and accurate work."

"Bender should be arriving any time now," I told him. "It would be better if he didn't see us."

Osborne rose and showed us out of his office, resting a hand on Alison's shoulder in what I assumed to be a fatherly manner. A favorable article in *Business View* wouldn't hurt either Heath Industries or his career.

The file room was almost as large as the anteroom. It was furnished with two wooden chairs, a table, and

148

three walls lined solid with charcoal-gray file cabinets. The fourth wall was all metal shelving stacked with varied but neatly stored office supplies. Alison took a chair near the table. I propped the file room door open at just the right angle and positioned the remaining chair so I had a view of anyone entering the outer office and approaching Osborne's bejeweled secretary.

My nerves took over, tapping my right toe in staccato rhythm on the cork floor, rubbing the fingertips of my right hand on the tabletop until they tingled.

But I didn't have long to wait. Five minutes after I'd sat down, at exactly nine o'clock, Frank Bender arrived.

He was a well-groomed and stylishly dressed man in his late twenties or early thirties, wearing a neat dark suit that went far to disguise the fact that he was overweight. He had an even-featured, handsome face with bright, small dark eyes narrowed by the fleshy padding around them. Holding his attaché case before him, he aimed exactly the right sort of friendly but impersonal smile at the secretary, and I heard him small-talking her as he gave his name.

Osborne's secretary seemed genuinely charmed as she got up and ushered Bender into the main office. She was still smiling at something he'd said as she walked back toward her desk.

Alison and I looked at each other. There was an anxious, super-alert expression in her eyes, and I wondered if I wore the same expression.

No, I was sure mine was tempered by worry and fear. The things that could go wrong! Might Gratuity be legitimate, a small or newly formed company not yet brought to the attention of the various agencies that had been contacted? Frank Bender looked like a thousand other insurance agents, didn't he?

Then I thought about the business card in Victor Talbert's jacket, in Chicago, on the back of which was

149

the name of a man who'd died a violent death in Los Angeles. As Victor Talbert had died. As Craig Blount, in Seattle, had died.

It was nine-twenty, and Bender hadn't come out. My stomach was vibrating.

He came out at nine twenty-eight, and by then I was on my feet, waiting. Through the crack in the door I saw him walk past Osborne's secretary and smile as he did when he entered. He said something I couldn't understand as he went out, and the secretary smiled and adjusted an earring. With a last look back at Alison, who was now also standing, I left the file room to follow Bender.

He left the parking lot in a light-tan sedan, probably a rental, and I trailed in the Avis Chevy. He wound his way through the streets almost as if he didn't know exactly where he was. I stayed three cars back, eating antacid tablets like candy.

Bender must have skipped breakfast. I watched him pull up to a hamburger restaurant, one of a chain, that had a sign proclaiming that they served eggs and pancakes. Parked in an inconspicuous spot near a discount store, I waited for him and thought of things other than food.

I hadn't carried a gun since I was with the department, and I wondered if I should have one now. Bender looked harmless enough, even amiable, but I remembered the deceptively peaceful death photos of Victor Talbert and the fear on Belle Dee's bloodied face when she opened her apartment door for me. And I remembered my own reaction to the sight of her injuries.

Bender finally emerged from the restaurant, his suit coat unbuttoned and his stocky arms swinging freely, the expansive walk of a well-fed man. I watched him get into his car; then I saw a hazy rush of exhaust fumes from the tailpipe of the tan sedan, and it backed from its parking slot and maneuvered in tight quarters to point toward the driveway to the street.

I started the Chevy and sat with the engine idling. When Bender turned the sedan into the flow of traffic, I reminded myself of Carlon's fifty thousand dollars and followed.

Bender was driving more confidently now, as if he knew where he was going. He was easier to follow.

We took a cloverleaf and were on Highway 67, where it was called Lindbergh Boulevard. Within a few minutes Bender made a left into the parking lot of the King Saint Louis Motel.

The motel was small and not very prosperous-looking, a series of duplex cabins. Bender must already have registered. The tan car made a sharp turn and parked in front of the end cabin. I watched as Bender got out of the car, carrying his attaché case, and let himself into the cabin through the door nearest me.

I sat in the car, parked on the gravel road shoulder off Lindbergh, and looked at the cabin's closed door. With a shattering roar, a jet passed almost directly overhead, so low it seemed the treetops flinched. The King Saint Louis was one of a string of motels directly west of the airport. I eased the Chevy forward, turned into the parking lot and, with a soft squeal of brakes, stopped in front of the tiny office.

I asked for one of the cabins nearest the highway. There were plenty of vacancies, as the sparse-haired elderly woman behind the desk informed me, and she was more than glad to comply. I registered under my own name and paid in advance.

The cabins were strung unevenly along a line diagonal to the highway. From my front window I could see Bender's parked car and the front of his cabin. All of the cabins were in minor disrepair, faded redwood

151

with patchwork shingled roofs. I could see tall weeds beyond the back corners of most of them, and outside the window of the back door of my own.

The telephone had a long cord, just long enough to reach the table by the front window. I set the phone down, moved a lamp aside and pulled a wicker-backed chair next to the table. Never letting the front of Bender's cabin out of my sight for more than a few seconds, I dialed the number of Heath Industries and asked for Tad Osborne.

There was something in the voice of the girl who answered the phone as she asked me again whom I was calling, then requested me to hold the line—a high edge of excitement. The next voice I heard was a man's, but not Osborne's.

"Who's calling, please?"

I started to speak, but an uneasiness, a subtle tingling of suspicion, bored into my mind.

"Hello, who's—"

I replaced the receiver.

For a long while I sat still, staring out through the dusty, slanted venetian blinds at the quiet, sun-brightened face of Bender's cabin. Maybe the girl on the phone at Heath had some personal reason to be excited. Maybe she'd given me the wrong extension and the man's voice was simply that of another Heath employee. Maybe nothing was wrong. Maybe it was.

I phoned Heath Industries again, got the same girl, then the same laconic male voice asking me to identify myself. Not office procedure—police procedure.

I punched the button in the telephone's cradle, dialed the Ramada Inn and asked for Alison's room.

No answer.

I hung up the phone and sat staring out the window. Another jet roared overhead, sending vibrations through the flimsy cabin. I had no way of knowing what, if anything, had gone wrong at Heath, or where

152

Alison was, or if Bender had somehow been tipped to my presence. Doggedly I told myself things might actually be going smoothly—nothing wrong at Heath, and Alison hadn't had time to return to the Ramada, where she was supposed to wait for my phone call. But the fear lay like a slab of lead in my stomach, and my chest seemed to be constricting my heart.

I was plagued by the feeling that events had passed from my control, that the tiger I'd had by the tail had finally turned around. But there was nothing I could do about it now; I could only go on with what I'd planned. I'd try the Ramada again in a while, talk to Alison and get some of the answers.

Noon arrived, passed, and Alison still hadn't returned to her motel room. And Bender's cabin—half in shadow now, peaceful, drapes closed—might have been vacant but for the fact that I knew he was inside. The tan sedan was parked, unmoved and baking in the sun, where Bender had left it.

My back began to ache, and I got up now and then to pace, occasionally sitting down to make another unsuccessful phone call to the Ramada. The intermittent overhead roar of jet engines was beginning to wear on me.

Then, at two o'clock, the door to Bender's cabin opened and he came out.

He'd changed clothes. Now he was wearing gray slacks and a pale-yellow sport shirt. Maybe he'd been asleep; he looked fresh. I stood at the window, leaning over the table and watching him.

I cursed silently as Bender walked past his parked car. At first I thought he was going to the motel office, but instead he turned left and stood on the shoulder of the highway, leaning forward, waiting to cross.

When there was a break in the traffic, he trotted across the highway, and I watched him walk south on the other side. I realized then where he was going. The

King Saint Louis didn't have a restaurant, and Bender was headed for the restaurant of the motel across the street for a late lunch.

I had to move to the side, hold back the drapes and peer at an angle through the window now to follow his progress. He passed out of my sight momentarily, but I picked him up again as he entered the motel restaurant. I relaxed my grip on the drapes and stepped back. My stomach said no to what I had to do next.

Walking to the back door of my cabin, I examined the lock. Simple, the sort that can be slipped with a piece of celluloid or a plastic credit card. But there was also a chain lock. I could only hope that the back door of Bender's cabin didn't have one; or, if it did, that it wasn't fastened. Parting the stained sheer curtains over the window in my door, I took a quick look out back, saw only tall weeds and a small gray trash container, and stepped outside.

Slipping the lock on the rear of Bender's cabin was no problem, but the door did have a chain lock and it was fastened. I saw what I'd have to do. If I punched out the door's small windowpane nearest the lock and cleaned up the broken glass, Bender would never know it unless he happened to look behind the door's curtains. My heart was pumping with labored wildness and my body was bent by the tightness in my stomach. I wondered how professional burglars ever got up the nerve to operate. With a fast, guilty look around, I rammed my elbow into the window, and the glass broke in four pieces but didn't fall from the frame. No damage to my elbow, and I was grateful there hadn't been much noise.

I removed the largest piece of glass, reached in and, with fumbling fingers, unfastened the chain. Then I added breaking and entering to withholding evidence and went inside.

It was almost as if I'd found shelter; I couldn't be

seen now. But the exhilaration and fear had entered with me. I could hear the sounds of my own breathing and rushing of blood, and only my rising anger with myself brought a measure of calm.

The interior of Bender's cabin was exactly like mine. A suitcase stood open on a luggage stand at the foot of the double bed, revealing folded white underwear and shirts. Bender's leather attaché case was on the floor, leaning against the side of the dresser. I went to it first, found it unlocked.

The case was empty but for a gold letter-opener and a thin packet of white business cards. The cards were similar to the card I'd found in the pocket of Victor Talbert's jacket, engraved only with GRATUITY INSURANCE.

I closed the attaché case and leaned it back the way I'd found it. Then I went to the suitcase and searched carefully beneath the folded clothes. It took me a while, and I found nothing but lint.

After rearranging the suitcase the way it had been, I checked the bathroom. Nothing there but a zippered travel kit containing the usual assortment of shaving cream, razor, spray deodorant and manicure set.

From the bathroom I went quickly to the closet. I'd been inside Bender's cabin for little more than five minutes, and I told myself it would be safer to slow down and do things right than to panic. He probably wouldn't return for at least half an hour.

The closet contained a suit, a sport coat and two pale-blue shirts on hangers. A search of the pockets netted me nothing but a postage stamp and comb. I straightened the shirts on their hangers, smoothed the lapels of the suit.

The blast of a jet engine made me take a step toward the back door; then I stood leaning on the dresser, waiting for the sound to subside.

In the first dresser drawer I opened I found a dollar's

155

worth of change and a set of gold cufflinks. The rest of the drawers were empty.

I stood in the center of the cabin and looked desperately around. There was nowhere else to search. I'd risked everything for nothing.

After making sure things were arranged the way I'd found them, I moved toward the back door. And that's when I saw the strip of white beneath the dark suitcase.

I stepped over, lifted the end of the suitcase and discovered that what I'd seen was the edge of an airline ticket. It was made out to Emmett Marshal, either Bender's real name or the name he traveled under, and it was a return-flight ticket to Chicago. The departure time was noon tomorrow. I replaced the ticket where I'd found it, letting the edge of white show as it had before.

When I left Bender's cabin, I removed the remaining broken glass from the back door's window frame and made sure the curtains hung completely over the opening. I dropped the pieces of broken glass onto some soggy cardboard in the gray trash container as I passed, and I entered my own cabin the back way and locked the door behind me.

The floor seemed to be made of sponge. I sat weakly on the edge of the bed and realized that I was practically panting, winded from doing nothing more than holding my breath.

After a few minutes I involuntarily laughed out loud, and that seemed to drain me of my tension. I got up, crossed to the telephone and dialed the number of the Ramada Inn, knowing it well enough now to dial it without thinking. When I asked for Alison's room, her telephone was answered on the first ring.

There was anxiety and weariness in Alison's voice instead of the usual crispness.

I sat down in my chair by the front window. "Alison, where were you earlier?"

"Talking to the police."

"The police? . . ." My fingers were suddenly slippery with perspiration on the smooth receiver.

"Tad Osborne's been murdered."

Fear rushed into me. I didn't know whether to curse my bad luck or my stupidity.

That I should curse my greed never occurred to me.

22

Twenty minutes after leaving the King Saint Louis Motel, I entered Alison's room at the Ramada Inn.

She was on the phone, her lips compressed in exasperation. When she spoke, it was with the brittle self-control of someone who'd rather be screaming. "I will," she said, "you can count on it."

When she hung up the phone, she sighed. "My editor," she explained. "He thinks I'm on another assignment and I have to stall him."

The police must have been thorough with her. She wasn't her usual composed self. Some of the shrewd confidence was gone from her eyes, and a stray wisp of auburn hair hung over the center of her forehead.

"How did it happen?" I asked her.

Alison brushed back the strand of hair and paced off some of her nervousness. "After you left to follow Bender I went into Osborne's office to talk to him. He was sitting with his head resting on his desk, his eyes open, as if he were looking toward the door. . . ." Her face was pale wax.

"Only he was dead," I finished for her.

Alison nodded, swallowed. The strain was pulling at the corners of her mouth.

"How?" I asked her.

"He was . . . stabbed, in the chest."

An iciness dropped through me as I remembered the gold letter-opener in Bender's attaché case.

"Did the police find the weapon?"

"No, the killer took it with him."

"Bender. . . . " I said.

Alison gave me an intent look. "It had to be him, but the police don't know who or where he is."

I could imagine Osborne's mistake. He knew we were onto Bender and reasoned that he was in no danger, so he must have pushed too hard, maybe lost his temper, underestimating the ruthlessness and deadliness of Bender and whatever he represented.

"Did you tell the police I was following Bender?"

"Not right away," Alison said, "but I had to eventually. I told them what I knew."

I walked to the window with my fists in my pockets. If I told the police where to find Bender, they'd pick him up and, with that, end my hopes of tracing Joan Clark. I was certain that she was somehow connected with Gratuity Insurance.

"Suppose that Bender realized I was following him, and that he lost me," I said.

"But he didn't."

"From this point on we pretend that I told you he did."

Alison gave me a nice eyebrow arch. "But you can't withhold evidence in a murder case."

I didn't tell her she was too late with that advice or that Carlon was paying me fifty thousand dollars to follow his advice.

"We're too close not to," I told her. "I searched Bender's motel room while he was out. He's going to be on flight five sixty-two tomorrow at noon, bound for Chicago, which is where he came from."

158

Alison appeared dubious. She touched the flame of her lighter to one of her long cigarettes and glared at me through the smoke. "Nudger, what have you got in mind?"

"I intend to take an earlier flight to Chicago. I'll be at O'Hare when Bender's plane touches down, and I'll follow him from the airport."

"To where?"

"That's what I'll be following him to find out."

I watched Alison take another desperate drag on her cigarette, glad I hadn't confided in her completely. She seemed to relax, letting the smoke filter thickly from her mouth and nostrils.

"What if Bender changes his flight plan?" she asked.

"The Benders of the world don't change their carefully laid-out plans unless they have to. You can bet that killing Osborne was in Bender's mind as an alternative before he walked into that office. And now he knows that if he ever does come under suspicion, it would be best if he left a record of having behaved normally after leaving Heath Industries. Remember, he doesn't know he was followed."

Alison stared at her cigarette and seemed to weigh the logic of what I'd told her. "I'll go to Chicago with you," she said.

"It might only implicate you further."

"I'm not implicated at all yet."

The message was communicated clearly. If I didn't let her accompany me, what was there left for her to do but cover herself by telling the police what she knew?"

"You *are* asking me to break the law," Alison said. "And remember, I'm the one who steered you onto Bender. We agreed to help each other with an exchange of information, so don't expect me to back away from this story now."

"I don't want you complicating things. I don't want anyone else to get hurt."

"And I want my story."

I knew I had no choice, really. If Alison called the police, I'd never be able to leave St. Louis, and I'd be in hot water a mile over my head.

"All right, but there's a condition," I told her, pretending to have a few bargaining chips. "I'll be in charge in Chicago, without any interference from you for the sake of a good story."

"If it will help your ego," she said.

I told her to make the reservations.

23

At eleven thirty the next morning I was in Chicago, sitting behind a bourbon and water in the airport lounge, waiting for the minute hand to make another circuit. Alison and I had arrived on the ten-twenty flight from St. Louis. She had gone to check in with her magazine, and I'd instructed her to meet me later in the day at the TraveLodge, on South Michigan Avenue. I'd already rented a car and had my luggage in the trunk. Bender's flight wasn't due to arrive until twelve thirty-two. It was waiting and thinking time.

Alison was the subject of my thoughts as I sat waiting for the liquor to calm me, to numb some of the fear in me. There was fear, but not to the degree that I'd be careless. A thin line there, increasingly hard to discern.

What was there about Alison? What inconsistency was stirring, invisible in the back of my mind? She ever threatened to become a dilemma in the case, and yet it was she who had gotten me this far.

160

And though I'd pursued the investigation in the only direction I'd seen open to me, would it actually lead to Joan Clark? Collecting the remainder of my fifty thousand dollars depended on that alone. Again I experienced that foreboding, that gradually heightening perception of a drawing nearer, an inexorable movement toward the vortex.

What if Alison was right about the possibility of Bender's having changed flights? It wasn't likely, but unlikely things happened all the time, and to me. Where would I be if he had changed flights, slipped away?

I knew where. I downed the rest of the drink I'd intended to nurse.

At twelve thirty-five I watched Frank Bender pass through security, wondering if he still had the gold letter-opener or if he'd disposed of it in St. Louis.

Weighted down as he was with his luggage, it was simple to follow him through the crowded terminal. But he did what I'd hoped he wouldn't and headed toward the taxi area.

Things got less simple then. I had to run to where my car was parked, and the damned thing refused to start. On the fourth try, when the starter was growling like a record played at slow speed, the engine turned over and I gunned it in frustration before jamming the shift lever into drive. Luck was the big reason I was able to get behind Bender's cab as it turned onto the expressway and headed for the city.

Inside the city limits the cab turned right onto Fifty, drove awhile, then made a left and began to wind through side streets. I followed well back in the light midday traffic. The cab had a mud-splotched liquor advertisement on its trunk and a limber whip antenna, and that made keeping track of it easy.

We passed through an old and doomed area of the city, then on into a marginal neighborhood of small shops and brick apartment buildings, and suddenly things began to look familiar.

The cab veered to the curb and parked beneath a block-lettered sign: EXECUTIVE TOWERS. I looked at the recently face-lifted apartment building as I drove past. Jerry Congram's former home.

Parked down the street, I watched in my rearview mirror as Frank Bender got out of the cab with his luggage and entered the building. The taxi's battered grill moved to the left in my mirror, and I turned off my engine as the cab shot past me with its backseat unoccupied.

I kept an eye on the building entrance in my mirror for about ten minutes, then I got out of the car and walked back along the sidewalk.

There was no Frank Bender on the Executive Towers' mailboxes, no Emmett Marshal. Bender must have been living here under a third name. I considered asking the manager about him, but that might only serve to tip Bender. One thing I could be fairly sure of was that, after leaving owing three months' rent, Jerry Congram hadn't moved back into the Executive Towers. I crossed the red and white tile floor, left the lobby and walked back to my car.

I passed the time by sitting in the rental car and then in a booth in a little doughnut shop across the street, waiting for Bender to emerge from the apartment building. This was the endless, monotonous part of my job. The disc jockeys on the car radio began telling the same jokes, playing the same music; the coffee tasted like the cup before, only worse, leaving a bitter aftertaste and frayed nerves; and the pavement I occasionally walked along to loosen my leg muscles became a treadmill.

The sun was setting, angling long dark shadows and softening the sharp vertical edges of the buildings. Supper was two glazed doughnuts washed down with more black coffee.

When the sky was almost completely dark and I was sitting behind the wheel of the rented Chevy, enjoying the breeze between the rolled-down windows, Bender walked out of the Executive Towers. He was wearing a dark business suit and carrying his attaché case and a precautionary light raincoat.

I sat up straight, started the engine and let it idle. Bender walked to a small green sports car, a convertible with its canvas top up. He unlocked the car, tossed the attaché case and folded coat inside, then lowered himself into the front seat. The sports car jumped forward and edged into the sparse traffic, and with a gentle touch on the accelerator I followed the low red taillights.

We took side streets for a while, then got onto Fifty but soon made a left onto a wide street with a grassy median. Traffic began to thin out as we drove for almost half an hour, then the median disappeared. Soon we were in a suburbia of middle-class tract houses and strip shopping centers. The sports car led me left on another narrow road, and the subdivision houses were fewer and farther apart.

Brake lights flared red ahead of me, and I slowed and watched Bender make a right turn. When I reached where he'd turned, I saw an unmarked dark road leading up a rise. I got a glimpse of twin taillights as the sports car took the rise toward some distant yellow lights, then I drove past the unmarked intersection to a spot where the road shoulder was wide and I could turn around.

When I reached the steep side road I sat for a while. My stomach was quivering, not helped by all the bitter coffee I'd drunk, and my heart was hammering out a warning. But I'd come this far. And, dammit, it was a public road. I jerked the wheel to the left and accelerated.

The narrow road was blacktopped but in need of repair. Deep chuckholes rocked the car every five or ten seconds as I drove steadily uphill. I passed a small, faded wooden billboard that told me I was driving toward Devon Acres, a subdivision of "affordable luxury."

The road flattened out, flanked by woods. I rounded a curve, and scattered over a wide stretch of flat land was Devon Acres.

Most of the lots were empty, though there were a few houses under construction. The houses that were fully built and spaced widely over the area were all lighted. Judging by the faded sign I'd seen, Devon Acres was one of those big subdivisions that had started strong but fallen into financial difficulty. I spotted the low-slung taillights of Bender's car far ahead of me, saw them merge as the car slowed and turned. Then I watched the play of his headlights flash behind large trees as he went up what appeared to be a driveway to the most isolated of the long ranch houses.

I drove past without slowing, quickly studying the house. Lights were burning in the west side, and it was built as at the base of a wooded hill. There were several other cars parked about the house and in the long driveway.

If I could park in an unnoticeable spot, I could cut around to the back of the house through the trees. There wasn't more than a dozen or so houses occupied in Devon Acres, so the risk of being spotted by a neighbor was small. It was a workable plan, I knew. The question was, did I have the guts. The answer was no, but I had the need.

The street curved slightly, and I parked the car in the drive of a partially built house, where it was invisible from the house Bender had entered. I got out without slamming the car door and walked quickly into the darkness at the side of the skeletal-roofed house.

For a while I stood bent over with my hands on my knees. Fear was making me sick. In a few minutes the

164

sickness passed, but not the fear, and I entered the woods.

I didn't understand how anyone could move silently through the woods at night. Every step I took seemed to bring an explosion of crashing brush and splintering twigs. I told myself that the noise seemed louder than it was, that I was right on top of it. But I wasn't very convincing.

Suddenly the square light of a window appeared through the trees, no more than fifteen feet from me. I had been dropping downhill without realizing it as I moved toward the house. My right hand shot out to brace myself against a tree, then scraped rough bark soundlessly as I lowered myself to a squatting position. This was closer than I'd intended to get, but here I was.

I was looking into a bedroom that seemed unoccupied. The floor was bare wood, and I could see a made bed and the corner of a dresser. The walls were white, freshly painted and free of decorations.

Keeping low and backing a few feet into the cover of the woods, I moved to my left and the next lighted window. This window had drapes, but they were partly open. I saw a dim shadow movement inside, and I inched farther to my left and closer so I could see into the room.

There was Bender, standing at the end of a long polished wood table. His attaché case was open on the table and he was reading from a sheet of white paper, glancing up now and then to gauge the effect of his words on his audience.

That audience was five men and at least three women seated at the long table in the otherwise unfurnished room. They were all neatly dressed, sitting erect and listening intently to whatever Bender was saying. At the head of the table sat a man in his late twenties, almost foppishly well dressed, wavy dark hair in a short but stylish cut, keen blue eyes. He seemed to be in charge, and occasionally he'd interrupt Bender to ask a question, then jot notes in an open file before him. I knew I was looking at Jerry Congram.

Maybe Bender was reporting that he'd had to kill Tad Osborne. I saw a marked reaction around the table, bodies leaning back, hands in motion on the polished wood, heads turning slightly to check other responses. Congram was sitting perfectly still, with absolute calm. He rapped on the table a few times with the cap of his pen.

All eyes were focused again on Bender, and he began to read. Congram seemed to be taking more notes.

What I knew I should do was exactly what I wanted to do: get away with what information I had.

When I stood to back away from the window, my left leg was asleep, and I lurched slightly. A dead branch I hadn't realized was against my shoulder cracked and fell loudly to the ground.

Almost immediately a face was at the window, suspicious, angry. I was crouched again, motionless, as the man peered out into the darkness. I watched his eyes roam, seeking an object on which to fix themselves. The expression on his intent face remained the same as his gaze passed over me twice. At the slightest indication that he'd seen me I was ready to run for my car. My legs were even more ready than I was, and my heart was pumping as if I were already running.

After a final dart-eyed look around, the man turned, said something.

The lights in the room went out.

The man could see outside more clearly now, without the reflections on the window. I almost straightened and bolted. I could barely make him out through the dark glass, the same angry expression on his face, as if he wanted to find someone. More faces appeared at the window. At least I was wearing dark clothing, and I was almost completely concealed by some sort of viny plant. Their eyes still weren't accustomed to the dark, and I knew if I had the nerve to stay still I probably wouldn't be seen. I was glad the window was closed; they might have smelled my fear.

Then suddenly the lights came back on, the drapes swished closed. The house's occupants seemed to have decided the noise they'd heard was of nonhuman origin.

I remained where I was, without moving, for another few minutes, fighting my powerful urge to break and run, willing my tensed muscles to relax.

Then, very slowly, with the greatest of care, I moved directly away from the house. When I thought I'd moved far enough up the hill, I began making my way through the trees in the direction of my parked car. I walked faster as I put distance between myself and the house, putting more of a premium on speed than on silence with each step. The woods were thinner now. Low brush snapped and swished at my ankles, and I no longer had to constantly brush branches away from my face in the darkness. I was already squeezing the car's ignition key in my right hand, though I couldn't recall reaching into my pocket for it.

I got to the car, managed to open the door with a fear-awkward hand and clambered in behind the steering wheel. I was careful to close the door without slamming it. On the second try I hit the keyhole with the ignition key and thanked assorted gods as the engine turned over. After backing from the driveway, I forced myself to drive slowly—simply someone passing through the subdivision who had innocent reason to be there. I knew now that I'd make it if no one heard my heart.

The car bucked as it took the steep, chuckholed road, then seemed to be grateful for smooth road as I made a left turn and drove for the city.

What I had witnessed, I realized, was a Gratuity Insurance business meeting, and the topic of business was Tad Osborne's murder. No doubt it had been Gratuity "agents" who'd beaten Belle Dee, trying to erase a link between the murdered Victor Talbert and the company. To have killed her, too, might only have triggered a deeper, more dangerous investigation.

And how much did Gratuity know about me? Was it my presence at the Poptop Club and at Belle Dee's apartment that had prompted her beating? I wished I knew more about Gratuity Insurance and Jerry Congram. I understood enough now to be really scared, maybe enough on which to act.

Bender, at least, would be a sure-fire suspect for Osborne's murder, and he could probably be made to talk in the process of plea bargaining. I thought about Osborne and the shock it must have been for him to realize his fatal mistake. Maybe he'd gone further with Bender than he would have, to impress Alison.

Then I remembered something about the conversation in Osborne's office, and dominoes began to fall.

When I reached the city, it occurred to me that I might actually have been spotted back at Devon Acres and that someone might be following me. For about fifteen minutes I drove aimless patterns on bleak side streets, breaking traffic laws a few times to see if anyone would break them with me rather than be left behind.

By the time I was satisfied that I wasn't being followed, I was lost. But my pulse was comfortably slower. I was about to stop and consult my street map when I found myself on Fifty once again and regained my sense of direction.

When I registered at the TraveLodge, they told me at the desk that Alison had left a message. She would be waiting for me in the cocktail lounge until ten. The wall clock behind the desk read nine fifteen. I thanked the clerk, and he told me where the lounge was and gave me a room key.

I entered the dim, quiet lounge and walked to where Alison was sitting, sipping a tall, clear drink. Her eyes widened slightly as she looked up at me, and I smiled at her and sat down.

"Where have you been?" she asked, somewhat in the tone of an irate wife.

"To a place called Devon Acres, one of those partially constructed subdivisions with more hope than houses."

"You look like you had some trouble."

For the first time I realized the evening's activities had taken a toll on my appearance. My hands were dirty and scratched and there was a small, jagged tear in the right sleeve of my sport coat. My hair was mussed, and no doubt there was grime on my face.

I ordered a double bourbon on the rocks and told Alison everything that had happened.

When I finished, she sat surveying me with a look of narrow-eyed intelligence, a white curve of smoke drifting like an ethereal question mark above her cigarette in the ashtray at her elbow. "Now are you going to the police?"

"Yes," I said, "but not right away like I should. First I'm going to claim the right that I've earned to nail down my end of this business. I think it's time for you to take me to Joan Clark."

The surprise passed from her face in an instant, but an instant was all I needed. I knew Alison was too smart to deny knowing Joan Clark's whereabouts.

She picked the cigarette from the ashtray, absently replaced it without drawing on it. Now that I was bringing the police in on the case, Alison had little choice but to do as I asked.

"Joan's in my apartment," she flatly admitted. "How did you guess I was hiding her?"

"Dale Carlon mentioned that you were a family friend," I said, "and that you knew Joan. Where would Joan go for help in her predicament, afraid for her life? Not to the police or to her father. Not to a private investigator, one of a bad type and a total stranger. But you, a family friend, another woman and a trained investigator in your work, could understand and have a professional interest. And more importantly, you could work on the case without attracting suspicion. You could arrange for the arrest of the people who wanted to kill her, and maybe she thought she could stay out of it."

Alison toyed with her tall glass, nodded. "At first she thought that, then she wanted me to find Congram so she could try to buy her life with her father's money. Joan has faith in me. I was sort of her big sister–godmother when she was younger."

"Does Carlon know where she is?"

Alison snubbed out her cigarette with short jabs. "No, Joan never talked to him. The seriousness of her situation dawned on her by degrees. Now she realizes money can't guarantee her safety. She simply wants her potential killers off her trail, in the hands of the law. I thought she was safe with me; I guess I made some mistakes."

"Not many," I said. "I knew someone was touching bases before me at times and thought it was whoever had killed Talbert, but it was you, working the same trail I was. I was searching for Joan Clark and you were working for her, searching for Congram. When you got the call about Osborne, it came from Chicago; I figured that for some reason you'd routed some of the calls through your office. But yesterday you were on the phone with your editor, conning him into thinking you were chasing another story. You'd already had feelers out for a Gratuity Insurance appointment, to be called to your home number, where Joan would always be waiting to forward the message to you. It was Joan who phoned from Chicago about the Osborne appointment."

Alison played her lighter flame over the tip of another of her long cigarettes, leaned back. I enjoyed the frank admiration in her green cat eyes. "You pieced things together neatly, Nudger, I'll admit. What about Osborne's remark in his office?"

"Now who needs ego boosting?" I asked her. "I knew you were too sharp not to have noticed when Osborne mentioned that Dale Carlon had arranged the appointment for us, but what he said didn't register with me until later. I never told you who'd hired me, and you let Osborne's remark go by without question. Not like you at all, Alison."

She'd wanted to hear that last part. She smiled at me.

"I think we should go," I said, and she agreed with me.

24

Alison's apartment wasn't the worst place to hide. It was on the seventh floor, and large, filled with modern furniture that somehow managed to appear comfortable. The pale walls were graced with multicolored inkblot paintings that seemed to be there more for the brown and yellow color scheme than for art. Two wide glass doors led to a garden balcony, the ledges of which were lined with narrow planters of tangled green vines.

Alison looked around, glanced at me as if surprised not to see Joan Clark in the apartment. Then she walked to a closed door and knocked on it.

"Joan? It's me, Alison. You can come out."

Alison was about to knock again when the door opened slowly and Joan Clark stepped out.

When she saw me, her slender body gave a slight backward jerk, and her large dark eyes darted sideways to question Alison mutely. She was wearing a wrinkled gray pants suit that distorted her slender curves, and her hand raised as if by helium and clutched her jacket closed in woman's universal reaction to distress.

"This is Alo Nudger, Joan," Alison said gently.

Joan stared at me, without surprise now. She looked worse than her photograph. The upturned nose lent her a wary, haunted expression that matched the hollowness of her eyes. Her hair was much lighter than in her snapshots, cut short and carelessly tousled.

"Alison's told me about you," she said in a calm voice. She was about to say something else, then caught herself and stared at me with cautious appraisal.

"You don't have to worry now about Congram or Gratuity Insirance," I said.

Something flared in her eyes for a second, something I couldn't decipher. "You know about them?"

"Just enough," I said. "I'd like for you to tell me the rest. It's the only way now, the best way."

She seemed to withdraw to someplace beyond me to consider that, walking absently to a chocolate-colored sofa and sitting lightly.

"You're working for my father," she said, as if it were an accusation.

"And for you, Joan. At this point your interests are the same."

Alison sat next to her, rested a soft hand on her arm. "He's right, Joan. You should see your only way out of it now. Do what he asks."

Joan laughed, almost a bitter sort of cough, and looked up at me. "You're not going to tell me my father's concerned with my safety?"

I shook my head. "I'm not going to pass judgment on your father. All I said was that your interests coincide."

"I don't have to go back."

"No, and if you do go, you don't have to stay."

Joan leaned back on the sofa, breathed out her uncertainty and tension in a long sigh. She'd reached a decision; for everybody's sake, I hoped the right one.

"All right," she said, "what do you want me to do?"

I sat opposite her in an armless chair. "From the beginning, tell me about Victor Talbert and Gratuity Insurance."

She didn't move; her dark eyes locked on something low and invisible on the other side of the room. "I loved Vic. . . . We loved each other. And things were beautiful until he lost his job." Now she did look at me, frowning and haggard despite her youth. "You have to understand what losing the job meant to Vic, what a crushing thing it was to him. He was ambitious, hard working and dedicated—not just to his job but to everything he did. The idea that he might fail never entered his mind, because he wouldn't let it. Nobody wanted success more, or feared failure as much."

I waited for her to continue and didn't say I could have introduced her to more than a few Victor Talberts.

"Vic tried to get another job," Joan continued, "and he could have had several with starting salaries and responsibilities below what he considered his level. He refused them, out of personal and professioanl pride. Then he decided to go into business for himself, and he went all over trying to get financing, but no one would give him a loan. That's when he began to get sour on himself, really depressed, and that's when Jerry Congram came along."

173

"Had he known Talbert before?"

"No, Congram said his 'research and recruiting department' had recommended Vic to him. Vic was impressed with Jerry. So was I and so was everybody. Jerry can tell you things, make you believe in yourself, make you believe almost anything. When he was gone, sometimes you'd begin to wonder. . . . But then he'd be back, with all his fire and all his belief. I'll admit, Vic and I were dazzled, and Vic had hope again, and something to suit his abilities."

"A position with Gratuity Insurance?"

Joan nodded her head, kept it bowed.

"Joan, I need to know how Gratuity Insurance works, how many people are involved."

She didn't hesitate. "There were fifteen, including Vic. I wasn't actually an employee, but I was going to be and Congram trusted me. Congram recruited junior executives and other strongly business-oriented people to work for him. He was very careful; he'd learn everything about someone before even considering approaching them for recruitment. Everyone has to be loyal to him, ambitious, aggressive, and believe in the system."

"What system?"

She looked at me curiously and moved an arm in an encompassing wave. "Why, everything . . . the way things work. Only without the hindrance of self-doubt. Jerry believes in realism without rationalization, self-honesty and the decisiveness to act on fact and not fancy. . . ." She seemed to realize that she was parroting someone else's words and thoughts, and her voice faded. Her jaw muscles flexed and she swallowed before continuing.

"Every Gratuity employee is extensively trained," she said, "before actually being used in the field. A trained agent will gain audience with a carefully chosen top executive on whatever pretense will work best. Then, in private, the agent implies that one of the few in the business hierarchy above the chosen executive has sent him, and if Gratuity's instructions are followed, certain obstacles to advancement will be removed."

She was parroting again, but telling me what I wanted to know.

"If the executive doesn't follow Gratuity's instructions, he'll suffer the consequences. Sometimes that would be an arranged accident, or even a false suicide complete with a note the victim was forced to sign. The agent instructs the executive to bring about some minor policy changes that will in some obscure way benefit one or more of his superiors. All this is used for is a convincer. Then the executive is assured that what is happening to him is now common practice, and surely he must understand, as did his superiors, that if he goes to the police or in any way fails to comply, not only will he destroy his career, but he must be killed as a matter of minimizing projected risk factors. The names of other Gratuity subjects like himself are mentioned to him and he's warned not to contact them. These are names of subjects who are classified as risks. When some of these names appear in the obituary columns, it serves as the clincher on the deal. At that point the executive is instructed to send large sums of company money to an anonymous address, which is how Gratuity Insurance derives its income. When a predetermined sum, which only Jerry knows, is reached, the company will be liquidated."

"It boils down to simple extortion," I said.

Joan's eyes were vague and dark, somehow innocent. "It's simply business, Mr. Nudger, business without hypocrisy." She seemed to realize what she'd said and looked away. But there was nothing to look at but extortion and murder, and her own fear.

"How many 'projected risk factors' were actually killed?" I asked.

"I don't know. . . . A small percentage, according

175

to Jerry. After the initial contact, the subject is watched closely for a while. Sometimes, if he does anything suspicious, Gratuity breaks off all contact with him rather than eliminate him and use him as an example. And if a subject goes to the police, he won't be killed. Too much danger to the operation."

"The operation, the company, was everything, wasn't it?"

"It was more important than any one of us," Joan said with fervor, despite the past tense. "Jerry held meetings as often as possible, and each meeting began with a short oath of allegiance to the company. There was no way not to be caught up in the zealousness and the feeling of purpose."

"What made Victor Talbert want out?"

"Jerry was away for more than a week, long enough for his personality and his ideas to lose some of their effect on us. And Vic got his loan. It was too late then—Jerry would never let him go. But Vic knew he could have made it without Congram and Gratuity, and that seemed to change him. We decided to run."

"From the apartment on Oakner?"

She seemed surprised as she nodded, raking her fingers through her mussed hair in an oddly careless gesture.

"Why did you choose Layton, feeling as you do about your father?"

"Vic and I knew what would happen if Gratuity found us. We thought that by giving the impression we were under my father's protection, even if we really weren't, it might stop them or at least give us time. So we moved to a little house in Layton, calling ourselves David and Joan Branly, and kept it a secret from everyone."

"How did you sell that idea to Melissa?"

"We let her continue to call herself Melissa Clark, and we told some of the neighbors I was divorced and she'd kept her father's name."

"But Congram found you," I said.

"Yes, and he tried to talk us into rejoining Gratuity. Jerry promised Vic everything—money, position. . . . He was convincing. But Vic refused and I chose to stay with him. We swore to Jerry we'd keep our former affiliation with Gratuity a secret, and he pretended to believe us on the basis that we'd be incriminating ourselves if we talked. But he showed us a newspaper with a story about a Gratuity-arranged death, and he had the back of the house sprayed with bullets that night to demonstrate how easily he could deal with us if we did talk. I think he really did all that just to convince us that he thought we were scared enough to remain silent, and to make us think he was sincere about leaving us alone. But all he was doing was trying to figure out the best way to get rid of us without suspicion. Vic and I didn't believe him, and we decided to move again. Then Vic. . . ."

"I know," I said, thinking of the photos of the young man in the blood-spattered jacket.

Joan clenched her fists hard enough to whiten the flesh. "I didn't know what to do. . . . I was terrified, for myself and for Melissa. I packed what I could. I didn't dare take Melissa; I was afraid she might be killed along with me. So I left her with the next-door neighbor and took a bus to Orlando."

Probably that was what Congram wanted, I thought, to get her away from Layton to where she could be killed without an intensive investigation, just another unidentifiable corpse in the bowels of some large city.

"I didn't know what to do," Joan said, "where to go. I left Orlando. Then I stayed in New Orleans for a while, but I never felt safe, and I was running out of money and hope. Finally I thought of Alison, the things she'd done for me, how she'd told me to come to her if I ever needed help. And I remembered what she did for a living."

And wound up here with very little hope, I thought. I

177

felt sorrow for Joan Clark, for whom a lot of things had ended, if not her life.

"You have to understand, Mr. Nudger, Gratuity employees don't see themselves as criminals. We—they are ambitious and aggressive business people, in a close-knit enterprise, who simply are carrying the precepts of business to ultimate reaches, where they're headed anyway." The autonomous voice had taken over again, the rote excuses for exploitation and murder. "Visionaries ahead of their time," she added, "no more criminals than the manufacturers of unsafe but profitable products that endanger life, no more extortionists than the lobbyists who twist the appropriate arms with personal knowledge to gain favorable treatment. Vic wasn't evil. He became what Congram told him he was—a genuinely honest businessman, a pragmatist without rationalization or apology."

"Do you believe that, Joan?"

Her body was trembling. "I did . . . and some of it I still do."

I understood her lingering belief. Gratuity's success depended upon its victims' believing that someone above them in their organization would employ polished potential killers in the course of business. And with relatively few exceptions, like Manners and Blount, the victims believed—and paid.

I couldn't blame them. I'd have paid. Manners and Blount and Tad Osborne should have paid.

"Melissa is with Gordon," I told Joan.

"I know. Alison found out for me. I was afraid to try to see her."

"You'll see her shortly," I said. "Then I'd like you to see your father."

"Is it safe? Is it over?"

"Almost. The dangerous part."

I could see that something in her mind rejected what I'd said while every other part of her wanted to accept it. Her thin body squirmed on the sofa, and she began to cry away the part that rejected.

Alison hugged her, appeared close to crying herself. Wouldn't that have been something to see? I got up, paced, and casually brushed the moisture that threatened my own right eye.

I used Alison's phone to call Dale Carlon. After explaining the situation to him and accepting his thanks, I let him talk to Joan.

Whatever his reasons, Carlon must have expressed heartfelt relief to Joan at finding her safe, because by the time she'd hung up the phone I could tell that things were at least bearable between father and daughter.

"What now?" Alison asked.

"Now you stay here with Joan," I said. "For the time being, this is still the safest place for her."

"Where are you going?"

"Where you wanted me to go in the first place. The police."

I told Joan and Alison that I'd be back and left the apartment, thinking of my soon-to-be fifty-thousand-dollar bank account. The drop in the elevator was somehow soothing, like a dropping away from my problems.

It's that way sometimes after you've punched the down button.

25

I got directions to the nearest precinct station, an old brownstone building with arched and shadeless windows.

The inside of the building was similar to that of a thousand other precinct houses, caged booking counter, interrogation cubicles, several steel-gray desks supporting typewriters, wire baskets and telephones. From a receiver somewhere, the ever-present crackling voices of a dispatcher and the answering cars read like a litany. Familiarity with this scene was a part of me.

At the desk a sergeant was talking to a plainclothesman. I walked over and identified myself as a private investigator, bringing about momentary interest, then polite boredom.

As I told my story, I could see that Sergeant Hartenstein was my main obstacle. He refused to believe that any matter was urgent or actionable without predetermination of every insignificant fact. He was a ruddy-faced, gray-haired man with a perfectly trimmed mustache, a slow and correct thinker. I was reminded of Sergeant Avery, in Layton.

"You say they're an insurance company?" Hartenstein asked, rolling a broken-clipped ball-point between sausage fingers.

"They say that," I told him.

His blue eyes shifted to the right and looked past me at a tall, broad-shouldered man in a lieutenant's uniform. The man had straight black hair, watery, sensitive dark eyes and an oversized nose that hadn't been set after a break.

Sergeant Hartenstein looked relieved, his facial muscles noticeably relaxing. "Tell your story to Lieutenant Morri," he said.

I did.

"That's beyond our jurisdiction," the lieutenant said, looking inscrutable and scratching the side of his neck.

"I figured that. Don't you have a cooperative arrangement with these other departments?"

"Sure, under certain circumstances, or if they request it."

"Who's your superior?" I asked him.

The lieutenant didn't care for the question, but he gave me the name and phone number of a captain.

I asked if I could use the phone, and they pointed to a black wall phone near the interrogation cubicles. On the gray-painted wall around the phone were penciled dozens of phone numbers, most of which probably belonged to bondsmen or lawyers.

Lieutenant Morri seemed worried, but he didn't have to be. Instead of phoning the captain, I called Dale Carlon.

The situation enraged Carlon. He said he wasn't sure what he could do, but that he'd do something. Money speaks louder than words and usually has the final say. But we were a long way from Layton. When I hung up, I mentally gave Carlon a slightly better than even chance of being able to make things happen.

One thing Carlon definitely hadn't made happen was the arrival of the press. But nobody's flawless. The press was with us at Devon Acres, equipped with cameras, recorders and mobile TV unit vans.

Lights still glowed in the windows of the house of the Gratuity meeting, as they did in the windows of the other completed houses scattered about the graded development. The night seemed darker, and I tried to stay out of the way while the operation took form.

I remembered when, years ago, my brother had sold life insurance and I'd helped him work on his sales approach. The company he sold for had used, on tough customers, a tactic they called "the hard sell death knell." "If tomorrow you die . . ." was the salesman's opening line of the horror story. Gratuity Insurance had assumed control of the "if" of that opening line.

Within minutes, exits from Devon Acres were blocked, and men were stationed in the wooded area to cut off a retreat in that direction.

Several unmarked cars drove up slowly to park around the house, then four patrol cars rushed to block the driveway and park in strategic positions along the street. I saw several dark shadows move swiftly to the rear of the house. Car doors swung open, figures crouched, and I saw the thick barrels of riot guns. Police from three departments were ready for a shootout if necessary.

Cued by a radio command, dozens of spotlights popped into brilliance and were trained on the sprawling ranch house, giving it the unnaturally bright, unshadowed look of a movie set.

The law had provided the lights, the press the cameras. Whether or not there would be action depended on Jerry Congram.

The major who was in command asked, in a polite but professionally firm voice, for the occupants of the house to come out unarmed. He then explained to them that they had no choice. But for the lights that shone in the windows and the cars lining the driveway, he might have been talking to an empty house. Beside me a man braced on a patrol car fender kept a portable TV camera aimed at the spotlighted house while he murmured something I couldn't understand under his breath.

The major with the bullhorn repeated his instructions.

Around me there was talk of tear gas, of high-density firepower.

Then the front door opened, and Congram led them out.

There were ten of them—six men and four women—all walking with hands raised to shoulder height, squinting at the brightness concentrated on them. Some of them appeared frightened, some baffled. Congram looked like a man whose worst suspicions had been confirmed. His expression was resigned, enduring, distantly amused.

As the line of Gratuity employees reached the police, there were flurries of motion and the clamping on of handcuffs. Several armed patrolmen rushed into the house through the front door, seeking more prisoners. Everyone around me began to close in on the now-diffuse scene.

The press sensed right away that Congram was the leader; he had that about him. He was leaning against the door of a police car, his wrists handcuffed behind him. I heard him patiently, even condescendingly, explaining to a reporter that a man is guilty only if established as such in a court of law.

"You maintain your innocence?" the reporter asked.

Congram addressed his answer to the half-dozen microphones thrust at him. "Of course. I'm as innocent as any of you. The only *wrongdoing* one can commit is the mistake that leads to his conviction and labels what actions he's taken as unethical or immoral. Until that conviction, no *wrong* act has really been committed. In the truest sense, the crime is in being caught. You all know that."

They acted as if they agreed with him.

"Innocent until proved guilty is the basis of our society . . ." he began, but his lecture was interrupted by the arrival of the police van to transport the Gratuity employees to holdover cells. They cooperated with the police in brisk, businesslike fashion so that the van was loaded in less than a minute. Congram was the last inside, and he nodded pleasantly to the officer holding the door open and climbed into the van without hesitation. One of the reporters yelled something about

183

another Manson cult, but Congram ignored him, sat down and seemed to order the officer to close the van doors.

In a way I had to admire Congram, which was what made him dangerous. He was the ultimate and inevitable extension of the system itself and, though he would deny it, the product of compromise.

One after another, engines roared to life around me, as if at the beginning of a race. I started walking to where my own car was parked. It was time to return to Alison's apartment.

"How do you figure in this?" someone asked me.

I pretended not to have heard the question and walked on, unsure of the answer.

26

The day after Gratuity's unexpected "liquidation" Carlon arrived in Chicago with a battery of anonymous-looking lawyers. I talked to some of them, filling them in on what the police might have missed telling them, and found them to be sharp, cold individuals. They pondered legal angles that sounded ridiculous until they discussed them so seriously that they became serious.

During the course of the day, I managed to break through to Carlon once, for a brief and interrupted phone conversation. His lawyers accounted for his inaccessibility with explanations that sounded reasonable when said fast.

Carlon did manage to have his daughter free within hours. Whether Joan Clark was out on bond or hadn't had charges brought against her I didn't know and didn't think to ask her when she phoned to thank me. I accepted her thanks with a humility befitting one of the finest investigators in the country, not mentioning the exorbitant fee her father had agreed to pay me for risking my life.

For a while, the police gave me a hard time about withholding evidence, but some old connections I had put in some words for me. Carlon also interceded, though in this instance he couldn't be of much help. It could have turned out worse. I escaped prosecution and was sure I'd be able to retain my investigator's license, but I'd never operate again in Chicago. I could stand that. Before Joan hung up I asked her to tell her father I was on my way over to thank him personally for his efforts on my behalf.

When I got there, Carlon was out.

It was past noon the next day before he deigned to see me in his suite at the Continental Plaza. I didn't know whether to be angry about his inaccessibility or grateful to him for helping to get the police off me.

When I walked into Carlon's opulent suite, he shook my hand enthusiastically and bared his teeth in his PR smile, making me more confused. One thing I wasn't confused about was the remaining forty thousand dollars he owed me.

Carlon was wearing leather slippers and some sort of patterned blue silk lounging robe. He sat down slowly in an overstuffed chair in the manner of a king situating himself on a throne. "I can't thank you enough, Nudger," he said earnestly, "and neither can Joan."

"Fifty thousand dollars is more than adequate thanks," I said. I found myself ill at ease in the luxurious suite, with my wrinkled bargain suit and the scratches from the Devon Acres woods still marking my hands and face.

"Actually I've been trying to contact you to talk about that for the past few days," Carlon said, and I felt a chill of suspicion dance up my spine, catch in my throat as a lump.

I wanted to speak, didn't know if I could manage it or what I should say.

"I've had my accountant draw up a check for you," Carlon said and held out a pale-blue and beautiful rectangle of paper.

Letting out my breath, I leaned forward and accepted it from him.

When I looked at the check, I saw that it was for five thousand dollars, and I felt a weight settle in my stomach. I was afraid of the rage that was pulsing through me. My voice was strained and distant. "You're thirty-five thousand short. . . ."

Somehow Carlon managed to look surprised. There wasn't a hint of insincerity in his handsome face or concerned gray eyes. "Of course you realized the remainder of the fee was predicated upon certain circumstances in Joan's disappearance."

"It was predicated upon my finding her," I said tightly. Behind Carlon his male secretary had entered the room and begun to busy himself about a cluttered desk.

"Let me point out," Carlon said, "that the investigation has revealed nothing criminal, nothing legally actionable, in Joan's involvement. My lawyers and the police have questioned her extensively. She was never actually a part of that establishment Manson cult."

"That seems to me to be beside the point."

He appeared puzzled. "It was Joan's welfare that this was all about, wasn't it?"

"That and fifty thousand dollars." I was getting angrier now, feeling the loss I knew I couldn't avoid.

"That seems a rather mercenary point of view," Carlon said. Then his voice became tolerant. "You must see this for what it was—a business arrangement. There is, after all, not even any written record of our agreement—"

"Our agreement was about fifty thousand dollars," I interrupted, "and I was to collect it when I located your daughter."

He shook his head as if losing patience with a backward child. "Believe me, Mr. Nudger, the conversation wasn't exactly as you remember it. The full remainder of the fee was predicated upon certain conditions. Why, any impartial judge—"

"I know I can't sue you. There's nothing in writing. And since you've somehow managed to get Joan off the hook legally, I can't endanger her case in court."

"You seem to grasp those essentials," Carlon said. "Why can't you grasp the fact that you were involved in a very profitable business deal, though not so wildly profitable as your imagination had led you to believe? I wish you could recall the exact details of our conversation in Layton." He seemed to believe it. I don't think any polygraph would have tripped him up. "The five thousand dollars," he said, nodding toward the check in my hand, "is as much a gesture of appreciation as anything."

I knew what he meant. He could still stop payment on what he'd given me, which would be a considerable amount of money even after I'd paid my expenses. The weight in my stomach seemed to expand, driving the anger from me and replacing it with resignation. I was disgusted with myself for feeling even a vague gratitude toward Carlon for what he had paid me. Though legally he owed me nothing.

The desire to get really nasty with him, even violent, left me then. I did have ten thousand dollars in the bank. And any outburst would cost me five thousand, in itself more than I'd ever been paid for a single case.

I'd be damned, though, if I'd thank Carlon for his

"gesture of appreciation." Stuffing the check into my shirt pocket, I left him without saying anything.

Some small satisfaction.

It was winter and I was home in my house trailer, lounging on the sofa, watching the six o'clock news, when next I saw Dale Carlon. He was standing before richly flowered wallpaper somewhere, pleasantly and patiently explaining to a network newsman how a rise in plastics prices now would actually save the consumer money in the future. Gee, he was convincing!

Later that evening I thought I'd catch the Carlton interview again on the ten o'clock news. But during the weather forecast, the picture on my portable TV suddenly shrank to a tiny, brilliant square of light, revolved and disappeared.

I went to the metal box where I kept my important papers and dug out the set's warranty.

It had expired the week before.